CW01649708

Another Step Beyond the Stairs

An Invitation to Walk into Other Dimensions

SHIRLEY BATTIE

Copyright © 2022 Shirley Battie

The Moral Right of the Author has been asserted.

All rights reserved. Apart from any permitted use under UK copyright law may be reproduced or transmitted in any form or by any means, electronic or mechanical, including photocopying, recording, or any information, storage or retrieval system, without permission in writing from the publisher or under licence from the Copyright Licensing Agency Limited. Further details of such licenses (for reprographic reproduction) may be obtained from the Copyright Licensing Agency Limited, Saffron House, 6-10 Kirby Street, London EC1N 8TS.

ISBN: 978-1-9995949-5-4

DEDICATION

I dedicate this book to my Earthly family who allow me to be who I am, and to my Space friends and Spirit family who have taught me so much and who have never lost patience with me when I have not stayed in contact as much as they would like.

CONTENTS

	Acknowledgments and Thanks	i
1	Introduction	1
2	The Stairs Method	Pg 4
3	These Journeys are Ongoing	Pg 7
4	Meditation Training and Exercise	Pg 205

ACKNOWLEDGMENTS AND THANKS

I thank all my spirit helpers for their patience and teaching. There would be no book without you.
My grateful thanks to my son, David Green, for his proofreading, cover and advice throughout to get this published.
My thanks to all those friends, known and unknown who have urged me to get this book out there for all to read.

I have brought this book to light again in response to many who were not able to get the first edition due to a minimum print and who have been asking me to bring it forward again. All these journeys have been written exactly as given by spirit and have not been altered, except where the wording has not been clear. I have deleted a few of my early journeys to include later ones which are relevant to recent times. As I include these connections with spirit it is becoming clearer and clearer that although these are my meditations, they are messages to mankind to accept or not. Discard or ignore what does not help you in any way. You may decide to read the meditation exercises at the end of this book to understand the process through which this important information has been given. I strongly recommend that you do. It will reinforce the knowledge that you too can do what I have done. It is that easy. Reading or trying out the exercise will not diminish your enjoyment or understanding but may enhance it. Much of the input from my journeys may inspire you; make life understandable..

1 INTRODUCTION

Friends come forward from another dimension to assist in self-discovery and purpose. Are you ready to take a ride with me? At the time of writing the meditations and urgings from the spirit world have led me to go to Zimbabwe, Kenya, and South Africa more than once. I also went to New Mexico, Canada, several cities in America, all over Australia and New Zealand and Brazil, (what a journey that was). Antarctica and Alaska were amazing. There are many other countries I visited but mostly without financial recompense, but always for the work of spirit and our Space friends. They are explicit about what they need as the occasion arises, often at the last moment. Imagine, without meditating I would not have gone to any of these countries. Was it worth it? You decide.

The journeys have moved into a wider field of interest and covers world changing events. I asked why they did not do the things they asked of me themselves? Why ask me to do them?

Their response: "You are very well aware that if change is to come about on your planet the change must come from those who inhabit the planet, whether they use their minds or their physicality. You Human Beings must make the changes, not us."

We are all about to enter a new gigantic advancement of the human race, an enormous leap for us all. Are we ready? Much of what follows here will assist you to see yourself in a different way.

Hold on tight. What follows later may stretch your belief. The most important and exciting experiences you can ever imagine all began with meditation. I urge you to take a leap and jump in. I did and have never for a moment regretted doing so.

First here is a little background just so that you know that if these events can happen to me, an ordinary person going about life the same as anybody else, then it can happen to you too. It was 1989, I was in my mid-fifties feeling a bit lost having returned to England after an unhappy divorce and starting a new job. I enrolled in a course on counselling where they meditated at the commencement of each session. I had previously thought that people who meditated were a little weird. The beads and bangles brigade I called them. Little did I know. They were nice normal pleasant and intelligent individuals. Nothing weird about them I decided.

Sitting at home one evening I gave meditation a try and had instant contact. What I did not expect was to have information and pictures concerning the planet and the future of the human species. I took notice. For more read *Love Being a Human.* To say it got my attention is an understatement. I did not know then what was expected of me and that all the information I would be given had to be passed on and acted upon. They made that abundantly clear.

Soon I had so many exciting visits from other existences and intelligences that I was hooked. I have come to call some of these journeys to other worlds and other times '*Mind Walking*' or '*Mind Reach*'. All that is required is that you go into meditation and let the mind take you where your spirit and soul wish you to be. You are there in those other places and feel as alive and real as at home as you are in your time. Meditation is the key that opens the door. Get ready for the ride.

We all have mind journeys. That is for certain. We journey when we dream at night. We journey when we daydream. We journey when we remember past experiences. More importantly we journey when we meditate. Our inner journeys are vital to our wellbeing and may for some be a safety valve from everyday life. These journeys help keep a balance between a spiritual and physical reality.

Journeys through dreams can and often do provide solutions to problems. Many of the world's inventions have come through dreams. Sudden understanding can come while daydreaming. Do you allow time to daydream in your rush through your daily routine? Things we cannot face in everyday life are often presented through dreams, interacting with a subconscious desire to find solutions to life so that the soul can go forward smoothly and without baggage. Dreams sort things out in a way that does not damage us. Dreams will often point the way for our path through life and show us what our purpose is. Scientists and doctors agree that if we are denied dreaming time for too long we may go mad.

This is not a book on dreams, but it is about journeys into another world. Through meditation, by using intention and earnest desire to learn, you not only have control but can interact and work with what is presented by your own soul consciousness, and by your guides and teachers. To do this it is helpful to use the Stairs Method which is similar to self -hypnosis and as described in my book 'Channelling'. This is not at all difficult. Forget the misconception that you must empty or still your mind. How many can do that? Using the stairs technique set out at the end of the book it is important to have your mind operating at full stretch, noticing, and registering everything that happens. It awakens your inner senses. The mind then gets so intrigued by what is going on that it does not stray onto mundane matters. It will not have time to get bored.

2 THE STAIRS METHOD

The journeys described throughout use the Stairs Method, which allows you to go deeper and deeper. It is very similar to self-hypnosis and bypasses the conscious rationalising mind. You go downstairs, turn left into a passage and then go right to enter your space. This is as brief a description as I can manage without going into full teaching mode right here. I have included the Stairs Method at the end of the book in full. I recommend you give it a try. You can do this before you read on, or at the end.

All these journeys have been recorded as they happened. It is a method that spirit has taught me, without which the experiences would have long since been forgotten. Recording has the advantage of not having to try to remember. This way it is possible to stay in the moment, truly be there and feel the emotions of each journey. It also has the enormous value of being able to listen again and transcribe from the recording later to read and absorb the true meaning long after the experience. The subconscious mind will never lie and often works in picture form, this being a universal language.

Even with today's meditations, if I do not record as it happens then I do not receive as much in the way of information. Worse still there is little memory later as to what has taken place. Having to speak does not allow time for the logical rational mind to interfere and change things according to how one thinks it ought to go, or how you want it to go. With no idea what is coming next each one is a real journey into the unknown. I share these journeys with you in the pages to come.

Occasionally, various people are asked what they think a particular message is being given through these stories. It is amazing how different the interpretations are. From that, I feel that spirit intend that others draw from the stories what they each need. It is for this very reason that I have put them into this book so that you may decide what they mean to you.

Imagine you are taking these journeys yourself. Spirit has often said to me that messages are deliberately presented in ambiguous form so that it might encourage debate and waken up a few minds. I truly feel that the journeys included here are for everybody to take part in and be inspired by. If we are one consciousness, then everything that has happened and is still happening to me is also a reality for you. The challenges are there for you to take up if you wish. Maybe we will meet during mind travel. Intrigued?

I have given titles to some of the meditations when there appears to be a message. You, dear reader, may feel an alternative title would be more suitable. This too is an indication of where it 'hits the spot' with you. Sometimes the grammar and phrasing of the sentence is inaccurate. I have left most as it is bearing in mind that when one speaks it is often not in good writing order. I have only changed where it is difficult to follow and to make it more readable. The term '**Being**' is used to describe a spirit of high celestial spiritual energy when the identity is not known. Much can be viewed as little tales, like parables with a message for all.

The journeys are in chronologic order to show progress as time moves on. The journeys included here are meant to inspire and encourage you to have them for yourself.

My early experiences depicted in the first book Beyond the Stairs were valuable baby steps in comparison to what followed. During my connections with spirit helpers, I learnt to travel further and further. They are now taking me to heights I had never dreamed of before. I travel to other worlds, space stations and within the Earth itself. I am able to cross time using the mind, and it all began with meditation. Please try it yourself. You will discover who you truly are and how you may prepare for the coming changes and huge leap for the human race. Use the method I have described at the end of this book. Try the exercise before reading further if you wish. When using the STAIRS technique, you will discover that you are actually channelling information you could not have any other way.

I promised I would give an account of a weeklong *meditation*, if that was what it was. It gives validity to my belief that meditation is the key to opening other doors to other realities. I give this here to make it clear that journeys using my method can be continued even if it is interrupted.

As this episode was not recorded I cannot now remember the date. The memory of what happened is as clear now as if it were yesterday.

I was in meditation 'tune in' when I found myself in a large oval room. The walls were not high since the ceiling sloped down to meet them rather like an oval shaped dome. Benches or slabs acting as beds were set all around the walls of the room. In a dream state I lay down on one of them and became aware of a slim figure standing at the doorway watching. I knew immediately who he was and that he was overseeing. Serapis Bey of The White Brotherhood was with me. Waves of coloured light began to stream up my body, wave after wave.

Time passed and at last I had to say; "I have to go because I have an appointment, which I have to keep."

His reply was: "We will continue this evening."

I faded in and out until at last I came back to my home reality and got ready for my appointment.

True to his word he returned me to the room that evening which amazingly became smaller each time and held fewer beds. This continued for an entire week, morning, and evening until there was just one bed left. Colours streamed over me each time. I knew that what was going on was a preparation on my form. I had no need or desire to know any more than that.

My next meeting with Serapis Bey was when I was taken into a room with one solitary bed such as you would get in an operating theatre. As I lay down a stream of extra-terrestrials surrounded me. What I noticed and surprised me most was that each of them had different coloured eyes. They were striking since our general expectation is that their eyes are usually black.

I have seen Serapis Bey a few times since that time, but this book is not the place for those accounts, especially as they were not recorded.

3 THESE JOURNEYS ARE ONGOING

1996
PYRAMID OF LIGHT

I descend my stairs to see a little girl out in the countryside who is skipping, jumping, and laughing. Every so often she stops, listens and then carries on. She is happy and enjoying herself in the open air. She comes to a hole in the ground. The little girl is me. I lower myself and slide into it. Underneath, below ground is a passageway. I bend down even though I am a little girl and not tall. I follow the passage and as one would expect there is earth, bits of tree root. It is underground but not deep. I come to a cave. All around is rock, glistening and reflecting back. It is not dark in here. I don't know why or how but it is quite light. I can stand upright now. I look around to see what I can see.

Standing over to one side are two figures. Two human shapes, though I can't see them clearly. They are holding hands. I can see they are humans though I can't see features. Because I can't see their faces I don't know if they are looking at me or not. I go up to them and being a little girl, I am not afraid. I put my hand out and touch them. As soon as I do this they become clear, light and bright. Beautiful! They are bright and shining and have faces now. They look at me and smile, still holding hands. They put their hands out to me and take mine so that we form a little ring.

I wonder why these two people are standing here under the ground. I am thinking as a child, not as an adult. They sit down on the ground still holding my hands so that I am obliged to sit down with them. I don't mind this at all. They bring out some objects from somewhere on them. One is a very large crystal, multi-faceted like an enormous diamond, huge. It is reflecting light and shining in the most beautiful colours. The other one fetches out a clear glass-like pyramid and places it over the top of the crystal, covering it completely. The light from the crystal fills the pyramid with light. The whole thing becomes a mass of light. It is like a generator, contained and glowing white hot. It is so bright I can hardly look at it. I stare at it.

These two people still holding my hands put them on either side of the pyramid so that they touch it. I lean forward to touch. As I do that the light from it shoots up my arms and shoots through my body. I am lit up completely by the charge, like being connected to electricity and receiving a shock, but it doesn't hurt at all. I look and watch myself glow as these two people are doing. I have the same form as they have now, and I know that anybody looking at me would not see anything but the glow. They would not know if I was wearing clothes or not.

They speak. "The light is in the earth and in products of the earth. The light is in all things. To see it clearly you must go below the surface of your being. You must go into the deeper recesses of your mind and heart. It is necessary to look within for the source of the light. Your outer covering throws a blanket over this, smothering it so that it is not easily seen. When all that is within you is disclosed then may the light shine out for others to see. So my dear child, show what is within. Bring it out, allow yourself to be seen, throw off the outer covering, throw off the veneer that you have plastered on yourself and stand free and naked before all humanity."

I, the child does not know how to do this. "How does one throw off the outer casing? How is this done?"

"Discover yourself and when you have done that you will have no difficulty."

"I need you to show me how to do this."

"Keep that objective in mind and request with all your heart that you be revealed so that the light within may come forth. The way will be shown to you."

My hands are still held against the pyramid. I know I cannot stay like this. As if picking up my thought they release their hands from mine. I remove mine from the pyramid but still they glow. I am beginning to feel the cold around me which is making me come back here. I thank them and thank all my friends for what they give me and for the love they show me each time.

***

1996
SPEAK FOR ALL

I am all in red, bright red. It is a flame. My surroundings are in red, thickly carpeted. The walls are red and covered in a soft material. There is a golden rail, a soft cord threaded through loops. I am reminded of a theatre. I walk down wide stairs, soft and luxurious. They sweep around, very grand. It keeps on going. I am alone on the stairs. The energy is building up in me so I ask to be shown what I need to see, in all senses of the word. The wall at the side is soft to the touch, like velvet. Relaxed I go down to the bottom into a big hall. It is like a theatre. I see one passage which I go along. Eventually I come to a door. Again it has a theatre feel. I push the double doors open with both hands and walk through.

It is very quiet and dim. I sense there are others here with me though I can't see them. I tread softly over the carpet, feeling soft pile beneath my feet. This is an aisle between seats. I move down the aisle. People are in their seats waiting. There is a man on the stage. He sees me coming. I am a latecomer for everybody else is seated. He beckons me on and I keep walking until I reach the stage. He invites me up. I go to the side and up the steps. I can't quite distinguish him. I can't fix what he is like for he keeps changing. Different costumes, different nationalities. He doesn't hold still. The minute I think I have got him he is something else. He is a kaleidoscope of people, all in the one. I am a little confused.

He continues to beckon me. I go up to him. He puts his hand on my shoulder. There is heaviness and warmth at the same time. I can feel the weight of his hand. He tells me to face the audience. With the weight of his arm across my shoulder I feel quite secure. I am to speak.

I am to speak to all these people, on the behalf of all nationalities that this man represents, of all that he is and all that he has been. I am to speak for him now as one personality. A spokesman for many lifetimes.

I ask him, "What am I to say?"

"For as long as we maintain contact with you, you will speak our words. For as long as you retain the connection, you will speak what it is we wish to say. As a whole we will speak as one although our knowledge comes from many areas of existence and parts of the world and covers many lifetimes of varying nationalities. You will speak as one voice that is able to be heard for as long as you maintain contact. Maintain the connection."

"Am I to be in trance or conscious?"

"You will be conscious of our presence for you will feel the weight upon your shoulders. You will be aware of the collective mind and with this awareness will speak what flows from us to you."

"That is not an answer."

"We do not wish you to join us. We wish to join with you through the voice and the connecting line. We will unite with you in a totality. You will be present at all times for we unite with you and pass through you. So in that sense you do not remove yourself from us but become one with us."

I ask again: "Should I not try for deep trance?"

"You will speak from a greater depth of your being. You will subordinate your conscious mind. You will submit your conscious mind to the greater expression that will flow through you from us. You will submit and allow us access."

I tell them I am happy to do this. But will they train me how?

"We wish this to be and having your permission we will arrange for it to be so. Do you understand us?"

"Yes, I feel I understand you and am happy to have you speak through me in order to help the understanding of others."

I had been asking for deep trance abilities, but it appears from their answer that this is not to be.

***

1996
RECORDS KEPT

Everything is a nice deep restful spring green, soothing. I wear green, draping heavy material. I can't see where I am going. I move forward. There are stone steps and I feel the influence of a monk. We are in a monastery. The steps are cool and curve round to the left in a broad sweep. I am in the centre of the steps. There is no need to hold onto anything. I am confident as I go down deeper. I am going to where the records are kept. This I know. I am going to where all books and manuscripts are kept away from the light of day to preserve them so that they will endure. I come to a flag floor at the bottom now. Cool and restful. I look to see which direction I should go. I should know. I should know. Yes, there is a door leading into the first passage. It is the first time I have had a door leading into the first passage. I open it.

This is an Abbey. I go along and turn into a little passage leading into a room. There are small steps going into it. I must be on a hill, for although I have been going down I see through a window which looks out on to the countryside. We must be high up, set into a hill to be able to look out onto scenery in spite of going down. There are wooden benches round the room. The sunlight is streaming through the window lighting a patch on the floor. The whole of the right wall is faced with books, dusty but well ordered. Like archives. There is a table and chair in the middle of the room, so it is a reading room.

Which book shall I take? There is one marked 1938. I didn't expect that. I take 1938 down. I was 4 years old then. Odd! Why? I put it on the table in the middle and undo the ties on the side. I open it and it is a pop-up book. How weird! I open the pages and figures pop up. What is this telling me?

"The figures are of a family. Parents, family, even a dog. Even your present life is contained within records from beginning to end. The records will be there for any to see, those who venture down to the past. You are making your past as you proceed, and it will be there for all to see. It is not only of value to go back to ancient times to learn what you can, but others ahead will also go back to your time to learn what they can. We point this out to make it known to you that your current life, method of thinking, believing and your deeds will be looked to by others who wish to gain wisdom and something of value. Do not discount this time. Put into it all you would wish to pass on. Indeed what you learn from your seeking of the past, you may take forward with you to make it more accessible to those ahead."

"Why 4 years old? Why 1938?"

"Up to the age of 4 you had no knowledge of who you were. From the age of 4, even though you were unaware, the awakening had begun and was already started into action."

"It has taken me a long time to bring it to my consciousness."

"Work goes on within your soul being, your higher self even though you were unaware of this. Instruction was given, journeys were made, and communication was frequent, even though as a child you did not know this. We watched to see how events surrounding you were dealt with in a conscious state as a direct result of our guidance. We were not disappointed."

"I am thinking that over."

"You may retreat here at any time when you feel the need for reflection. Sit quietly at the window and look over the sunny plain below. Take peace and know that all will be well. You have surmounted many obstacles, gone to great lengths, and placed yourself in difficult situations to enter, and now we say there is no need to overcome the obstacles, for you may enter freely through the door with ease."

***

1996

FATHER IN HEAVEN – A very special experience.

I am in green. I am walking along a path covered in green leaves. Not autumn leaves but fresh, young, spring green leaves. But they are not on the trees and they don't rustle as I walk. They are soft and tender, juicy with the sap, yet I am not bruising them. I walk over them lightly with bare feet. They are not damaged at all. It is as if I am not physical anymore, the weight of me doesn't make any impression. You might say I am passing along this way rather than treading heavily. The path divides, both ways covered in green leaves, and I don't know which one to take.

So I stand at the fork and hold my arms out like a Y figure.

I know I must go to the right and follow the path upwards. I see myself as if from a distance walking up, as if I am viewing me detached from a part of me. I come very quickly to an archway which is all green, plants, flowers, like an arbour in a garden. I walk under this and as I do a shower of petals falls over me, on my head. A bird begins to sing somewhere. I can't see the bird, but I can hear it. It is sweet, so sweet.

As I walk along the arbour of leaves and flowers, I come across a seat at the side. There are two children sitting there and there is a space in between them. I sit in the space with a child on either side. They take my hands, one each. They hold my hands as a child would hold the hand of an adult, trusting. It feels good to hold them. It feels good.

We sit there a little while not speaking, simply trusting. They jump off the seat, still holding my hands and pull me with them off into the greenery at the side from where they have come, into the bushes and the greenery. They are smaller than I but they know the way. I go with them for I can't do anything else because they have hold of my hands. I am pulled along quite willingly.

We come to a very old man. I know that he has sent these children to fetch me. He is a very dear old man and I feel a great, great love for him. I have an enormous love for him, almost overwhelming. I get down on my knees and bury my head in his lap. The love and feeling, and emotion between us is strong. It is as if I have been waiting all my life to meet this man. He bends his head over mine and puts his arms round my shoulders, comforting me. We sit there, held in each other, still not saying a word. I feel as if I have come home. I feel I have been reunited with somebody very special to me, yet I don't know his face. I don't know him in person, I know him as an emotion, as a feeling of great love. He feels the love in the same way back. It is a joint thing. Eventually he and I stand up. He is not as old as I thought. He stands straight, not bent. He is strong, not frail. He holds my hand and we walk together. He the elder and I the younger with the two children trailing behind, following us.

I ask: "What I am doing here and who are you?"

He says, and I can hardly believe it. He says: "I am your Father in Heaven. I represent all that you aim for. I represent your striving. You might say I represent mankind. You might ask how this can be? How can one person represent mankind? I say that One Person does represent mankind. The love between you and mankind is strong. I am The Father in Heaven representing mankind for you."

I know what He says is true, even though He is not anybody's idea of the Father in Heaven. He is representing. Now I can understand the feeling between us. The children are His messengers. We walk on until we come to a large gathering of bright souls. I say bright because they are all bright, all glowing, all merging with each other's light, hardly distinguishable one from the other. They are all standing there, glowing in a mass. We walk up to them and into them so that we are both of us surrounded with the light from these Beings.

In answer to the question in my mind he says: "These too are all my children. I am their Father in heaven too. These Great Ones are all my children. These Great Ones do my bidding out of love and with the love that I give them. These Great Ones journey wherever they feel it is necessary, wherever they feel that love is necessary, wherever they can shed their light. They do this out of love for me who represents the whole of mankind. You are now part of them for you too will do my bidding for mankind whom I represent. For I am The Father."

I feel very tiny and insignificant in the middle of all these Great Beings. I know I have a long way to go, and I have a lot to learn and there is a lot of growth to be made. Yet I am in the presence of These Great Ones, and I know they will sustain me. I know that my own guides and personal helpers who have been with me are among this number. I know they are there, merging with the others, for they are part of the whole. They are all doing the bidding of The Father. I know this too. I feel overwhelmed but inspired at the same time. I know I can come to no harm. I feel uplifted.

I find myself standing alone once more as I come back to this life.

Even fifteen years later the memory of this journey still moves me greatly.

***

1996
PATIENCE

"Be easy Little One, over the minor irritants of your day, over the little matters that cause you so much concern. Take a larger view and rest easy in your mind for it is only your own conduct that has any importance, your own state of belief, your own state of serenity. That is what has importance for you. All other things are merely testing. Do not concern yourself so greatly. They are not even major obstacles, but minor ones. All things will even themselves out. They may appear important to you, but in truth they have no importance, none at all.

You know dear one, we are safeguarding you by not allowing you those things which you desire so greatly, for these things, were they to be given to you now would cause you stress and anxiety. You are not yet strong enough to take the pressures that having those things would bring to you. Allow yourself a little longer. Do not be in a hurry."

***

1996

INTO NEW LANDS

The colour is green. I am standing in a tunnel of leaves, in a wood. I can feel the leaves. Some are leathery and some are fine delicate ones. I am surrounded on either side by a tunnel of greenery. There is just enough room for me to stand. I begin to walk along and can feel the scrunch of undergrowth and the snap of a twig as I step on it. I feel the crunch of an acorn as I go. It is obviously well trodden, so it is a path that is well used, probably by animals because it is well cleared but with undergrowth on either side pressing in. I keep walking. The path goes up slightly and winds round. I am going gently upwards. I wonder where it leads because all I can see is the tunnel. It is very secluded and safe.

The tunnel winds round to the right, like turning a corner. I follow the direction and come up against a high wooden construction. I can't see if it is a gate or a fence. It is old, heavy, and is right across the path. This doesn't make sense, because the path leads to it and has been well trodden before, it must lead somewhere, or people wouldn't use it. I ask why the path stops here? I know the path does not stop here and carries on the other side of the fence.

I push it to see what happens, not hard but just to see if it will give way. It does. I can see the hinges now that you can't see when it is shut, but only when it is open. It is a very big gate. You could get a wagon through it. I walk through and pull the gate shut after me. I realise it is not intended to be known by all and sundry that it is a gate. It is only for those who would persevere. On the other side it is much smoother. The undergrowth has been cut back as if to allow for a greater passage. The path is firmer to the feet. I am on a gravel path which crunches as I walk along. I have no idea where this is leading. It's still upwards. The undergrowth starts to thin out until eventually I am standing on open land.

The path goes up over a rise. As I stand at the top of the rise I see a vista of countryside. It is a vast horizon, so vast I can see the curve of the earth. It takes me by surprise, and I still don't know what I am to do. Everything is open to me, no doors to go through. I can go in any direction.

I ask, "What am I to do? Why am I here?"

"Go down into the world. Go down into the vastness. Whichever way you go will be surprising. New people, new ideas, new challenges. Do not limit yourself by remaining on the known path. Venture outwards now."

"I thought that was what I have been doing over this year, this last year."

"It isn't to stop there. You have a tendency to return to the land of known adventure. We say go on to yet new lands. Continue the process. Do not return."

"I don't know how I can do that. I need to be told where to go, the same as before."

"When the time is right we will tell you which land. Maintain your contact with us and we will advise you which land to go to and will set your direction."

"It is all very vague. What have I got to offer anyone? I still don't have the clairvoyance for platform work."

"You have healing, and you have the ability to speak. Wait for the openings. They will be there."

"I haven't seen Andreas (*my guide*) lately."

"He is with you at all times."

Someone takes my hand and we walk down steps, down the hillside towards the vast horizon together. He is starting me off on the journey. We keep on going down and down and down. It seems as if we are never going to get to the bottom. I feel like a pioneer going into the unknown, it is so big.

***

1997

I am at the top of my stairs in thick warm clothes, thick trousers. I am really padded up. Everything is cold, like ice on the way down. I have thick gloves, thick mittens on. I feel as if I have been transported to arctic regions. Thick studded boots. I feel very clumsy going down the stairs. I clump my way down knowing I must go on this particular type of journey.

I get to the bottom feeling very heavy with all the gear on. It is like an underground cave. It is a little warmer down here but I'm not taking my outer gear off. It is not warm enough for that. I go along and turn off. It is like going through an ice tunnel, just big enough to get through. I can stand up. The passage is just wide enough for me. If there is an opening I will surely find it because I am hemmed in so tightly here. I do come to an opening, cut into the ice.

I turn into it and once inside it is different. It is warm, it is light. There are colours, it is another world. I begin to take my things off. They are out of place here. There are tinkling little sounds, and little lights. It is like fairy land. I see people sitting at tables, talking, laughing, chattering. They are really quietly enjoying themselves. I wonder why I am here.

I see a man beckoning me from the other side. I go to him. I thread my way through the others. They are not too tightly packed. They give me an occasional glance. They are not interested in me. But he has seen me. He seems out of place because he is what we would call a spiritual master. I am not even sure the others can see him. He reminds me of Jesus though I do not think it is him, for I would know. This figure is a biblical figure.

"I want to know why I am here, what am I going to learn?" Will you tell me?

"There are so many different worlds, so many and so vast. While you must focus on the one you are living now, it is only a minute portion of what there is. Do not place so much importance upon it that you cannot see the overall picture. The little things you have been worrying about are so insignificant as to be almost laughable if you were to look at them with a wider view. Take the grander view and see how you personally can affect the life and environment in which you live. Look to see how you and your actions can improve life for others, without being overly concerned about insignificant matters that do not make a difference one way or the other to anybody else, including yourself.

"Focus on those things that do make a difference. Focus on those things which will be lasting in effect. If you do this then all the other little irritants will fade into insignificance where they belong. In all your actions and all your work applications, consider first, will this have an impact and beneficial effect on the life and the lives of those who share your time? Or will it have no bearing on the matter at all? Then your way will be easy. Then you will know the direction to follow. It requires but this question. You must think long and hard and think ahead to where the consequences of actions taken come in, and what they might be.

"Much work is involved. It is not easy. It is not easy to work in this way. We do not promise ease. We promise work. We promise results following dedicated application that will benefit not only your own soul but others also. It does not come about without your effort. It does not come of itself. It does not lie in complacency or giving up your energies. Remember to contain your energies for this work and not for other insignificant matters."

"Why was I dressed in all that ice gear?"

"You have travelled from the cold, unfeeling areas of your life, the elements that freeze into inaction. We wish you to emerge from inaction into a more fluid, warmer, more encouraging environment. Whenever you feel you are frozen in time, in inactivity, visualise your presence in this room where there is warmth, laughter and chatter. Where active minds dwell, and indeed where I dwell. You will see there is light and there is laughter. There is interchange between minds. Come out of the cold; come out of frozen time where nothing can be achieved."

"It is not quite clear, for I am doing things."

"Yes, my dear but you are doing things and getting nowhere. Put your mind to what you must do to have an effect."

"Interaction with others will help me to achieve. I feel I am very much doing everything on my own. The others in this are interacting with each other. I am on my own."

The figure pats me on the head. "You know you are not alone, even though you cannot see us. We move the chess players on the board."

***

1997
PREDICTION?

I am in red. The staircase is a peculiar one made out of rough wood planks, or tree trunks, anything to hand, scavenged from the countryside, as if there were no tools there. There are all sorts of branches and boughs, scraps here and scraps there to make a way down the slope. I am holding on to bushes at the side. It has been cut through the undergrowth, not cut but bent and pushed apart, using whatever is to hand. Somebody has done this.

I keep going down into what seems to be a hole. Not a hole in the ground but a hole through undergrowth. I do not know where this is going. I am in red which means some energy for me, strength, passion too. I feel nothing. I almost feel nothing for something is welling up in my throat, a tightness. There is emotion, a great emotion of - I don't know. It is the sort of emotion when one wants to cry, but I do not feel sad. Yet this is coming so strongly. It is as if something has me by the throat, but they haven't, it is my own feelings, something very deep, very emotional is about to happen. I know that but I do not know what it is. I can hardly speak for the tightness and ache in my throat. Perhaps they are shifting something in my throat. It is all centred round my throat. The deeper I go the worse it gets. It is so hard not to cry here but I have nothing to cry about. Nothing to cry about.

I still keep going down. Eventually the tunnel opens out. I find myself on a flat piece of land. Open clear countryside. I must have been going down a hill. Where are we? I can feel the presence of spirit very strongly with me. Where am I to go? I look around, no clear path. I go forward, directly ahead of me. There begins to be more undergrowth, as if I have gone across a clearing. There is purpose in this. I can still feel spirit very strongly with me, guiding my thoughts. I turn off to the left.

I can see a whole city laid out, an entire city. It is huge such as one might look out over Birmingham, it is that big. But it is silent, nothing is happening in that city. It is like looking at the past. Only this is not the past that I am seeing. It is so quiet, no smoke anywhere, nothing, nothing, it is dead. No sound of traffic, no lights, no general hum that one gets with the city. Nothing. The tightness in my throat comes again. The feeling of spirit with me is stronger than ever. Why, why, why is there no sign of life?

"This is the future that you are seeing. For that one portion of land. This is the future that you are seeing."

Where have the people gone?

"Some are still around, but not there. They have vacated themselves elsewhere. Some were too late, for they did not believe."

I am trying to take this in. They give me time to absorb it. I want to know about other places. I can only see this one place. What about other areas?

"It is a pattern which is repeated elsewhere. It is a pattern in all parts of your globe."

Why am I seeing it? I want to know why. Why are you showing it to me? my throat still aches.

"You can do something about this. You can alert men's minds. You can prepare them, give them serenity before the event so that serenity carries them through. You can do this. Give them the connection with their own beings, for this is what will carry them through."

"How am I to do this? How am I to do this? Nobody listens to me."

"This is where your book comes in. This is how you must angle your book. This is the bias you must follow. This is the thread that must run through it. Give serenity to men's souls so that they may not be frightened. So that the calm they receive remains with them."

"It is not easy. It is not easy to reach the man in the street. How do I do this? How do I do this?"

"You will receive assistance. You will receive expertise, both physical and nonphysical."

I am so very pleased about that, but I have been told it is alright many times and I am still struggling. How much more, how much longer do I have to struggle with this? It is interfering with my life and the work I do.

"This work is more important than all the other connections you have made in your life. This work has more importance than ever you would believe possible. Give people serenity in their hearts, not by telling them that these events will not happen but by giving them the strength to face them. Give them the strength to face even their own daily lives with calmness."

"How can I ease this throat so that I can actually stay within? This physical interference brings me back to consciousness each time."

"Do you not know that your consciousness and your inner being are one now? One cannot disrupt the other for they work together. You do not lose the contact when your physical condition interferes. You have reached the point where the two are one. Do you not know this?"

"No I did not know it. How was I to know this?"

"Please accept our word that this is so. You will find that you have the contact with your own being. When you feel our presence it is merely an addition. Not always required, but there to give you comfort, to give you confidence, to reassure you that you are not acting alone. For even while you are in physical form, you are acting in spirit, with your spirit and with the spirits. Can you understand what I have said?"

"Yes. I wish I could feel more confident about this. It is so difficult, so difficult."

"Trust yourself more."

"Yes. I feel better. My throat has stopped aching. Why did it ache so much?"

"There is grief in you. There is grief in you over so many things, both in your present lifetime and in the past. When you touch spirit more closely this grief surfaces. Serves as a reminder."

I do not feel I want to delve into that. I do not think I could manage it right now. Maybe at another time. That is all I can take. I take a last look at the city that is dead. I look at its sprawling roads, motorways, buildings absolutely silent. All in one piece but silent. I look at it and begin to hear again the sounds of my room. I bring myself back quite deliberately. I can still feel them. I thank them for being with me. I withdraw, something I don't normally do.

***

1997
GET GOING

I am standing at the top of the stairs. I am very cold, especially around the legs. The colour is ice blue. It is very clean but there is coldness about it all. I have to go down backwards into a stairwell. It is steep, almost a ladder. It reminds me of a well because I can see a glint of dark water down there. It is obviously where I must go. But if there is water at the bottom how do I stand and how do I go from there?

In fact when I get to the bottom, it is not deep and it is not cold. It seems to be alright. I paddle through it and swish my way through. I can hear the water lapping on the sides as I push my way along. It is echoing sound, everything is echoing. I can't see where I am going, but there must be light for it is glinting on the water. I go ahead and then turn off. There is water running all along the bottom. I don't understand why this should be.

I have a feeling that I am in a ship, a ship that has - - I don't know. It has water in it and has obviously been abandoned. I come to an opening. It is a ship's door with a threshold that one has to step over. It is raised to stop water coming in. I step through the door which opens inwards because the passage is too narrow for it to open outwards. The floor is wet but it is not too bad. I look around me now to see what I can see. It is definitely a ship. I must be in the captain's cabin for there are charts, maps, and all sorts of things scattered about. It is not a seaman's cabin; it is an officer's cabin. It is a bit untidy, deserted, bits all over the place. I know before I ask, but I must ask anyway.

"What is this all about? What must I do?"

The voice comes and says: "This ship is going nowhere in this condition. You must dry it out. Raise it up and make it fast. Put things in order then set sail. Plot your course and get moving for that is what ships are for. They are not meant to be at anchor. You must take the captain's role, take command and get the whole thing moving."

I feel this is referring to the book again. I have let it go, not out of mind but certainly not moving. It is all very helpful and all very nice, but it doesn't tell me how to get it moving. It is not as easy as it sounds. I need help. I need help please. Somebody has thrust a great big pen in my hand.

"The first thing is to write."

I am despondent over the task. I stand and look at the pen. Through the door comes an officer and with it come the words: "The captain doesn't sail the ship by himself. He has a team, a crew and he gives them orders. He merely does the planning, sets the sails, but his men do the work of moving the whole thing. He cannot do it all on his own."

"I need a crew then. I don't have a crew."

"What does the captain do when he needs a crew? He goes out and recruits one." Easier said than done.

***

1997
DIFFERENT LIFETIMES

I am going upstairs. It is a steep climb. It is quite hard work for the steps are high. Huge steps as if they are made for a giant and not for somebody like me at all. I keep going up. They don't appear to be attached to anything. What a climb!

I have been going for a while now and am at the top, the top for me anyway. I am helped off the step for I am quite worn out by this time. There is an air of jubilation that I have managed to climb so far without giving up and going back, which I could have done. There is a feeling of celebration that I have managed it. I am being carted off now to somewhere else. I do not know where. I am sat down in an amphitheatre. There are lots of other people here.

I am told that I have merely come to join myself in all these other times. I have come to join with the other experiences I have had as other people. If I saw them in the street I wouldn't recognise them, but they are all me in different times, in different guises and both sexes. They are all me, it is strange.

"We are trying to put things into perspective for you so that you don't get too worked up over your present life and its difficulties. We are trying to give you a more balanced view so that you work through this one more calmly. While it is important, do not attach too much importance to it so that you throw out of balance the equilibrium. In having lived all these lives we would expect that you would have learned much that you will have the wisdom of retaining your sense of balance, your sense of purpose without being flummoxed by the experience. You would say, without being thrown into dismay.

There should be no dismay for much has been achieved. While your time has not yet finished and there is yet more to learn, were you to leave the Earth plane at this point you would be contented with what has passed. So do not spoil this now, no matter what events occur around you or how they touch your heart strings. They are really of such small consequence in the overall plan. You have endured far worse things than this. What is now required is a stronger sense of purpose and a stronger application to the deeds in front of you yet to be accomplished. You require yet more discipline and dedication for your purpose." Whew! That is telling me.

***

1997
AS A CHINESE

I have red. Do I need red? The carpet is like a living flame, deep red. It is soft and comfortable. I am wearing slippers, not sloppy slippers but rather smart, stylish for occasion type slippers. One might call them soft shoes. I am wearing heavy clad brocade clothes right down to the ankles. I am reminded of the Chinese heavy brocaded coats. It is heavy with the brocade and the silks and embroideries in it. It is Chinese.

I walk. I am not sure if I am me. I feel as if I am a Chinese man, an older man. I am not me as Shirley, yet I am just starting on this journey. It is odd. I have a moustache. It is difficult to know how old I am. It is always difficult to feel your own age. Possibly I am early forties. I am not sure. I go down the soft red carpet. I am very much a man and very sure of myself also. I belong here. This is my place. This is my home, my domain. As I go down there appear to be servants on either side of the staircase. They bow their heads to me as I go. I seem to be somebody of importance though I do not know my name. The stairs sweep round to the left. It is very grand, like a palace. I do not know where this is taking me or why this has happened. I have no idea.

At the bottom it is difficult to make out the covering of the floor, not that it matters too much. It is smooth, marble like. I had half expected carpet. It is very wide, very open. I don't know where this is taking me. I walk straight ahead where there is a door. It is typically old Chinese style, mandarin style, whatever that is. I go through the door out into a courtyard. This is all very nice but what is this telling me?

"You seek for a cure for all your ills. You continuously seek and yet you have not tried the one thing that is natural to you. Why do you not try this, as it is effective in your case? From then on you will not have the disturbance that prevents you from working to your fullest capacity."

"Why all the build-up just to tell me that?"

"We wish to remind you of your roots, the part of you that is strongest in you, the part of your existence that has had the greatest influence on the quality of your soul. Why do you not tap into this source, for this source is strongest in you? We say this because we are speaking of this Earth time, though we would remind you that there have been other Earth times. Here your influence and foundation of being was somewhat different. Here we are referring to your memories of Earth times."

"That is intriguing, very intriguing. There is confusion now in me."

(Sighing) "Let us put it this way. There have been other Earth times. We are now speaking of this Earth time's recorded memory, recorded by your historians. Does that help you?"

"Yes, indeed it does."

"You see my child there have been other times which have not been recorded by your historians, of which they have only a glimmer of knowledge: an inkling of understanding and no more. No facts only intimations of memories lurking in their minds."

If I follow this route and I feel you are referring to acupuncture here, I am against Chinese medicine where they use animals. If I use this and become fully active again, will this help me with the book? This is where I need help at this time. I need help.

I get no response to that and my hay fever is getting worse so I can't even think now so I will have to close.

***

1997

I ask to be helped. I am dressed in silver, in a long slim silver sheath type gown. Very glittery. I walk along a path strewn with silver shards, all pointing in one direction. I can't quite describe it. It is a bit slippery. It is all flat, not going down; a narrow pathway of silver, like a silver thread, only the thread itself is composed of many things. I step forward with very small steps because the sheath I am wearing is rather tight. It is glamorous and I must be glittering as I go because the gown is like thousands or millions of sparkles. I am quite taken up with this. It is extraordinary. I feel as if I have a lot of hair, a halo of hair. I don't know where my hair ends and the roundness begins. It is as if my hair is enveloped in a bowl, golden, silver, all sorts. It is not heavy just that it has something around it. It is not a hat. I don't think it is my hair as it is all around my head. I don't know what this is telling me. I have to give description as I go. (*as instructed*)

I am getting near the end of this now. I know that I am and put my arms out in front of me as if to feel the end. It will be the end but I won't be able to see it, only feel it. I am right to do so because I feel an energy wall which I can pass through. There is a distinct division between where I have come from and where I am going. I walk very gently into the wall of energy so as not to damage myself. I pass through as if it isn't there, but it is.

As I get through to the other side there is a distinctly different feel. It's like being in a vacuum, though I've never been in a vacuum. It is as if there is no atmosphere. It is light as there is no influence from the Earth. It is free falling or being in space. I float onwards from here, no effort required. Free, no pressure on the limbs, totally free. I am floating all over the place. It is like being in space, though I have never experienced that either. I float my way along the tube, for that is what it appears to be. It is quite a wide tunnel, the size of a room in height and width. The length I don't know because I just keep going along it. Moving along using arm movements, like swimming though I don't do too much of that because of the tight garment I am wearing.

I come to another invisible wall. I know it is there though I can't see it. I push my way through this one as well. Soon I am standing on firm ground and am free of this free fall thing. I am back in pressure and normal atmosphere. I stand there and look around me. There are all sorts of shadowy figures moving about, very tall and very thin, and indistinct too. One of the shadowy figures, that is all I can call them, comes up to me and takes my hand. He is almost not there but he is at the same time. He pulls me forward; it is a long journey this one. He is very unreal and yet he must be real for he is pulling me forward. I feel his feelings. He is very welcoming, smiling. I am feeling his thoughts and feelings. I know what he wants to do and say. I know it.

He takes me before what I can only describe as a Jesus figure. I don't know if it is Jesus. It is the type of figure that one sees of pictures of Him, sitting down with his kind gentle face. He is very relaxed. I stand before Him and don't know what to say. He puts his arm and hand out in a greeting; no it is a blessing. It is the sign of a blessing on me. I still don't know what to do. I am tongue tied. I feel as if I am frozen in time, a long period of nothing but this picture. He has to be Jesus. He looks like Him. Everything is frozen and great energy comes into me. I can feel it as I speak. It enters my head and I feel the difference. A part of me wants to record this and the other part is going off - away - away.

I ask Him to help me with my endeavours, to help me be a pure channel.

He says: "Hush, my child. Be still. We know of your endeavours, and we are pleased to see where your heart lies. Hush and be still."

I feel very moved and very still. After a long period my thoughts come back to the builders due to arrive any moment and the need to eat something. I still feel very lightheaded and swimmy. These thoughts are stopping any further progress. Life continues and others don't know.

***

1997

I am going down a steep grassy hillside with no path. It is steep and I skid and slide a bit, almost on my back in parts. It reminds me of the Welsh hillsides. It is exhilarating but I don't know why I am doing this. I dig my heels in so that I don't slide all the way, to have a controlled descent. At the bottom there is a stream. It is really only a little brook, sweet and gentle, not turbulent at all, a gentle pleasant place to be. I sit down on a dry patch of grass at the side and gaze into the water. It is just nice and reflective and peaceful after the journey down the hill side.

A man on the other side of the stream comes from among some trees. He is wearing a broad brimmed hat and heavy coat, long and flowing. He reminds me of the French Bergers, the mountain men in the old days. I want to talk to him. He is waving to me trying to catch my attention as he draws nearer, as if I would go away. He draws closer so that he is within earshot. He steps across the stream using the steppingstone that is in the middle. He sits beside me. We both sit staring at the water not rushing by but gurgling by. We are lost in thought.

He says: "Yes, life goes on whatever we do. Everything goes on. Nature goes on whatever we do. It will find a means of expression, expressing itself into life. Whatever we do nature will express itself, it will express the joyousness of life. It will always find a way in whatever form."

I look at him because he had voiced my thoughts.

I say, "We must make an influence on our kind as we pass through as a human race. We go on no matter what happens, we find expression? We ought, didn't we, make that expression as good as possible?"

He nods. "You are talking about your book now, aren't you?"

"Yes. I want to make my expression so that will have an effect on the race of human. So that it will benefit. I need your help. I need everybody's help for it is a joint effort after all. I am part of the flow of humankind. It is up to me to be a good part in that flow, to add to it and not detract from it."

We both go back to being lost in thought, his thoughts and my thoughts side by side. I also sense the presence of spirits. I don't feel that either of us here are alone. The minds of spirit beings are with us too, watching.

1997

I am dressed in purple and there is a chute. This is like a children's playground. When I get to the bottom I land on sand. It is soft dune like sand that one gets at the seaside. Although the way is soft and comfortable it is also hard work. I plod on looking for something. I see a beach hut. There is somebody standing in the doorway waving and beckoning me to come forward. I make my way laboriously across loose deep sand and go up the steps. The door is held open for me. I go in and find it is larger inside than I expected.

There is a group of men sitting at a table. They are gathered there like an assembly, a council or something. They are all looking at me. As I pass down the line each one in turn gives me a rolled-up document. By the time I reach the end I have an armful of them. The last one doesn't give me anything. He holds it in his hand, but he is not giving it to me.

He says, "This one you have yet to earn. You mustn't give up now for you would not be able to complete. You would feel unfulfilled. So you must persevere with this last one for it is not more important than the others but the completion of the others, and where they have led you. You need to complete before you pass beyond these doors. You have all the other experiences behind you to help you. Do not give up."

***

1997

I have gone up this time, not down. The first part was quite hard, and then I was whisked up. I have arrived and am walking on beaten earth. The Earth is up here as well as down there. I come to a flight of steps up to a building. There is an ordinary door on which I beat my fists. I want to be let in. I am hammering away at the door when somebody opens it from the other side. I go through. Inside it is palatial. That is the correct word for it. Enormous, polished, and clean and yet it is simple as well. Clean lines everywhere. I walk, with my feet not making any noise for I am not wearing shoes. I pad across. I wouldn't want to mark this floor for anything. There is another door at the far end. I make my way to it. It is a small door. I go through.

Behind the door it is very ordinary, like a working area. Books, tables, like a big office. Lots of chairs, comfortable chairs. This is a sort of library. A man asks: "What have you come for?"

"I don't know. I have just come to see where I might end up."

"I would say, you have come to see your book."

"But my book isn't written yet."

"You have come to the future. Your book is here on the shelves. Not one, but many. Which one do you want?"

"I want the one I am writing now. I want to see."

He goes up a little step ladder. I see a whole row of books. All in blue and all with my name on it. He fetches the first one in line. It is '*The Communicators*'. (*this book was later titled* **'Being Human'** *and has now had a name change and is republished as* **Love Being a Human**. It is not very thick. I want to see inside it. He hands me the book.

"You can't take it away," he says, "for this is from the future and you are in your present. You may look at it."

The words at the front 'We were having a picnic when the thought struck me. What would it be like if I was living in the future? A stupid thought for I was living in the present. All the same I wondered. What would things be like in a hundred years, two hundred years, three hundred years from now? What I didn't know was that thought brought to me a response, from where I do not know. A response I was to have. I was to step into the future. I didn't know all this then. It all began with a thought, a wondering. People say you should have investigative minds. Maybe we get responses to all our questions, to all our thoughts. Maybe these responses come much later, long after we have forgotten the original thought. That is how it all began. A few years later I was in Calgary. I would never have guessed that I would ever be in another country as far away from home. I still didn't make the connection. I had long since left behind that day, having a picnic.'

That is totally different to the way I have begun my book. Now what should I do?

Wow! As I write this entry from December 1997 when I had no idea of what was to follow the beginning of the book published in 2010 is exactly as predicted way back then.

"Just let your mind roam free my dear and it will pour out of you. Which is what you have been asking after all. This is your response. Can you not recognise a response when it is given to you? Do you not wait around for the answers to all your questions, or like a child you ask and then run on, not waiting but impatient to ask the next question? Just like a child."

***

1998
SOULS WAITING FOR BIRTH

I am standing at the foot of stairs all in white. I have a long flowing gown, very full. I have to go up the steps. I must pull the skirts up because it is so full. I go up without holding on to a rail. It is quite steep but it is not an effort. I go up easily, very upright, very stately. It is strange because it is just the staircase, nothing else, no foundation to them. I am reminded of a piece of paper folded into a concertina shape and then spread out. These are just steps and nothing else. Nothing below them, nothing above them and nothing around them. As I climb my mind is brought back to the present with hundred miles an hour gusts outside.

A tall narrow door is in front of me, double doors. I push them open, they open in the middle. Once I am inside it is quite different. There is a lot of green, a lot of laughter, a lot of life. There are many children here pulling my clothes to make me go with them. They are happy but want me to go with them. I am very tall amongst these children. They keep pulling so that I really have no choice but to go with them.

I go slowly, calmly and we come to what appears to be the edge of something. We look down, we all look down and see far, far below - we seem to be looking at the world. We are not seeing it as a globe in its entirety. We see activity and what is going on down there. There's a lot of smoke and dust. It is confusing as there is a cloud over it so that you can't see clearly through the clouds, through all the white stuff. I know it is the ground, land, the cities. It is covered so that you can't see clearly. I hear the sound of gunfire. It is war. There is war going on down there. It is fighting, violence. We are far removed from that up here, but it is a hell down there. It is a hell.

The children don't want to go down there. They look at me and say, "Can you change this before we have to go? We don't want to go when it's like that. We are not looking forward to going into that."

I can understand their viewpoint, but I don't know what I can do.

One of the children says: "We have free choice. We don't have to go into that, so we could wait until it improves."

Another child says: "Well, if we all do that there will be no more children. If we all do that there will not be a generation for us to follow. We have to go sooner or later."

Several of them are saying, "Well, I'm not going until it is better. I'm not getting mixed up in that stuff."

I look at the children. "It's not all war. There are a lot of lovely places down there. It's not all bad. There are some beautiful calm and happy places on the planet."

A little boy from the far corner says: "You show me then, because I haven't seen any."

At that I ask my spirit friends to find a spot that is happy and calm. The land below rolls to one side. I see the tops of hills, not high mountains, just hills, similar to what you get in Wales, the rounded hill tops. I look at the hills and it is peaceful up there. Just the sheep. It is so peaceful, too peaceful.

The children ask. "Where are the people and where are the houses? There don't appear to be any. While it is peaceful there are no people. What is the good of that? Don't you know it is the people who have created disorder and war? Where there are no people it is naturally peaceful. It is the people who have created the disorder, it is not the planet, it is not the gods. It is the people themselves."

A little boy says: "How can I go there if there are no people. I can't be born where there are no parents."

"It is a problem, isn't it?" I tell them: "Why don't you ask for people to begin going to the peaceful places. Ask for the peaceful people to go to the hills. Speak your mind only to the peaceful people. Your thoughts will reach them and you will find that people will travel to the peaceful areas to escape war. Then you will have a family to go to."

"I'll give it a go," he says. "I'll give it a go."

One after the other the children pipe up and say: "I want to go to the peaceful places too. I don't want to go to the towns and cities and where there is fighting. I only want to go to the peaceful places too."

I tell them: "You can't all go there."

The one who said he wasn't going, digs his heels in and says: "Well, I'm going to wait. I'm not going. I'm going to wait, so there."

I look around me. I know these are all young children and are representing young souls. There must be some mature souls, some evolved souls here. They too may re-incarnate. I look around to see where they are. I see over to one side, a large group, quite a large gathering of mature souls, bright souls, evolved souls. They are all talking together, discussing and debating, talking of mighty matters. They are in a debate.

I leave the children and go over to them. I say to them: "How about you? Are you going to re-incarnate and are you only going to choose the peaceful areas?"

One of them looks at me and says sadly: "No we have allotted to go into the war-torn areas. We have allotted to go into the dark places on your planet and see what we can do to change the situation. We have chosen to be the pioneers, to go down and see how we can change matters so that these young souls have more space in which to reincarnate, have more peaceful areas than there are at present. We have a difficult job to do but we have decided that there is no alternative to this. Somebody must go and so we are going. We know it is not going to be easy and we know that not many of us will survive a full earthly span. We may have to come back before we are ready to. It does not really matter for we know that when we return we will have done as much as we could possibly do."

The question in my mind has just arisen. I must ask them. "Are you going to be born as new babies or are you going to go in as Avatars, Wise men, or simply become Walk-ins and take over another body?"

"Avatars are few on the ground. We have but few who can make this claim to be such a one. Of the others there is to be a mixture, so that there is a spread in time. Some of us will be born as babes. Others of us will become Walk-ins. We must arrange things so that there is a spread over time."

As I talk to them I can see a flickering of flame, lights. As I turn my head to look I see it is coming from the edge where the children are looking. I go back to them and look with them. They are looking at fires. The fires are alight on the planet. It is on fire in the troubled places. This too has a beneficial effect for it is a cleansing fire. Where there has been fire there can be rebuilding. Maybe there is hope after all, even in these places.

I say goodbye to the children and turn from them and turn back to the evolved souls. I put my arms on their shoulders. I give them a hug and wish them well. I turn from them also and walk back through the doors and back to the staircase so that I may return down to the earth below. Down to the troubled sphere.

***

1998

I have orange. I am an orange flame, like a burning flame. I am walking on flames, all being blown in one direction ahead of me. I come to a steep slope. The flame sweeps down the slope, I follow. I keep going down. I am not hurt at all. For some strange reason my ears hurt and begin to sting. One ear in particular. My throat is tightening and aching. I am filling up with something, I don't know what. I watch myself as a column of flame. I pass through a door. I don't bother to open it as there is no handle. I pass through as would a ghost walking through walls.

I see a goblet, a silver cup on a table over to the left. I go to it. There are handles on either side of it, tall handles. I look inside and see it is golden, like a bronze gold. I try to pick it up but I can't as it is too heavy. It is as if it is fixed to the table. I can't budge it. I was going to lift it and take it with me. I try to drink from it but I can't, it won't move and I don't know why. It is fixed. I ask why.

"The cup hasn't been won, not yet. You can't take the cup until it has been won."

That is a little depressing. I walk on. There are corners here, passageways which go in different directions. I feel as if I am underground. I go down one of the passageways. It is very narrow and rocky. It is like being in an underground cave, but I can walk upright and I can see, which is strange. I can see all the rock face. It is so narrow that if it gets any narrower I won't be able to go any further. It is like going deeper into a crack. Just before the crack comes to an end and I can't go any further, I see an opening on the right, like a large hole. It is too narrow to turn round and go back the way I have come. I go to the hole and almost fall into it. As I get through I have to be careful not to fall right down to the bottom, for it is a deep hole. I stand looking at it and thinking there isn't anywhere else I can go, except back.

Knowing that nothing can hurt me I jump into the hole. As I go I am caught up by currents of air. I float down like a feather in the wind. So there is no danger at all. I float downwards and wonder where all this is leading me.

A voice says: "When you go into the unknown you will always be caught. You will always be held safe no matter where you jump, especially into the unknown. You will feel as light as a feather and the feather will be blown by your friends to the place it was intended to go. It is rather like a child would blow a balloon in the direction it wants it to travel. We too do this to you whenever you jump into the unknown. Don't be afraid of new experiences. Don't be afraid to try new things. Don't be afraid to go where you have not been before. All these explorations will lead you to exciting things. It will also lead you to people who have a need for you so that you may continue to fulfil your pledge to humanity. You will be directed by us. First you must jump into the unknown and take that courage in your hands."

I ask about the book.

"The book has diverted you from further learning. The book has been a distraction. It will find its place in due course of time. There is more learning for you and more experience. This must take priority for the moment."

I am shown a picture of hands joining mine and others across the chasm.

"You will join hands with those across the seas. There will be a joining of souls."

I feel I must come back now. That is all I need for the moment.

***

1998

FIGHT THROUGH TO LIGHT

I am standing on pine needles. I can smell the sweet pungent smell of them. I feel the softness of them, spongy under the soles of my feet. Lovely, pure heaven. There is a pathway through dark undergrowth. I must bend low at some points to move along. I can't see very far ahead because of the denseness. As I step forward, and there is always another step I can take, it twists and winds a little bit. Pine needles are still there, which is strange because I can't see any pine trees, only dense undergrowth. It is as if the pine needles have been collected and laid down specifically to make a path, for nothing will grow on the needles. So it leaves a path clear for me. It is very clever really.

I keep pushing my way forward through brambles now, all sorts. It is not the easiest way to go through. There is warmth here as well. It is comfortable warmth, exciting. I keep pushing and come out into a wider, clearer higher space. I can stand up easily and see the sky above. It is spacious here. It is like a circular, open circle as if it has been trodden down many times. The undergrowth is all flattened. It is a perfect circle, perfect.

I move to go and stand in the very centre of the circle. I raise my arms and slowly turn clockwise with my face to the sun. Oh, it's lovely. There is nobody here but myself. I can do daft things like this and nobody is going to take any notice, no public around. I turn full circle. I have had my eyes shut, but now I open them.

Ahead of me is a clear path and at the end of the path is a light. Daylight, but a light just the same. It appears to be the only path apart from the one I have just come down. I follow it. It is clear easy walking this time. No bending down, no brambles catching on my clothes. I move very quickly, swiftly, regally towards the other end of the path because something is brighter there. The light is shining brightness not ordinary daylight.

Suddenly from somewhere comes a wind, a strong wind, fighting against me. I have to push very hard against the force, as if something or someone doesn't want me to get to the end. It is a very strong wind. It is as if I am in a wind tunnel and I have to fight against the force to get my way through. I am determined to get through. I push, push and keep going. The wind gets stronger. I will not be blown backwards.

At the end of the path, where the light begins, suddenly I am through. It is like pushing against a door which suddenly opens and you fall in. I have fallen into the light. I pick myself up from the ground. I can't see clearly; it is so bright. My eyes are blinded, I can't see clearly. The brightness is really great. I try squinting, trying to make out something through the squint. It is not as if the light hurts, it is simply blinding. I keep my eyes squinted.

The light comes from one source. I know that inside that source is a figure. The light is radiating from the figure. I can feel the presence of a person, a being. It moves and is talking but I can't hear what it is saying. I can hear sounds, but they are not sharp. My ears are not accustomed. He is talking to me and I can't hear, can't make it out. It is incoherent to me like hearing an overheard conversation. Hearing voices but not actually what is being said. I ask to understand and to see. I stand and wait. A shiver goes all over me, a deliciousness. The voice settles into something I can understand.

"To be comfortable in this brightness, to see and hear clearly, it is necessary to keep your mind on your objectives, your spiritual attainment. Focus your mind on what it is you strive for in your own spiritual growth. What are the values you have set yourself? When you have decided the values and the quality of your being that you are striving to attain, may all your actions be to gain this attainment, to become the one you wish to be. May all your endeavours be geared to this end. It is not sufficient to be available for others, to assist them.

What is required is the quality of your being when you are making yourself available. Being there is not sufficient. Being of spiritual endeavour while making yourself present adds to the results and to the benefits that others will reap from you. Keep your goals for your own self in mind and the rest will fall into place. You will not have to seek to help, because those who will require assistance will seek you. So you can see, my dear the importance of looking to self. Do not neglect this aspect of your endeavours. Seek to grow. Seek to understand and by your very nature you will pass whatever you have gained on to others. Have something to give."

***

1998
TEXAS?

I am walking down a wide path with rough stippled walls on either side. It is stippled rendering. I go quite determined. There are wide gates which I go through. They are very wide and large. A big driveway. Keep walking, keep on. There is a way to go yet. It is gravel underfoot, not uncomfortable. It is very well kept, this place, like the grounds of a big house. I come to the house with big imposing steps. I go up the steps and into the front door which is open, big of course. It is no ordinary house door. There is a hall inside. Polished floor. An enormous hall. In the middle of it is a table, a round table.

There are men sitting at the table, talking, discussing. It is a round table so some of them have their backs to me. I walk up to them and look over the shoulders of the ones who have their backs to me to see what it is that is on the table. There is a big layout plan on the table which they are debating and discussing. I feel this is my layout, my movements. There are big criss-cross lines all over it. It doesn't make any sense to me whatsoever.

I recognise it as America, where I shall be going. Lines crisscrossing. They are showing me the lines more clearly and pointing, there, there. I shall have to look it up on the map. From my scanty knowledge it does appear to be Texas which would seem I am going to after all. I can see where the line ends.

***

1998
CREATE BY THOUGHT

I have green; There are leaves, big leathery jungle type leaves. Leathery and shiny, not the sort we get in England. I seem to be in the middle of all the leaves. It is thick around me so that I can only see leaves. I push my way forward with my hands. I have big strong hands. I am not looking at the rest of me for I might receive a surprise. I am not ready for that yet. I keep pushing my way forward as if I have done this many times before. I feel this is routine, as a pathway around one's house is routine. It is familiar. I am in the jungle. I come out to a clearing and as one would expect there is a hut. It is not a native hut. It seems to be built on stilts but doesn't have the look of a mud hut but one that is constructed by a civilisation, even though it is wood. I am not a native. I am white and not of this land even though it is familiar. I am still a visitor to this land. This abode, this dwelling has a veranda. I go up the steps and in through the doorway. It is not even dark inside. There are things on the table. It is well lived in. There are things hanging around. It is full of things.

As I look around a voice: "Man has taken his mind and his creations into the very heart of nature. Nature has intelligence but does not think. It behaves intelligently without conscious thought. Mind of man has created and thought about its creation, it has a purpose for its creations. There is a purpose behind all his actions, his intentional actions. That is the difference, which is the conscious difference between nature in its pure form and man with the thinking mind. The message here is clear. If you would have creations which are to your liking then think before you act, so that you create what you desire and for the best possible reasons. Man is not intended to be haphazard in his development. The soul of man is intended to develop on a deliberate conscious level, aiming for the highest."

***

1998
ENJOY LIFE

My passage down is roughhewn rock, boulder rock. I go down rough stone steps, narrow stone steps cut into the rock. It is going down into the solid core of the earth. It echoes. It is steep. I am getting deeper and deeper in, isolated from the world. I am leaving the world far behind and entering a totally different world, totally different in every way. My feet touch the bottom, loose rubble, loose stone. I doubt if anyone has been this way before. Very narrow, only one way to go. I keep following, I don't know if it is turning or not. I keep moving step by step. I squeeze my way through in parts. It is as if the earth has been split, not by man but by nature. It could just as easily close up again. It is a fissure I am walking into between split rock. It must go somewhere.

To my enormous surprise I see a little green shoot, so there must be air and moisture. I can see, so there must be light, though where the light is coming from I have no idea. It is a little weed of some sort. I don't recognise the plant. There is a current of air. There is a current of air coming from the other end. I can see now the light from the far end. There is a soft breeze blowing into it. I arrive at the opening and squeeze out into sunshine, warm, bright on the eyes. I am standing on the edge of a cliff face. There is no way down that I can see. I am halfway up the cliff face. I look around to see if I can find some way, some way without having to go back and retrace my steps.

To the right of me there is a little ledge, wide enough. I climb on to that and begin to work my way along holding on to the wall face. I mustn't fall for I'd have a long way to fall. I mustn't fall. Gradually I come to an easy slope which goes upwards. I climb. The rock is a little loose so I must be careful. I climb and hold on. After a while I arrive at the top. It is a grassy bank, like on top of a cliff. I crawl over on to this on my hands and knees, away from the edge. I look up and see a sheep looking down at me. I feel a bit stupid. I crawl past the sheep and then stand up. I feel safe now. No more trials.

A man who has been looking after the sheep walks up to me. He seems to come from another time. Old. His clothes are not of my time. He is not at all surprised to see me. He comes to my side and takes me by the arm. I let him. He walks me over to where there is a wooden bench, and we sit together. We look out over the grassy plain. It is a plateau for I can see we are high up. There is nothing to see but sky, grass, and sheep. It is very peaceful with skylarks.

He looks at me - blue eyes. "Isn't this wonderful?" he says. "This life, isn't it wonderful? All you have to do is enjoy it. Don't worry about anything. As long as you have life and the sun and are healthy, what real cause is there for you to worry?"

"I have many things on my mind," I tell him. "many things, challenges, finances."

"Keep your mind fixed on the sun, the fresh air, nature. They are the good things of life."

My throat dries up and I cough. This takes me away from him. It is difficult to continue. I am waiting.

"You shall live a long time," he says. "As long as you are of the same mind then you will enjoy your life."

"What about my mission?" I ask him. "I am not supposed to just enjoy my life. I am supposed to work and achieve what I have come to do. I can't just sit back and enjoy life. If I could have done that I would have done it years ago. I wouldn't be pushing myself now."

"Your life would be very empty too, for you do have a purpose in life and you are striving to achieve success in that. We will help you. We will be with you. Just keep a sense of proportion about things. Don't let worry interfere."

***

1998

TACKLE THE FEARS

I am walking down a very steep slope, as if the ground is falling away from me. There is nothing to hold on to. It is a bit precarious. Very unsteady. It would be easier if I turned round and faced the surface. But I am facing outwards, digging my heels in and just going. I am out in the open, there is nothing to hold on to. There is nothing around me, nothing at all, just emptiness, a vacuum. At the foot there is a shingle path. Loose stones. Again not a very easy surface to walk on. I go on slipping and sliding a bit. The stones are quite big, not small. One could easily twist one's ankles here. I keep going, turn round the corner. There is still nothing on either side of me and I can't see anything at all. The gravel path goes into a hole. It is as if I am stepping through a hole, a blackness, an entry point. I walk through into the black thing that is in front of me. I can't see where I am going.

As soon as I step in there is a different scenario. I hear scurrying, a lot of movement. There are a lot of people, not people as we see them, but beings of some kind. Life, life, that is what I need to say. There are things here. I can't see them, but I can hear them. A lot of movement, touching, touching. I can feel them touching me. I can't see them, but I can feel them touching me. I feel quite safe because I know that nothing can hurt me. I don't think they intend me any harm anyway. They are just curious.

They have never seen anybody like me. They are curious. They are not malevolent. They are prodding and pulling and feeling. Pulling at my hair, touching my feet. How do they touch? I don't know. I can feel pressure on my feet. I can't see anything.

I move forward hoping I am not going to tread on anything. I don't want to hurt anything. I don't understand.

"These are your fears, your anxieties, your worries. They touch you and pull you. All you need do is say 'boo' and they will scatter and run away from you. You know there is nothing to fear. You know your anxieties are not real, not valid. Send them from you and go forward as the person you are."

I do and say 'boo, be gone,' to them. Instantly I am alone. I am standing in a meadow, sweet meadow flowers, birds singing in the sunshine. I am on familiar ground. This is the Earth. This is my existence, this time. I feel good to be alive. The good 'can do anything' feeling. That is all I have to do when I feel anxious and nervous.

"Say 'be gone' also to the cough and the little physical irritants that beset you. You can also dismiss them as easily as you have done with your fears."

"I have tried that one and it didn't work. I will try again."

"Don't expect to succeed at the first go. Try again."

***

1998

HUGE PYRAMID GENERATING ENERGY

I have yellow with a tinge of green. I stand straight and tall looking down at my feet and at the hem of my gown. I am standing at the top of rough concrete steps. They are thick, narrow, not wide. Cellar steps with rough walls on either side. A very enclosed space. There is a cold damp chill to it. I descend into darkness. I don't need to see my way for I have my hands on the walls. My feet can feel each step. My legs are tired because I am not used to going down so many steps.

Thankfully I reach the bottom where the ground is fairly smooth but is rubble. It is not comfortable to my feet for they are bare. I am not accustomed to the rough edges.

I have to walk carefully. I feel my way along and turn off. It is easier now. The ground is smooth as if it has been swept. It is quite comfortable, warm. I can see and drop my hands from the walls. I can walk easily now, still with my gown flapping round my feet. I daren't look upwards to see what else I am wearing. I don't need to. I can see my feet and I know it's me. Big feet. I stride forward, flicking the hem of my gown with the movements of my legs as I go.

I come to a door, as I knew I would. It is shiny like a Perspex shine, not glass. It is a brilliant colour, iridescent. I put my elbow to the door. There is no latch, no knob. It opens easily as if it is a board put in just to close the gap. It is not fixed. I walk inside and find myself in a huge, can't call it a room. It is huge, like a warehouse but it isn't a warehouse. It's a big building, it echoes. It feels empty but it can't be. I must find something here.

Over on the far wall I notice there are books lining the wall. It is quite some distance off. I walk purposefully. The wall is the only thing I can see to focus on. I move strongly forward to get to the books; they are packed in very tightly to the point where it could be very difficult to get one out. There is a stick on the table nearby. I pick the stick up so that I can reach. The books aren't meant to be taken down. I run the stick over them as one would run a stick along railings, making a noise. They are not meant to be taken down. Why are they there, then? I can't see the point of that.

I look around the huge empty building, like an aircraft hangar. I don't know what to call it. It is empty. It doesn't echo now. You could hold a hundred dances in here and there would still be room. I look around trying to find something that I can focus on. I see in a corner, a little crystal. It is glinting. I follow my eye to another corner which is a long way off. I see another little glint. I look all around and see a crystal in each corner. I realise for the first time that this is the base of a pyramid. It is so big I didn't notice the roof, the shape, because it is so big. It is inside a pyramid but completely empty. It is the shape of a pyramid.

Knowing pyramids I go to what I feel is the centre. As far as I can judge I am in the middle of the base. I am not quite sure if it is in the middle because it is so big here. I move around in a tight little circle and hit the spot. I know it is the spot. As I stand on it immediately a shaft of light comes down directly over me, as if I have set off some mechanism by being there. It is a gold light just big enough for me to stand in, no more, no less. It is a little blinding, wonderful. The light as it shines over me is like liquid gold. Around the floor I see the light keeps pouring and spreading across the floor and is pouring over me and spreading across the floor. The whole of the floor, the base is covered with light. Rather magical.

It does more than that. As it fills the base it begins to rise up as if somebody is pouring in the gold and it is going to fill the entire pyramid. I am in the centre. I have triggered it. I don't know what this means at all.

"It is necessary to trigger the beginnings. It is necessary for you to be the catalyst so that the input can take place. The input will fill this generator of energy so that when it is full it will generate sufficient energy and light to encompass the entire world. It will continue to generate for it is self-generating. An enormous powerhouse that is inexhaustible for as long as you remain at the centre to trigger this input."

I ask: "What do I do exactly?"

"You will continue to pass the knowledge that you receive by making your entry into our world. As the receptor you will then have what is required to extend this input beyond this generator."

"What does it mean, this staying in place?"

"Keep firm to your ideals. Keep firm to your purpose. Keep firm to your pledge to the spirit world and to humanity. Do not wander away from the centre of your ambitions and your goal. Stay focused upon your purpose and the input will continue to flow. Waver from it and the process will cease."

"That's clear enough."

"Do not doubt that the input is taking place. Do not doubt your abilities. Do not doubt that we are near, ever nearby. Do not doubt the synchronicity, the placements. The doubts of others should not affect your own purpose. The doubts of others are just that. They should not be taken upon yourself, for this would be the equivalent of one apple damaging a whole box load if you allowed this to happen. So continue in your work with confidence and trust in us. Make your contact more in trust than you have been of late. Renew your purpose and your intent."

"Who is speaking to me now?"

"We speak to you as a group of those who have united with each other to focus our minds upon your thought process. We focus our minds so that what we wish to give to the world will pass through you."

NOW I CAN GO STRAIGHT IN WITHOUT USING THE STAIRS METHOD OF GOING DEEPER INTO MYSELF. ***Sometimes I still need to use the stairs but more often do not.***

***

1998

ENTRY INTO THE WORLD OF DEEPER LIGHT

I am in a swirl of green. There are two figures ahead of me, both of them stretching out their hands for me to take. They are merging together in the one colour. I reach my hands to them and they take hold. Their hands are rustling, like taking hold of leaves. Strange, not what I expected at all.

I take hold and it is O.K. just a bit odd, weird, like taking hold of nature itself, two of them. I am not asking questions at the moment. They draw me in between them. With the hands closest to me they put their arms around my back, supporting my back and guiding me forward, as one would a blind person. They make sure I am encompassed. I am being taken, protected, and safeguarded at the same time.

We all move forward. They know where they are going, I don't. I am like a blind person for I can see nothing ahead. They keep on. I am blind for all I can see is light and shadows. We go into some difference in light, a deeper light. How can one have a deeper light? That is the only way I can describe it. It is more intense and yet deeper. Odd! We enter the depth of light, richer, more vibrant, more profound. I don't know the words. I don't know the words to express the feeling. They have still got me fast, gently, and tenderly now. We move forward and I am reminded of care assistants at a bathing place where handicapped people are guided into the water. A feeling of care and attention comes from them. I still don't know what this is all about. It doesn't matter. They are not there to talk to me. Wonderful, wonderful love coming from them. We move on into the depths of this light. We come to a sudden halt as if waiting for something. We are waiting for something. The wall of this depth of light is in front of me, I feel it more than see it. I feel it for I am in it and am merging with it. If I were to be observed, I wouldn't be seen. It is --- I don't know the words. I am standing in the light, of it, for you can't distinguish me in it.

Two doors swing open and there is a blinding flash. The depth suddenly changes. The brilliance makes me stagger. Now I know why they have got me held hard, why they have got me held quite tight. If they hadn't, I'd have fallen. They have got me hard and fast so I remain standing. I can't describe the feeling of the other light. I can't feel anything. It is not hurting. I stand there adjusting, being held upright and moved forward. I step very gingerly to the brilliance. I feel faint. I feel faint.

I am dimly aware of hands holding me. I am in a blur, confusion and yet I must keep talking for the words are my link with my conscious mind. (slowly). T h e w o r d s keep me safe, not that I am in danger. I must keep my thread, my connecting line. I feel so faint. Lost in it. I must keep talking, must keep talking. A hand is put on my head now, holding me, fingers outstretched covering my head. It is light and yet firm. I am charged, charged. The faintness begins to disappear. I feel stronger and can stand on my own now. I can stand without support. They still hold me, firmly. I can feel the grip. I feel their strength but now I am stronger than they. If I wasn't courteous I could release from them. I know they have helped me this far so I wouldn't do that.

I must listen. I don't need to talk to keep the thread. He is doing something with my feet. I feel a liquid over them, warm and soft and silky. It runs between my toes. I can't see anything.

"Welcome. Welcome to the world of light."

I am overcome with emotion.

***

1998
CRYSTAL WOMAN

The colour is green. I am standing on loose pine needles. Soft and spongy. Very comfortable. I can feel them beneath my toes and the soles of my feet. Like walking on a spongy mattress, rather nice. I come to what appears to be a very steep slope, almost vertical. It still has an outdoors feeling. I must go down here. I slide down and the pine needles make it easy to slide. I slide quite comfortably down. I land on both feet at the bottom, down into myself, my innermost being.

I have landed in another world, another time. There is a lot of activity with people going about their various tasks. It is as if I am an observer. Nobody takes any notice of me. It is very strange, very different to our time. The clothes are different. I can't quite describe whether it is future or past. If it is the past it is beyond our knowledge. Everybody seems to have efficient, practical clothing. Sleek and uncluttered, not like our clothing in the past. It is modernistic. Everything is practical. That is the feeling, practical.

I step into a world with clean floors. It is like stepping into another country, no, another world. I walk into it. I must find somewhere I can go in and meet who has the knowledge I have come to seek. That is the purpose of my visit, to meet with the wisdom I have come to find. I want to resurrect knowledge, to bring it back with me, to bring it back in my daily life in my own time.

Two people come up and hold me by the arms for they have seen me. They are not ungentle but are firm. They walk or guide me, one on each side, through the crowds. The crowds can see me now. I am an object of curiosity, unconcerned curiosity. I am walked firmly through a doorway into a front courtyard, up some steps into a rather large door. Yes. I am indoors now, inside. The two men holding me release my arms and allow me to walk where I want. I look around seeing what I can see. There is a woman dressed very tightly, she has a hat. Hat is not quite the right word for it. It a head gear.

She is a very strong woman, very upright and unbending. Before her is an enormous crystal, huge. It is nearly as big as she is. It seems to change shape as I look. One minute it is fat and the next thin. I don't know how she does that. She is controlling this crystal with her mind. Her mind is intensely focussed, and I can see rays coming from her, from her face and from her mouth. She opens her mouth and a blue light like a laser towards the crystal. She does nothing but open her mouth. I know it is done with intense focus of her mind and thought power. She is doing something that only she knows in her mind, only she can see. With sending the light to the crystal, it in turn sends it back, for it is linking. It is connection, like touching a probe. Once touched the current flows both ways. It is a conduit, no more. She receives as well but has instigated the action.

She appears to feel nothing. She appears to feel nothing, so intense is the focus. I am just watching. She will not take her concentration off the crystal to see me or greet me. I don't know what it is she is doing. I don't know more than that. Then she stops. The light stops. The laser beam of blue ceases. She shakes her head as if to free herself. She goes limp, not so upright, not so intense. She leans back in her chair, closes her eyes and then opens them again, normal.

She looks at me for the first time, says nothing. I look at her and don't know what to do.

"Come and visit me whenever you wish. Come and see my work whenever you wish," she says.

"I don't know what you have been doing, so it means nothing to me. It looks good but what is it doing? What is the purpose? What is the purpose of what you have done? I wish to know your motives, your abilities. I wish to know what it is you do and why you do it. What is your objective? That is what I wish to know. How and why? Maybe you can tell me these things. How and why? I will meet you face to face, for you would tell me how and why for the benefit of those in my present world, for the benefit, not of yourself but for myself and those in my world. You will tell me what, how and the purpose so that I will know all that you know. You will awaken in me the memory, the knowledge and the ability."

I don't know what she is doing now. Listening?

***

1998
IN AUSTRALIA – BE OF THE LIGHT

I have red and yellow. It is the colour of fire, active, not static. I am walking over fire, over hot coals. I can see a glowing, just a glow of red and yellow. It pours down like lava. I don't know why I have this colour or where the stream is flowing. I am flowing with it, down and out of the mouth of the Earth, out into the fresh air. I have risen with the embers of the earth. I need to know. I am flowing into all areas of cracks and crannies. I am flowing beneath doors into the houses. As I enter each place, I become solid, real and tangible. I am immovable and cannot be erased. I want to know why I am here in Australia. Why? What do I have to do?

I am now me as I am usually, standing free, looking around in a great hall, vast, huge. An enormous expanse of space but enclosed. If I were to raise my voice it would echo, it is so big. I look up at the vast dome above me, like a vaulted ceiling. I feel very tiny and insignificant. I know I am not alone here. As an observer I am alone, but as me the observed I know I am not, for I feel things around me, pressing me and touching me. Spirit forms surrounding me, spirit beings of all kinds, all kinds, spirits of green, spirits of the rock. There is a word I am trying to get, it won't come.

"Speak to me, Spirits of the Earth, spirits of the Origins of man." I look up and see my dear Andreas, standing there calmly and glowing as always. Smiling gently as he always does, he holds his hand out to me to go to him. I shake myself free from the spirits who are clinging to me, nicely but clinging. I walk towards him calmly, knowing it is right. I put my hand in his in a greeting. He smiles and we walk onwards together through a door he is to show me. He is taking me elsewhere.

I see light, another world, another existence. It is white light, deep light. We walk into it and as we do are lost in it. We become the light that we walk into and can no longer be seen, for we vanish into it. My mind is still active, as is his.

"I want to know what I am doing here, what practical use can I be on this journey? Tell me, what am I to do?"

"The only thing you have to do is be as the Light example. Be of the Light and let others see. To achieve this you must think no wrong, do no wrong. Regard others with no judgement. Regard others as yourself and see them also as of the Light. Trust that all is well. The vibration of this Light in itself has a power to heal, to make well, to rejuvenate. The vibration of this Light consumes all ill, transmutes all dark into light. Being in and off this vibration light transforms all within range, at whatever state of readiness or awareness, all are transmuted. There need be no conscious effort except to think and act according to the highest principles of love and light. It is so simple. You do not need to strive to be, for you are. You cannot help but be."

"On the practical side, why here? Why Jenolan Caves and is that right?"

"The caves are of the Light and they will enhance yours, for their vibration transmutes, transforms and have a beneficial effect. Just to be is sufficient. Simply be."

"What about the psychic surgery, the meeting with - - - and the others?"

"Follow the threads that are given you. The threads will unravel. Follow the threads and you will arrive at the point that was intended for you. Observe, notice. Do not disregard any lead or any information.

Follow all leads. Negative leads will not be given to you. There is a purpose."

"I must finish soon for I am going to be interrupted. I thank you. I thank you."

I knew instinctively that I was to be interrupted in my meditation and so I was.

***

1998
A PORTION OF ME BACK TO THE PAST AND PSYCHIC SURGERY

It is odd that I have a three-way staircase with big broad steps, wide. It splits into three. I have never seen that before. I don't know which one to go down. I decide to use the middle one, it seems more direct. It is a narrower stairway with a rail on either side. I can touch both sides. I decide to go with my right hand on the rail. I can't see anything on either side, just the rail. There is a carpet in blue, like the carpet I have at home. I go down slowly, uncertain. I am not certain of myself anymore.

At the bottom there is the same blue carpet. I walk ahead expecting to find a turn off that must be there. Again there are several ways I can go, all of them looking identical, all of them looking exactly the same. They are spread out like a fan before me. There are seven. I decide to take the very first one on the left-hand side. I walk down trying to get a feel for the place. It is interesting that the walls appear to be made of hands all reaching out. It is made of hands reaching out, not for help but to touch. They just want to touch, no more, no less. It's a greeting by hands all wanting to say hello and wanting to touch. I am confused by this. I don't know what that means. It doesn't matter.

I must keep walking. Soon I come to an opening. No door, just an opening with a curved top to it. I don't have to push a door as it is just an opening. You couldn't put a door into this anyway as it wouldn't fit. I walk through and as soon as I do I am on a glassy surface. It is shiny and quite dark. It is not transparent. It is polished like black marble. I can feel it with my toes for I have taken my shoes off. I look around.

"What is there here? Show me Father what there is for me to learn from. Show me the way forward. Please show me."

I see before me a tunnel, still and inert. It is big enough for it to take me. I go to it and although I can't see what I am stepping into I step in. Inside it is just the right size for me. It is eerie and echoes. I can't see a thing. I go forward into the tunnel feeling with my feet, for I don't know how it goes, up, down, straight? Suddenly there is a whoosh from behind, a push. I am shot forward by something from behind, like a great wind.

Shot into the tunnel. I am now an observer of me as I hurtle down. I watch myself being hurtled down and yet not down, just along, lost, lost in time.

I am still standing here watching and yet I know I am gone. I can't understand that. "Show me what this is about."

"A portion of you has gone back to the past. A portion of you has gone back to relive, to re-experience." I know he is talking of my time in Atlantis.

"Why only a portion of me? I need to have this knowledge here in this consciousness?"

"The portion that has to re-enact will return to you and re-join with you so that you will know. It may take a little while. Be grateful that here and now you are not that portion, for you would be changed by the experience."

"Surely to be changed by the experience is the objective?"

"We wish to add to what you are, not convert you, one life to another. This is the only way that we can add to your current lifetime by sending a part of you.

"How will I know when this has been achieved? How will I know?"

"Re-stabilise yourself my dear. Settle your mind. Be at peace once more. Get your things in order and when you have done this then may you be re-joined. If you are in a state of unease of distress you would not be able to withstand the knowledge. So we say, put your things in order. Re-stabilise yourself. Settle down and be happy. Know that all is in order. You do not need to fret about it."

"I thank you for that." I wonder how long it will take me to re-stabilise. The part of me that was the observer is now walking away from the tunnel. I am still in the place with the black marble floor, or black granite. I don't know the difference, but it is beautiful. It acts like a mirror. Wonderful!

I walk around, not seeing. There is a table, a bench at one end, slightly off to the right. Ahead and to the right. I often see things in that direction. I go towards the bench with my arms outstretched with a feeling of 'at last I've found you'. On the bench lies a body. Head to the right and feet to the left. A body. I can't see who. I can't see an individual face I know. It is simply a body.

Somebody from behind takes my arms, takes my wrists and pushes them forward so that they rest on the body. I am slightly bent over with my hands on the body. What am I to do? The body is inert. It might be dead for all I know. The hands came from behind, though how it manages to reach I don't know. The hands are holding mine in place and all kinds of energies are streaming through, really streaming through hard, not soft, but hard, purposeful. They shoot through the palms of my hands.

My hands are alive. My hands are alive. They sink into the body. The whole hands, both of them are sinking into the body until they are inside up to the wrists. I can't feel anything except the energy. I wriggle my fingers. It is like putting one's hands inside jelly, moving easily and freely. It is not a problem to move. I don't know what I should be doing. I don't need to know what I am doing for the fingers are being guided by the hands that hold my wrists. The energies come through and move my fingers independently. I enjoy the experience of it. There is sharpness and tingling in my palms, like little knives, not unpleasant, just sensation.

I know now that the body is not a body of a human, a living human. It is just a dummy of some kind. It is there to demonstrate for me what is possible. It is an object at this point. I know this is training, reassurance. I am reminded of the mouth-to-mouth teaching where they use a dummy for this. This body is just a dummy for me. I breathe a sigh of relieve for I don't know what I am doing here.

The hands that are holding my wrists pull me out of the body. They appear to be the same, though I can't feel them at all. I can feel energy from the hands that hold me. I stand more upright. The hands that held me release me. I don't know what to do. I have a pain in my chest and my head aches. There is tightness in my chest now. I don't feel good. I must release from this. I feel faint. It is over.

***

1998

In Minnesota. I am told to say these things. "The damages of the Earth will be removed and the Earth will run sweet again." I stand very stiffly at the top of the stairs. I move forward very jerkily, stiffly. Like a dummy, mannequin. I jerk my way down like a doll. I don't understand why. I've been wound up so I can keep going. I go with difficulty. I reach the bottom. I turn my head this way and that as if I am not me. I am not in control. I am simply a physical manifestation, directed by remote control, a toy that is being manipulated. I turn down the passage the controller knows. I go along and find a door. I don't hesitate. A hand comes out and turns the knob. I enter. As soon as I enter the artificial restriction on me drops from me in a heap. I am left standing free, the real me.

My eyes are searching everywhere, seeking something I can fix on. The walls are high and domed. I am in a kind of a dome shaped room, big. There is something over the far end. I must go to it as it is the only thing I can see. It is a long couch, soft and comfortable covered with a beautiful purple cloth. It is the only thing there so I sit on it. It is so long there is plenty of room for others. I am bidden to put my feet up and rest my head on one end. It is a chaise longue.

I lie there and drift. A voice is speaking to me, taking me back, back in time. The voice is taking me. I can hardly hear it for I am drifting back – back – in time. Back to Atlantis. I am drifting, drifting back. I wish to be as I was, with that knowledge now, for me to remember for all time, the assets and the learning. Take me to it. (*Time passes and I have no memory of what happened because there is no recording*)

I can't stay for my physical body is bringing me back. I can't carry on.

***

1998
PSYCHIC HEALING – ALL WORK TOGETHER

I have been given leafy green. I am an observer of me. I am dressed in fresh green. My hands are long and delicate. The pathway, the descent before me has a rail on either side. It is a walkway through the forest. It has been put there specially to take me safely through dense forest. It is made of natural elements. It is all nature. I am reminded of the rain forest in Australia. It is like a swing bridge, not over a chasm but over rain forest. I hold onto both rails, ropes, and walk across. I enjoy it, although it swings.

It is crossing over one area of existence to another. I reach the other side and there is a figure waiting for me. It is impersonal. A guide, just that. He is to lead me down a path. I keep following behind, single file. At least I know I am being taken somewhere. I am being taken. Suddenly we come out from the trees. There is an enormous expanse of sky and beach. It is gentle. The seagulls are crying. The waves are breaking gently on the beach. It is warm, not too hot. We begin to go down onto the beach. The sand is a little slippery, soft and dry. It is not so easy to walk on. I follow, trying hard to keep up. I wonder where we are going.

I come to some steps which go away from the beach. Wooden steps, five or six of them. I go down these at the back of the beach into a little dip. There is a house, a wooden house on stilts. I think of the huts in Malaya where the houses are raised on posts to keep them off the ground, for ants I suppose and other creatures. I mount a ladder, and I am shown into a doorway. Inside it is dark, not too dark.

There are a lot of people sitting cross legged on the floor. They are waiting for me. I have been brought to them. They are not primitive people. They are bright, intelligent, and full of wisdom. I know that their knowledge is far superior to anything I might have, in spite of technology. I ask them why I am here. They make me sit down. They ask me to sit down, for they are also courteous. I notice for the first time there are people lying all around the edges of the room, if you can call it a room.

They are sick. The men sitting on the ground point to them and they point to me.

They say, "Do something."

"I don't know what to do."

"Do something and we will provide the energy. We will provide but you do."

I know this is referring to psychic healing, psychic surgery, maybe.

I ask, "Will you, can you, and can I?"

"If we all work together, we all can. Know that we can and we wish to. Providing you are willing we will all work together."

I thank them for that was what I wished to hear. I get up and go and look at the people lying around the walls. Some of them are terribly injured. Some of them are wasting away. I shake my head and think; it will take a miracle to save these people. I ask for help from the Divine to be able to do something. I don't mind where I am sent.

I come back into the circle and sit in the middle. Each of the men here, shuffle forward so that they are close enough to touch. Each of them puts a hand on my head and on my shoulders. I sit quietly, I sit quietly feeling a change. A change.

***

1998
PROTECTION FROM WIND FORCE

I am standing on the top platform of a fire engine ladder. It is moving about but I am in the little cage, so I don't fall off. There must be a way down for it is a ladder. But there is not. The fireman's lift thing moves itself around to a tall building. I get off onto a balcony. This is most odd. What do I do now? I must go along the balcony till I find a door, a green door. It opens easily for it is not locked. I go into the building. No sound, nothing. No sound. In a room I find a baby, all wrapped up and asleep. It is the baby I have come for. Why did I have to do it this way? There is nobody else here, just the baby. I pick it up and carry it out to the balcony. I go back to the lift and get into the fireman's cage. I am taken down to the ground and the baby is handed over to some people. I don't know what this means or why I have been given this. It makes no sense to me at all. Maybe it has been left high and dry and brought back to earth? I don't know. I shall have to think about this.

It is quite clear that I haven't finished. It seems I am a busy little bee for I walk about. There are lots of people here. I find a shaft going down into the ground. I must go down in there. It is not too deep. I get to the bottom by a ladder. At the bottom there are lots and lots of people milling around. Lots of people being herded down here.

I get sudden realisation. There is a wind coming, a strong force and they have all gone underground to escape being damaged. The baby was left behind and there wasn't time to go up the stairs. The baby had to be brought down so that it too could go underground. Everything has gone below ground to avoid the wind that is coming. There is no time for long preparation though people are still working on the surface, getting people below ground as far as they can. The only safe places lie below the streets. There is not much space. The underground stations are all full. There are so many people, and they can't all get underground. There isn't space enough to get everyone below ground so they must take their chances. There is no time. I am just making sure that people are safe, that they don't start fighting. I am telling them it's alright, it's alright.

I ask. "What is this to do with my request to go back to Atlantis. What has this to do with it? It is not what I was asking for in this meditation. It is not taking me back."

I am told: "It is doing precisely that. It is taking you back to similar occurrences. It is doing precisely what you asked for. It is typical of scenes enacted in those times."

"Why underground? I understood that the ground split. It is the last place that you would want to go."

"All they knew was that there was a nuclear fallout. All they knew was that they should shelter from the blast and from the winds, from the searing winds that they had heard of in other parts. They didn't have much choice, either stay above ground and be seared or blown, or take the chance that their area would not be affected. They had only heard rumours. What else could they do?"

"Why give me a modern setting to tell me this? Why not give the view of that time? I want to know. Why?"

"We use whatever means we can. We also do not wish you to jump immediately to conclusions so that you feel you are inventing the story."

***

1998
MIND ONLY – TO SELECTIVE BREEDING IN ATLANTIS

I am going down steps very quickly, in a hurry. I am going down, down into my deep unconscious. As I go I can feel energies building up in me, as if I am losing myself and gaining another. These steps go down into the bottom of a hole, into another world. I am in a void. I am not on anything or surrounded by anything. I am simply there. A mind only. I am a mind only, a consciousness. My thoughts take me where I wish.

I wish to have knowledge awakened in my consciousness of the Atlantean time. That is my objective now. I see Andreas, I feel it is him.

My mind has been with him. Although I am simply mind, he can still reach me and I can still see. He takes me with him for I am protected by him. My mind travels back.

I am seated at a big heavy glass table. It looks like glass for I can see right through it. Spread out before me are documents and photos or drawings. Faces, people. I am sifting and spreading them all out. I am looking at them all. I am choosing, making a selection. I don't know what for. Some are being rejected and some of them are being selected. They appear to be men.

I am a heavy woman. Large, physically strong and heavy. I am bigger than most in height. I stand and tower over all. I am very tall, enormously tall. I move away from the glass table and walk around to the end. I come round to the other side. There is a flight of steps. Just a little flight, 4 or 5 steps perhaps. I go down. These are my private quarters. There I have sexual relations with somebody, who it is doesn't matter.

I ask Andreas to take me away from this. I want to go where I can do some good. He takes my hand and we go into another place. There are quite a few children here. They are my children, my children that I have born. There are many children, many. I produce them easily, but I am as a mother to them. I love them no matter how many there are for I do not have to look after them. There are people who do that, to attend to their needs. I have children almost like a machine. I have many children.

The photographs on the table were about selecting fathers for future children. Selecting them for their genes, for their abilities. This is selective breeding. I tell Andreas this is not what I need now. I need to know how to materialise and de materialise. I need these secrets and that knowledge.

***

1998
ON THE BOOK

There is rush matting on the floor, on the stairs. I am reminded of Singapore, of the jungle. It is hot and steamy outside. The rush matting goes all the way down. I don't have to go very far. Just a few steps and yet it feels a long way down. There are a lot of people at the bottom of the steps. They are milling around and making it difficult to go forward. I tell them I have to go forward and can't be waylaid. I push my way through them trying to ignore their hands. They appeal to me to stop and talk.

I move on into the jungle. I leave the path and go into the undergrowth. It is not easy. Why I am doing this I have no idea. As I go, I get a weight and an ache, a pain across my shoulders for no apparent reason. I am not carrying anything. It is as if something is pressing into my shoulders, hard pressure. It is quite painful. I keep going through the undergrowth, getting a bit scratched here and there, getting hot and sweating. It is steamy. I push my way through a very thick part here. I come out to a clearing, as I knew I would.

There is a stream. The undergrowth has been hacked away. It is not a natural clearing, it has been cleared specially. There is somebody by the stream, bending over, looking into the waters. Not that you could see anything in the waters for they are moving, not still. It is the movement that keeps them free.

I go to the man. He is dark skinned. I feel as if I am looking at the face of the aboriginal painting I have. If it is not him it is very much like him. This is an aboriginal which is a surprise to me. We are talking of jungle, tropics and yet I have an aboriginal face here. He is an old man, thin, bony and doesn't say much. He stands up and beckons me to go with him, which I do. He is going to show me something. He puts his fingers to his lips, telling me to keep quiet. We go along the path which leads to another clearing. There are children playing, play acting a role, which children do all over the world. Doctors and nurses, mammas and daddies.

They are engrossed in their play. He tells me to be quiet. He puts his fingers to his lips again. I can't ask him any questions, but I want to. I mustn't, because he wants me to be quiet. They are enjoying themselves and don't know we are there. If they knew we were there they would feel inhibited. We must keep out of their game so that we don't spoil it for them. The children amazingly turn into the pages of my book. All separate pages of my book. They are all playing, dancing about and enjoying themselves, it seems. I am told to keep quiet again and leave them to their play.

I ask, "How can the book ever get published if I leave it?" The aboriginal mentally tells me that when they are tired of their play they will settle down. They will settle into their correct order. Then I can go and pick it up and it will be O.K. I wonder how long it will take them to be tired of play. The aboriginal shakes his head as if to say, all these questions. Why don't you just let them be?

I ask now, in my mind, is this the first book or the second book? I am not getting an answer.

***

1998

NATURE ALWAYS WINS – THE POWER OF LIGHT

The ground is rocky, volcanic, hard on the feet. I pick my way over trying to get a firm foothold. I didn't expect this. I asked to go to Atlantis.

I didn't expect this. I am having to go down, bend over and hold on with my hands to stay secure on my feet. It is very hard going. There has to have been a volcanic eruption here. It is cool so it is not too recent. It hasn't had time to weather down. It is still extremely rough. I make my way across asking to go to smoother ground. I quickly come to the edge of the flow, for that is what it was.

I am on grass now, on the slopes of a hill or mountain. I am on slopes for my feet are at an angle. Keep walking. This is not what I wanted to see or where I wanted to be. I am told I must see this. I must know this. So? - I could find this scene anywhere in this time.

"What does it tell me? What are you telling me?

"Man has long had the power to create his world according to his actions. Man has long had the power to activate nature, to interact with nature, to affect nature. Man has long since, long past learnt how to manipulate nature, but we tell you that nature will win in the final outcome. You, Man, may think that you have all things at your fingertips. You may think that you have the ability to order things according to your wishes, but it is nature that has the last word. It is nature that is the master, even over man and his ways. Nature will not be subdued, will not be dominated. Nature's will is stronger than anything you can perceive."

"I want to know why this (meditation) is not answering my question and taking me where I wanted to be? I want to have the knowledge that I had in times of Atlantis so that I may use this knowledge. I want to know how."

In answer to that my mind is taken to my hands again. I look at my hands. There are lights coming from them, spears of light coming from every fingertip. The whole of my hand is glowing so that the glow is obscuring the hand itself. I put my hand out to touch the land. My hand disappears into the ground.

"The Power of the Light is strong. The Power of Light is the force. Remember that. The Power of the Light is the energy. The Power of the Light."

"Does the Light know what it is to do?" I ask.

"The Power of the Light has intelligence within it. It contains knowing. It does not operate in words. It operates in simply knowing the order of things. It knows the correct order of things. It knows the perfection of all cells and wherever it touches perfection reigns. Where it reaches, perfection reasserts itself. It can do nothing else but for it is touched by the Power of the Light. All you need to do is carry that light within you and direct it where it is needed. It is that simple."

I think about that one.

"To carry the Power of the Light you must be of the Light. To enable that Light to flow through you must be of the Light. By that we mean you must behave as of the Light. Be the perfect being that you see so often. Do not view but be. Do not be just the observer but become. Of course this requires dedication, and action according to Light's principles. You must earn the Power of the Light by being worthy of it. You will know, you do know how to be worthy of being a vehicle for the Power of the Light. All men, if they so desired and so acted, could be vehicles for this Power of the Light. Some have it already. You will know these when you meet them for there will be a glow that shines through the physical form and out so that eyes can see. If you will you carry the Power of the light within you will be perfection in mind, heart and in all ways."

"That is a very high thing to aspire to, not easy for us to have all of that. Is it possible to have some of that light while we strive for the wholeness of it?"

The Light that is glowing from around my feet, speaks. "Think of it as a darkened room and when one lights a candle, the light is there but may not fill the entire room. It allows one to see where one is going. If you place more candles within that room the light becomes brighter, and the going is easier. You may see more detail. When full light has been turned on you may see clearly. When full brightness is placed within that room then walls may disappear. You would not see them, for the brightness would obscure the physical, you would not see the physical. You would see only light, and the light would penetrate the structure that forms the room. That is an answer to your question. Whatever light you can arrive at, that you can achieve is of value. Whatever light you have within you is helpful.

Do not sit in darkness. Do not live your life in darkness for you would see nothing, you would know nothing, and you would interact with nothing. You may achieve the fullness of obliterating light, obliteration of the physical. Light is what should be aimed for. This is what should be aimed for at all times, not merely that of Atlantis, but for all of your existence in time."

"It is a lovely answer. How do I achieve that now? How do I achieve that vision?"

"We have already answered that question."

***

1998
HEAL CHILDREN OF THE PAST

This is very odd for I am wrapped in a palm leaf, an enormous leaf, huge. I am cocooned in it. I have hopped my way down the stairs for I can't do anything else. I look a bit like a penguin. I can't put out my hands to touch anything because I can feel my fingers held fast against my legs.

I hop down and before I get to the bottom I turn into a bird, a kingfisher. I fly off. I feel nature is having a say here. The kingfisher flies up and settles on a branch of a tree. It dives down into the water below it, underneath the water. It brings up a fish it has seen from a distance. I haven't got a clue what this is telling me. We have had nature and the water. I don't know. Am I wrapped up in things?

I don't know what this is telling me. I feel it must be a very symbolic message, one I must give attention to later. I am now transferred to a normal me, walking along, looking, looking to see where I can enter. I find an opening, which is a concealed opening. It has big leaves hanging down, jungle type leaves covering it. I can push these aside and enter. It is concealed but I knew it was here. I step in through them.

There are lots of native men, brown men sitting on the ground. Old men, young men. I can't see any women at all. As I go in they scramble to their feet. Why do they do that? They are all standing now. They come forward and pull me by whatever they can hold, my hands, my clothes. Some of them are behind me pushing me. They clearly want me to go with them.

They take me far back away from the entrance. It is not exactly a cave, an opening made, an enclosure. We move back, back away from the entrance to the far corners. Lying on the ground are children, sick children. They are too weak to get up. Some of them are dying. They are the children of these men. There is much wailing from the mothers. The children are there, helpless and hopeless too. The men and the women have tried and failed to help. They look to me and point, making sure that they can see. They wave their hands over the children. They don't speak but are trying to tell me this is what I must do. I must heal the children. I must heal the children. The children are of the past, as are these people. They are of the ancient times. I must heal the children.

If I heal these children now then the future that we are in will be improved. Very strange and I don't understand it. I must heal the past, their past, not my past. I don't understand, but I must do it. I walk around and through them, passing my hands over each child, even the ones that are dying. I do simply that, no more. I pray for them to be better. I pass my hands over the mothers too. All of them. That is all I do. I pass my hands over them, and I pray and ask for help and assistance.

As I pass my hands I am weaving a blanket of covering, to cover them. I am making it with the passing of my hands. I can see streams of vapour coming from my hands as I pass along. Vapour, something coming from my hands. I don't know what it is exactly, but you can see it. As it leaves my hands it drifts down and settles over everything, forming a film, a blanket, a filmy blanket over everybody. They are covered with this now, all of them. As I look the covering seems to dissolve into the forms, soaks in. Like water droplets on the earth it is absorbed by it until you cannot see it.

They begin to stir and show more signs of life. They begin to get up, to stretch and smile and to cry too, for they now feel whole and well. The mothers gather the children to them. There is a reunion. The fathers stand proudly around. There is rejoicing. The babies are picked up and hugged, fed, for they are rejuvenated, renewed, re-energised. There is rejoicing. I walk away from them and turn back towards the entrance. That is why I came. I still don't understand it but that is why I came.

***

1998
SOUL RESCUE

I am at the top of stone steps. They are quite deep, not very wide with sharp edges like concrete. It is outside. I can't see the bottom. I go down. There is a rail at the bottom. It is not meant for comfort, this. Each step is deep. It is quite difficult but not impossible. I can't see the bottom. There is no particular colour. It is just grey. There is greyness about everything here. As I do down it gets darker. Although I started outside I am in some sort of hole. There is darkness about everything. I get to the bottom. There are concrete floors again. It is smooth as if it has been laid especially and fairly recently too I'd say. It hasn't had time to get dirty or marked by a lot of feet or the weather. It is quite clean. The walls are very bare, again concrete. Very austere. No warm human touch.

I turn off to the left. The same thing! A corridor, freshly done, very barren and stark. I come to the only door. I am reminded of a barricade, very forbidding. It is not meant for just anybody to enter here, only those who know must enter here. It is like a safe door with bars across, reinforced. There is a padlock on it. The key is still in the padlock which strikes me as a little odd. I unlock it and take the key out. I go in.

I vaguely see people or shapes. There is something here. It is very dark. It is as if whatever or whoever is here is holding its breath. They are all a little scared. They are scared of me. They don't know who I am, or who has come through this door. I can almost feel them cowering back against the walls. I just feel them there. I can't exactly see them. They are just shapes, shapes. I can't tell if they are adults or children, people huddling against the walls. They can't get away any further from me than that. They are very frightened of me.

I walk very slowly. It is so dark in here. As I have done once before, I know I must get their trust. I sit down in the middle, on the floor cross legged. I lean forward slightly so that I don't tip back. I sit and I wait. I simply sit and ask for help. Meditate and ask for help. Meditate and ask and draw in the forces of light. The light is needed here. The light is needed here. I am drawing in the light and asking the Divine Beings to shed their light in this dreadful place. I ask that the fear be taken from those around me.

I sit and a wide beam gradually intensifying in light and strength shines down on me. It is wider than me and casts a pool of light around me. So I am seen and they can see me clearly, though I can't see them. I sit quietly with my eyes closed, waiting, waiting and asking for help from the angels. I feel little touches on my cheek and my hair, like little butterflies. I know that the beings of light are here, for it is a gentle and comforting, reassuring touch. I continue to sit and wait and wait.

I hear movements from those who have hidden themselves against the wall. They shuffle forward slightly. I can feel them coming on hands and knees, not standing but shuffling forward. I am surprised how many old people are here. Old and haggard. There are the young macho boys, rough characters. They are here too. We have the pious ones with their noses in the air, supercilious ones, and frightened ones, unsure now, where they were sure before. Because a few have moved forward the others do. They creep closer and closer, still not standing, still afraid.

I continue to sit and wait. I wait for them all to come and settle. They too wait. Movement continues as they move in closer. They are on the edge of the beam of light. They haven't entered it yet. Their faces are lit up with the glow as if sitting round a fire. They daren't enter the light; they are touched by it but are afraid to come too close. They draw a little closer and can come no more without entering the pool of light, without getting close to me. They don't want to get too close for they don't know who I am. They wait and I can see their faces. All kinds.

I turn my head to look. This frightens them, the movement frightens them. They are frightened, terrified of what will come next. I just look and smile at them, hoping the smile will reassure them. I wait and smile and ask again for help from the angels. Suddenly the beam of light that surrounds me widens. It expands into a larger beam and all those sitting around are caught in it now. They are blinded. This frightens them even more. They cover their faces.

They gradually realise that the light hasn't hurt them. It hasn't hurt them at all. Their eyes little by little become adjusted. They look at each other for the first time. They regard each other, some with interest, some with loathing, and some with tears running down their faces. But they are taking notice. They are taking an interest in something other than themselves at last. It has been a long time since they took an interest in anything other than themselves.

I stand. This takes them by surprise. It doesn't seem too bad for now they are interested. They stand for the first time for a long time. They stand up. The light expands even more. It is light from the angels. It fills the room and shows the bare walls. One by one the people there begin to fade. They dissolve, they disappear, fading and not to be seen. The room is now empty, and I am standing alone. The job has been done and I now can return. I thank all those Divine Beings and cry.

***

1998
GUARDIAN ANGELS

I have been given silver. I am going down steps which are ribbed, like reeds placed along the ground. There is nothing to hold on to. It is a little unsteady. The reeds, the ribs of which are dark green and very flimsy, almost not solid at all. It is precarious going down here but these are the steps I have. These are the steps I go down on in trust. I go down in trust, as I must. Nothing to hold on to. My hands are outstretched for balance more than for anything else. Eventually I am at the bottom. Now what?

There is a very steamy feel, tropical, very hot and humid. I can hear the insects in the jungle, the high-pitched screeching. I feel quite giddy. I feel very giddy as if I am going to go right off. My head is spinning, spinning- - - (faintly now) I feel weird.

I stand still for quite a long time. I can feel insects biting. My nose is running. I can't stand here forever. I begin to move off in any direction. It is just jungle. I move forward and find my way through. I don't know where I am going. I push my way through. It is tough, tough going. I come to what appears to be an easier way. It is not even a pathway. I push through the thickness which is everywhere and break through into a space. It is a natural clearing, not man made in any way. An open space at last. There is even grass.

I stand sweating and ask to be shown what I need. I ask for proof of what I am. Immediately two enormous figures appear before me, huge giant figures stand before me. They are fighting angels all kitted up with their swords. They are fierce. Lovely faces, but there to do battle for me. They are there to protect and fight for me. Why I don't know. Their role is to look after me. I don't understand. They have come to look after me and to protect me. I don't understand why, and I still don't know who I am.

"You are our little brother."

"Brother? I am a woman."

"You are a woman in the flesh. But you are our little brother."

"Oh. And what is my name?"

"Matthias. You are Matthias."

"Can you prove this to me? Give me proof."

***

1998

ANOTHER ASPECT OF SELF - conquer the world with love.

I have wooden stairs and am dressed in ordinary clothes. Wooden rail to hold on to, not even polished. There are bare boards on these stairs, like an empty house. I must go down. The walls are bare plaster, not even painted. I don't know if this is a new house that hasn't been done up yet or an old one that hasn't been lived in. I don't know. There are no furnishings at all. I walk forward and turn off.

It is surprisingly a long corridor, lots and lots of doors stretching as far as the eye can see. How am I to know which is mine, for heaven's sake? I walk along and feel for I put my hand out on either side. I feel them as I arrive at them. I come to one which has a different feel to the fingertips. It is silky, warm and silky. It is quite different to any others. This intrigues me. I look for the handle. It is a beautifully small ornate knob. Not a big thing, more for a cupboard door. I turn it and go in.

Over on the far side, hanging on the wall are gold chains, pendants, chains of all sizes and weights. They are beautiful, lots of them, as if this is a place where they are hung when they are not being used. I ask what I am to do. I see one which strikes me more than the others. It is a beautiful, heavy red stone. It stands out from the others. It is magnificent, a very deep bright red. It draws me. I take it off the hook and put it round my neck. It feels good. What does this mean?

I take a step back from the other chains and separate myself from them. I feel I am going to keep this pendant. It is alright to take it. I turn around, away from the others. I see a man beckoning. Beckoning! I can't see him clearly. As there is nothing else to see I walk towards him. As I approach, he holds out both his hands and grasps me by the elbows in a greeting. I know this is alright. I thought for a moment he was going to kiss me on both cheeks. He looked as if he wanted to, as if he might. I wouldn't mind. He doesn't do that. Why doesn't he do it? He Is warm and friendly.

We stand with arms held for a little while then he releases me and turns away. I must follow him. - - - There is a chair. Oh dear! This is a chair up on a little platform. I feel an investiture here. This is an investiture, whatever that means. Oh, to be invested with something. I am to sit on the chair.

I sit on it feeling rather embarrassed, rather silly in my ordinary clothes, out of place. My feet don't even reach the ground. They are swinging a bit off the ground. I must look rather silly here. He doesn't think so. He hands me a rolled-up parchment. He hands me a glowing globe. It is the world. It is lit up from inside. He puts that into my lap, not into my hands but on my lap. It is quite safe. It doesn't roll anywhere. Then he puts a blue cape over my shoulders. The blue shimmers, shimmers beautifully, as if it is alive. I feel better having it on while sitting in the big chair. It is more appropriate. He makes the sign of the cross on my forehead. As he moves his finger I can feel the energy from it. The energy impresses itself in my brow in the sign of the cross, an equal cross, equal arms. I feel giddy, I feel a little sick. I don't know if I can stay with this. I am going away----away.

(**In a new powerful voice**) I am transformed. I pick up the globe and hold it aloft for everyone to see. My clothes begin to glitter. Suddenly not ordinary, mundane. I am another being. I am transformed. I have a new energy. I must use this energy to greater purpose.

"You have become another. You have now a greater knowledge. You have ability to change things, many things, many forms, many ideas. Work for the Light and do not forget who you are. You are many things, many aspects of self. You choose which aspect you wish to present, to use. You have a choice of many aspects of self. Use them wisely."

I climb down off the chair with legs a little shaky, a little wobbly. I still feel me, ordinary, everyday me. The man, the Being takes my shoulders and kisses me now on both cheeks. He couldn't do it before. In some strange way I feel as if I am a man. I don't look like a man but I can feel, I can see a man being kissed here. The man is me. I am a strong heavy man, very powerful and yet this has to be me. For he or I have just come off that seat, that chair. He is like a knight in armour, invincible, invincible. Now what? Now what do I do?

"Go out and conquer the world."

"That's a bit strong."

"Conquer the world with love."

I feel a little sick and had better come back.

***

1998

BE WITH NATURE

I am bathed in a sea of sunny bright yellow. I am almost lost in it for I am of the same yellow. It is beautiful and fresh, sunny, clear. I have a great lightness of spirit. I trip lightly down the stairs, skipping, feeling joyous. It is not important what the stairs are made of this time. Everything is bathed in golden light. I arrive very lightly, like alighting at the bottom. Even here everything is bathed in a golden light. It is a glorious feeling. I move along and into the passage. It is like moving into gold. There is nothing of a texture anywhere. I could be anywhere. I keep moving forward, seemingly because I must move. I enter my space.

Here the colour is more of autumn, deeper, rusty colour. Golden but with a deeper shade. I quieten down a little, I feel a little more reserved. There is some feeling of awe. I look around. I am in a wood. There is a little fawn, creatures are around me. Nature, natural things. There is a quieter, quieter feeling.

A man steps out from the trees. I almost laugh for he is covered with leaves, autumn leaves. It is as if he is dressed up for camouflage. But he is always dressed up this way. He is a man of nature. The leaves are him though he is a big strong man. I am reminded of the Green Giant but this is not the Green Giant. The man is big and is a part of nature, mainly a symbolic figure. But he is very much alive. If I touched him I would touch the leaves. I know he is solid underneath. We stand and look at each other. He is amused. You can see the amusement at my impression of him. He won't laugh but he is amused, there is no doubt of that.

He turns and I follow. We scrunch our way through the leaves. We come to a little brook, just about enough water to go over the stones. He tells me to drink, to drink from it. I get down to the ground and cup my hands to the water and just about manage to fill them. I drink. As I do I change. I change somehow. I want to go away from me, out of me, leaving the physical me asleep somewhere. I am free. I am free now.

I seem to drift and lift out of me. It is rather nice. I am free. I can go where I want. - - - Something is happening. My physical body is feeling things. I have a headache and I feel sick and yet I am free too. I don't understand this. If I am free why am I feeling physical discomfort? I don't understand that. I don't understand what all this is telling me. It is very nice but what am I learning from it?

This man puts his hand out, touches me. I know in that instant that I must have more connection with nature. I have kept away from it. I need to be with nature more if I am to experience all things. I know what he is telling me now.

***

1998

IN ABADIANIA – Brazil – an agreement

High guides are with me. I ask to be with the spirit doctors, to see what they do. I ask to leave my body to be with them and remember. They take my right hand and walk me round the crowd meditating in the room. They wave my hand at several of them.

I get closer and closer to Joao's spirit, closer and closer to him and join into his body, entering his body along with the doctors. The line of people pass by. I watch several souls, all kinds. I feel great compassion, almost crying. I do not heal anyone but watch. One I remember was deaf – a lady. I am told to blow through one ear to the other. A cloud, a mist came out. To recognise her afterwards, for proof I was told she has a fringe straight across – shoulder length hair – dark brown. I straighten the fingers of one arthritic lady – old.

I even agree to use the knife if required. Several entities pass through me. Try to remember, try to hold onto it. Said I would do this work, was happy to do so. I see acres of people suffering. Need to help. I can't hold it any longer.

I must remember this is just one part of my mission. There is more, equally important, if not more. I am reminded on this journey, that the people on this planet are our responsibility, as we have created them and now must look after them. All peoples. We cannot create children and then abandon them while they are still young. We entered into this agreement.

***

2000

I am standing in red, strong brilliant red. It is not a weak affair. It is the colour of blood. There is a ladder in front of me. I can't see where the ladder is leading but I must get on it and start to climb. I feel the rungs beneath my feet and under my hands as I grasp the next rung. It is an ordinary ladder, but I can't see anything except the ladder, so it is a bit scary. I can't even see the wall that it is propped against. I get what must be near the top and find I am getting out onto a ledge or platform of some kind. I am up high but where I don't know. It feels spacey as if only the platform is there. I can't see anything around it. Total trust is needed for this. I am higher, symbolic I know, but much higher.

I hear the sound of music like trumpets blowing, but not Celestial trumpets – music, a tune, songs and things, playing something specific. As it is the only thing I go towards the sound, making sure I don't step off into nothing, making sure the ground is in front of me, something to stand on. Now there are voices calling me, calling my name. I head in that direction. I am blind to my surroundings. Head on, head on, keep following. The voices now. Activity beyond my sight. They want me to join in the activity. What is this telling me?

I come to an area that is brightly lit. I walk into it and see lots of things and people – active – lots of bustling and yet it is calm and peaceful at the same time. Everybody knows what they are doing. They are all busy but knowing what they are busy at. There is no confusion here. A man whose head was bent over something looks up and beckons a finger at me to come near. He is an old man but heavy set and broad, solid and dependable. I walk towards him knowing he is fine. He reminds me of Neptune. He looks at me with beautiful blue eyes, steady. So calm he is, so calm. You look at him and know that he knows everything. He knows what I am thinking. He knows me inside and out and it is not unsettling at all. There is love in his face and it makes me want to cry. Such love makes me want to cry. Love like this does not exist on the Earth plane. Love such as this is rare in a physical world.

"You will soon be in this world of love, though you will not die. You will experience the world of love while still in physical form. Wouldn't that be wonderful if all were to demonstrate this? How absolutely wonderful that would be."

"What can I do to help bring this about? I don't seem to be doing very much on a big scale but just organising my own activities."

"You are going to be given the larger work. Rest awhile for you will soon be plunged into the wider field. Rest awhile. You will soon be taken up into a larger plan. All that has gone before has been preparation for this. Don't be anxious. Open yourself daily to us. Open yourself to us daily. Do not miss for we have some information to give you on a regular basis now."

I must, I must, I must. I want to. I will communicate daily and carry on with trust. This lovely man takes my hands and raises them to his lips and kisses them. It is a gesture of affection for a child. I feel like a child before him. It is a wonderful feeling to be the child instead of the adult. It is nice to have someone who cares.

***

2002
BOTH SIDES OF VEIL

I am in a warm climate, feet in sandals and very skimpy short brown dress, more like rags. I walk forward for I do not have to go up or down. It is a dusty and dirty road under hot sun. I keep walking forward. I feel I am in Africa. A tall long lanky man comes to meet me. He is a tall African leader, a spokesman or whatever. He has come out to meet me. He shakes my hand. He has been expecting me, Mgulu. I don't know if this is his name or a greeting. That is what he is saying. We walk together with people all around us. It is a place I have to go to but it doesn't tell me where. The thought Mbuto comes in but I don't know if this is right or not.

I go down a very narrow path. Sometimes I have to squeeze through. I am very slim. Anything larger could not follow. I find another opening on the right which I expect to find for I know it is there…It has always been there. I have been here before. I go through squeezing between the rocks into what seems to be a big crack. Once I get through it is a big place. Nothing large can get through here and although I know this place like home I don't know why I am here now.

I look around looking for something, some clue. Two big men come from the back and greet me. They know me. They are huge, rough men. I feel I have gone back in time, back to time. They call me Hedwyn.

"You survived then in basic conditions, and you will survive again. So will many others."

"I don't understand. What about the new dimension? I don't understand. I need clarification."

"You will exist simultaneously in the next dimension and in this dimension. You will travel to and fro helping those that remain here. You will be aware of both sides of the veil. You will be invulnerable. Nothing can touch you for you exist in the next dimension also."

"Is this true for me now in this present moment?"

"It has been true for a long time. You are of another realm. You know this already. Your problem is that you have not made contact more closely with the other dimension. You are able to do this and travel freely from one to the other. Why do you not take the opportunities that are offered to you? What holds you here?"

"Maybe I can't return to here where I am needed."

"This has been set many, many years ago. You are here specifically to assist. You cannot be barred entry. You can travel to and fro. Do you not know this? If you do this you will bring gifts from the other dimension that you may use in your present one here. When you get the next opportunity to enter then do so. Do not fear that you will not return. Travel freely from one to the other."

This message may have come because I had an entry point shown me and was invited into while in Australia walking in national forest land. I was not expecting it and not in an altered state and ran from seeing the portal in the land. I have regretted it ever since.

***

2000

I walk along, underground between dark rock walls. There are rainbow glints here and there. I begin walking on an upward path and come out high up on a craggy mountain, well above the tree line.

A voice said: "Why are you looking for a way down? Why don't you stay awhile and enjoy the wonders here?"

I do and look at astounding scenes of beauty. Then a huge bird flies down to me. It is larger than I. It is a bird man with an eagle's head but a man too. My thoughts immediately fly to Interplanetary Being Horus and Osishoo. He speaks a language where I can't understand the sounds. He wraps his arms/wings around me and flies up with me. He sets me down high up in a hollowed out space – like an egg. We stay in this comfortably enclosed. He wraps me right inside his wings, like a mother bird does to her chick.

He said, and I understood: "My little one. You are always protected by me and many others and will come to no harm. Horus and Thunderbird and I are of the same place. We are the same." I knew this was Osishoo and that I was his child. I feel enormous love.

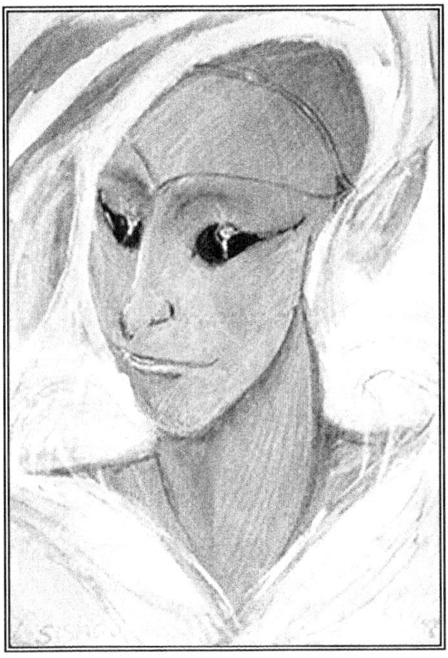

Osishoo

***

2000

I have been taken up to see Maitreya who looks rather different to my expectations. I ask about Solomon. I wish to see what he looks like for I know he is there. I am surprised to see he is a very large man, very imposing one. A good feeling but much larger than I expected. For some reason I always thought of him before as being small. He is imposing, strong and virile, a fine figure. Something is happening to my vibration and I hear the voices:

"Hold her. Hold her down. This is powerful stuff."

It is odd because I can view this. I can see my form undergoing this and yet I am still here watching. Transformation is taking place of my form, etheric body, I don't know what to call it. I go quiet. I stop resisting.

Those holding me, Solomon and Matreiya step back as there is no need to hold me anymore. I change before their eyes and before mine. I grow and am a space being. I am humanoid but not as I am as Shirley. I am not of the planet Earth. I have a large head which appears to be too large for the rest of me. I am changed. The eyes have clear vision. I can see differently now. My eyes are not as they were. There has been a reversal back to what I was. This is for the better. It is not deterioration. The deterioration came when I entered human form. Now I have taken back my form. I can now enter this soul wise when required. I don't understand the process here. I don't understand how I can be two things.

***

RA SPEAKS

I feel a great presence within me. He speaks: "All things are possible. All things within the mind are made manifest. You can manifest whatever it is that you desire sufficiently. There are no limits. There have been no restrictions put upon your mind. It is time that you realised that whatever you desire and put before you can be made in reality, is made in reality. If you desire peace for your world then construct it. Do not take the view that it is impossible. All things are possible. All things can be done. Know this to be so. You are with me on my beam of light.

"**I am Ra** and I speak to you as one who travels the light. You are one who carries the light, the one who assists me in my work for mankind. Know that you travel afar to many corners of your universe. Know that you travel far in your consciousness. Know that your soul has no limit in time or space. You will learn to take your physical form with you when you engage in these journeys. Believe this to be so and it will be. You are in no danger of losing yourself. You are in no danger from adverse realities. Do not give attention to those who would cast doubt and fear in your mind. While you have me within you are at all times safe. You will experience me again in Egypt. I will present to you Thoth."

***

It was while I was staying on Aruba in January 24th 2000 that I had a message connecting this incident. Again I was not meditating or in a deep state. I was trying to get ants out of my clothes. I was told to write, and this is the very powerful message I got:

> **Shifting sands, shifting sands. Smooth movement of land, vast land. Nothing is recognisable, nothing is left of former times. Move on, move on. The new is fresh, the new is welcoming you. Forget the past, forget the now. Look ahead. It is almost here. Can't you see it coming? Do not be caught unawares. Do not waste time. Get your mind settled in peace and readiness. The change is for you. You will do this with no company alongside except me. I am Ra, the greatest of all. Come with me. Be with me on my beam of life and you will know all.**

***

2000
AFRICA

I am standing in elephant grass. I am assuming that where there is elephant grass there are elephants. It is very tall but this is the path I must tread. I wend my way through since I can't see over it. I keep walking because it can't go on for ever, not even elephant grass. I clearly am in Africa for this is not India because I come to a round hut, typically African. The grass is all around it and is set in a clearing. You would never see it from a distance. You would have to be up close or in the air to see this hut, no, a collection of huts now.

I walk up to the first hut that I can see. No people are present, nobody I can see at least. I go inside. It is very dark. I can't see for the moment. Then I see two children on the far side, a boy and a girl. They are nervous of this white stranger. I don't think they have seen a white person before. Their eyes are adjusted to the dark and mine are becoming that way. They crouch against the wall of the hut. There are no adults, just the children.

It is no good me trying to reassure them for they don't understand. I sit down on the floor and wait. I wait for their curiosity to get the better of them. Time passes. Eventually they get up from where they are sitting and begin to come nearer. I see they are both crippled, maimed. They were not born like that. They have been maimed. One is minus a foot, the other one minus an arm. They are not in good shape. They make their way towards me, eyes big and round. Because I do not move they feel comfortable but are still nervous. I try not to look directly at them because it is too confronting. I look at the ground and see them out of the corner of my eyes if I can.

I put my hand out and look at them and smile. They are not sure. I keep my hand extended. The little girl puts out her hand and touches my fingers to see if I am real. She explores my fingers with her little hand, the one she has left and begins to feel my hand more, then my arm and shoulder. Because I don't move she comes closer and starts to touch my face. The little boy watches and doesn't want to be outdone by his sister. So he too comes forward, touches me and then becomes bolder for clearly I am not going to harm them. They allow me to give them a hug. I draw them into my arms and rock them back and fore. They start to cry, then they begin to sob. The sobbing gets louder and more intense, deep, deep sobs from the very core of their being.

I look up and find that adults are there after all. They have heard the crying of the children and have come to see what has caused it. They must be used to it by now. I am told they are not used to it for when there is deep suffering there is no crying. There is silence and patient resignation. They go beyond crying. I smile at the adults as they stand in the doorway and they come into the hut, as many as can crowd in.

(crying with emotion now) I don't know what I can do here, except to be here and give them something from the outside world that isn't going to hurt them. This is a place that is not reached by aid association, for this place is hidden and is not reached by the outside. I ask spirit if I can bring some hope, some light by being their contact. I ask for the rainbow bridge that has been suggested to reach down to this place and for it to be a bridge for the angels and the light so that they can travel this bridge when they wish. I ask for something better for them.

I am to take them. I am to lead them to this bridge and to encourage them to go over it to the arms of the angels. I am to go there.

***

2000
ANGELS/BIRDMEN

I am standing at the top of a hill looking out over vast plains. It spreads as far as the eye can see on a clear day. There are no mountains, but flat all the way round going off into the haze of distance.

"What am I doing up here?" A great bird comes flying out of the distance right up to me and alights next to me. It is a man bird, a bird man. He is taller than I am and speaks to me.

"You are to come with me. You are to go where I go."

Knowing I cannot fly I climb upon its back and hold on tight to its feathers. I lie down across its neck and put my arms around it holding on tight. I know it is a man and yet it is a bird that flies. Interesting! Maybe that is where the stuff of angels comes in.

Maybe. Now that is a thought that has not come to me before. It takes off and soars up higher before it flies off sideways into space. It flies over the vast plain, so high that the details below are not clear. It is too high;

it is too swift. We appear to be flying sideways which is strange. It is covering great areas, going a very long way. I don't know where we are going to arrive. I seem to be on the bird for a long time, so long I am getting sleepy. It is similar to when you are on a bus on a long journey you eventually doze and forget to look at the scenery. I have become comfortable and relaxed and still we fly. Still we keep going. I am taking it all as a matter of course now that we will arrive somewhere and at some time. I am very dozy now.

I wake up after a long time and realise that we have landed. We appear to be in a city of some kind but no city that I have ever seen before. There are tall shining crystalline structures, nothing but light and colour. It is beautiful, clean and smooth. There is nothing dirty or gritty here. It is clean like being in crystal that has no grit in it. It is pure shining, smooth, silky. I am standing alongside the birdman. He begins to walk for he does have legs, human legs. He is after all similar to the angels, like a man and yet with wings. Now I see and I walk with him. Where am I going? What is this all about?

We walk into what appears to be a crystal and yet it is a building. As we walk in I see other beings like him, lots of them. Are they angels or are they birdmen, bird people? I don't know the difference. It is difficult to tell the difference. I am the only one there who is not a birdman and yet I feel at home. I feel completely at home and that I have come home. (I cry with emotion) We walk through crowds of them with no problem. We are accepted as we walk through them, lots and lots and lots of them. I feel as if I am in the land of the angels, beautiful bright shining colours everywhere. There is a feeling of great peace and joy. Peace above all things.

We enter a room where some of these angel/birds are looking over a map spread out over an enormous table. They are pointing at various parts of the map. It is a map of our world, the Earth. They want to show me where I must go. They point to where I must go. One of the places is Africa, but not just one part of Africa as I have been told but all over Africa. That is a huge task. How can I do this?

"You can cover this easily for you too can fly. You too can cover vast distances in a few moments. You do not need to be physically present. You do not need to take an aeroplane to be there. You can cover vast distances in your mind, in your thoughts and in your deeds. You can work your magic wherever your mind takes you on your travels. You will also travel there physically but do not think you have to set foot in each of these lands that is Africa. You will do this in many ways. You will write about Africa; you will influence the minds of peoples through your writing about this continent."

I argue that I have no knowledge of this great continent. I have never set foot there. I have no knowledge so how can I write knowingly about somewhere I have never been?

"We will give you the knowledge. We will give you the information. It will come to you. You will find it. It will be presented to you in a variety of ways. Do not concern yourself about this. You must awaken men's minds to the importance of setting this vast land on a course that is healing. We will assist you."

"Hmmm! It sounds good but I'd like to see the evidence of this now. I ask now for you to give me evidence that this is about to happen and is not just within my meditation. I want some sort of proof to show me that what I am getting now is correct. This is not a doubting of you but a cross checking to make sure that I am not self-deluding."

"We will do what we can in this for it is an important mission, one that you need to focus upon for the present time. There will be more."

They ignore me now and continue to look at the map and pass hands over various parts. They are setting things in motion. They are organising with their own energies and directing their thoughts. They are able to do this. They are planning their own actions as well as mine. So I will have these birdmen with me I know that. When I travel I will do it with them alongside with them watching over me. I am quite content that this is so. I have no-one who will make this journey possible for me and I don't see how I can do it otherwise.

"It will have to be done over the next few years. It will not be immediate. Attention of the world is elsewhere but it must return to this land, vast though it is."

A great energy comes over me and I know I have someone mighty with me, giving me the energy.

***

2000

MANY PARTS OF A SOUL

Two figures have joined me on my journey. They have fallen into step beside me one on each side. Two male figures and yet they feel like angels, light beings. We go up the steps. I am slightly ahead of them. All I can see is a light before me but I can't see where I am going. I ask to be told who I am as I approach the light. All I can see is the light so I ask again, who am I really? I step into the light and am shown a mirror. I go and stand before it. I see a figure, a male figure, extremely powerful. It is very much a male. I look to see what I am dressed in. It is difficult to see for the figure merges in the light. I know it is a male. It is hard to see the outline for it shines. I am human in form and yet there is something not quite of the Human Race. I don't know.

I look around to see mirrors all around. Each reflecting this main one. Each looking slightly different, the same figure but not quite the same. I am a composite of many parts, many of my essence. It explains why a part of me can be in the Galactic council giving commands and yet also here on this Earth. How I can be elsewhere, working with the sick.

"Parts of you are playing many different roles, all for the moment, all in the present time, no past, present or future. They have all come together and are working in different areas at the same time. Whenever there is a need here the part of you that is required comes forward instantly and fulfils the role that is called for. The man steps back when that need is over, therefore there are many things and still you have not seen all for we have not shown all. The past of you has come forward into the present. The past abilities, the past knowledge and that which others see in you are these parts. That which puzzles you when others see you for many purposes are the parts which step forward and become one with you in this incarnation. That is what is seen. It is time for you to recognise that you are many things in one body, not many souls, not different entities but all parts of the same essence of you. All have come together in this moment, in this period of time. All have united with you so that you are now complete in your incarnation. You have united all aspects of you."

"What about the future?"

"These lie waiting to be discovered by the conscious you that is currently incarnated. You may with application and with dedication step forward into the future if it is felt to be of benefit. So often it is not of benefit and we would advise against this for the present time. Your actions today would be influenced to the extent that soul growth does not take place. It would be rather like having answers to the questions before taking an examination. We wish you to learn and to continue to learn as you progress through a series of events. However you have your past and the variations of you united. Now you can call on any one of you in any given circumstance. There is nothing that cannot be done now. When you are called upon for action you know that it is within your capabilities to call upon that part of you that has already learnt."

"Can you please tell me about my visits to the Galactic Council? I wish to remember my time on board the Galactic meetings. I wish to know so that I may act with knowledge upon this planet. I wish to know the connection with Solomon and the connection with the ancient gods of Egypt. I wish now to know my role in those areas. I am aware that I ask a lot but I ask so that I may conduct myself for the benefit of this planet, so I may give to those who come to me the maximum that I can. I wish to open the minds and to do my task with the DNA."

***

2002
A DIVINE STATE

This is a serious request to spirit. First I have been told to first make a link with them, before I ask a question. Otherwise it is like leaving a message on an answer phone before and not after the long beep. I had never thought of it that way before. I will repeat my questions once I have made a link.

Something else I have just discovered – gosh, after all this time. The reason I get more when I speak is similar to that when mediums in the church need the sound of the voice to help them give the messages. It is when I begin to speak that it is something in the voice, the vibration perhaps brings an opening, brings the connection. It is only when I began to speak that I got the link.

I am getting answers to my questions about the book and although it is contrary to my idea, it makes sense. It is to write the How To books, how to meditate, how to channel etc. how to do this that and the other. For these will be the most help for others and will pave the way for the writing that I really want to do on a deeper level.

"You have been given this opening and this recognition in order for you to go forward in confidence, knowing that you have the ability to do all those things which we have put before you. You have the ability to do all those things to which you aspire. That is the difference. You know that all things are possible, for have we not told you this? All things are possible also for other beings. They simply do not awaken themselves to this fact, to this awareness. So do not deny what we have told you. Allow this to be.

"Your next question is 'How do I achieve all these things? How do I put into practical manifestation all these things which you have told me?"

"We say to you just know that it is possible. The barriers which you have erected will crumble before you like dust. You alone can do this. You alone must know that all things are possible. You must feel, you must accept and all things will be possible for you."

"I want you to show me please, show me with pictures. Not simply words, but pictures for my mind's eye, my origin, my original place."

I walk to a brilliance of light. There are moving lights so bright I cannot see the source of the lights. There is brilliance of beings. There are no words for this. Divine light each. There are many beings here, each so bright that a form is not possible. It is energy form but you know there is intelligence in it. There is a being in the centre. I wish I could find words, it is just beautiful. The lights! I walk into it, one can walk in. The lights are all around so that I too am obliterated. It is like walking into a mass of light. Any denseness I have is no longer dense else I could not be here. I feel touching. I am touched but nothing solid but just a knowing I am touched and caressed. Warm and love, such gentleness. This is my source. This is no place. This is a state of being. This is no place in space. It is a state which has no fixed position. A Divine state everywhere, everywhere and at all time. Not even a moment in time but all time.

***

2002
EVERYTHING AND NOTHING

I feel the left side of me is being pulled up through the top of my head. My eyes are being pulled up out of their sockets. It is uncomfortable. The words of the Atlantean Sital came to me: "There is nothing you cannot do." I see my guides. Although the pressure is still there I am with them, I can see them. Osishoo is a lot taller than the others, head and shoulders above the rest. I can see them standing there and I am there too, looking very ordinary amongst them. Osishoo, my father sweeps me up in his arms as if I am nothing. I don't have a physical form – I am spirit. He holds my energy form to him. My energy goes into him. I am inside and yet I am aware of him as if looking at him from the outside. It is a hard thing to describe. I am now part of him and able to observe and be absorbed at the same time.

We are rising up. Everything is receding below us. It is like going up in a rocket, only slowly. All the others are still down there. We seem to be in nothing now. All we have is our mind, our consciousness, nothing else. We are nothing, nothing to see, nothing to touch, just our minds, just our awareness, nothing else. It is perfectly alright, for we are everything.

He speaks to me. "Why do you want to know?"

I answer: "Because what I know can help all those down there."

"Why do you want to know when being in nothing is all that counts?"

"It's all that counts for us. What about those all the way down there who don't know this and don't feel this? They need to be helped into the nothing too."

He agrees that that is my role. That is my job. He wanted me to experience the nothing and the everything. It is the same.

I ask if I can take some of the everything with me back down there. I want to give everything to those down there.

We begin to drop down and other things appear. I begin to feel colour, sensations, awareness of something more solid, awareness of breeze on the skin, awareness of sight, sound, awareness of the senses coming back. We settle gently back with the guides again – in form. We hadn't really gone anywhere; we had simply experienced not being in a form and just being a mind. Intelligence, energy. We hadn't gone anywhere except in this way. We had simply vanished. What is bizarre is that I don't think that those present knew. To them we were always there. Our vanishing, our going had no place in time, no time in space, it simply was. It was continuous to everybody else. We hadn't gone anywhere from their perspective or from the perspective that was a separate me.

***

2002
ETs SURVIVE IN THE EARTH

I am in a glowing orange standing at the top of my stairs looking down. Parts of the stairs are rough and parts of it are smooth, like the peel of an orange. It is a weird surface, dimpled. The handrail is knobbly. A peculiar rail – this is nature. The means of getting in are not stairs at all really. It is a means of getting down. There are boulders and it is more of a climb down, not a walk down. Down I must go to find myself.

It becomes easier as I go further. At the bottom it is shingle. I walk forward shifting on the shingle as I go. I follow my nose and turn off looking for some means to get in. There is a crack, an opening between two boulders. This is it. I climb through. There is no difficulty but I must climb over. This is physical.

I feel the presence of others here. I can't see anybody, but I know I am not alone. Show me what I need to see. I feel the others are from another planet. They are not of this earth. I can just see them now – shadowy. There one minute and not the next. I have to be quick to see them. It is like trying to see a shadow that is moving. If I am to communicate with them they must show themselves more clearly or stay still. They are inquisitive. They are all over me, little ones pulling, investigating, curious and not harming me at all. I do not feel frightened of them. They are just tasting me in a sense, feeling the vibrations of me and deciding if I am alright through a sense of touch. They use touch and vibration to decide. I realise now that they cannot see. They are blind. They sense me in the same way that I sensed them. They can't see me but can sense me, which is why they are feeling me much as a blind person would do. They operate through the mind.

"We will teach you how to survive in the earth. We will teach you not with words but with knowledge and ideas. A knowing so that when the occasion arises you will simply know what to do."

Wouldn't it help me to know in advance?

"No it would not help you for you would tell your mind and your subconscious that it is impossible. But when the occasion arises, you will know, and it will be possible. It does not help to have advance knowledge of this. Information will be there when you need it. We did not always exist inside the Earth. There was a time when we lived on the surface also."

I am confused now. I can't think clearly. Something is going on. Maybe input is taking place now. I can't think of anything else. Is the message for future times to come?

***

2002
PIXIES AND ELVES

There are round smooth pebble stones. The walk is through trees, dried crackly leaves and brittle twigs. It is autumn or winter. Everything cracks and the air is dry and thin. I am walking through a winter forest. Because it is winter I can see through the trees. I come to a slope down. It is off the path. I slither down the slope into a great pile of leaves at the bottom. I can't stop the slide. It is like a funnel for I slide into the spout of the funnel and fall out the other end. It is warm and cosy – underground. There are people here. Not normal people for they remind me of elves and pixies. I don't understand this at all. Show me what I need to see.

"Although we are human looking we are another species, a completely different species never to be mingled or matched genetically. We will always remain separate in form. We belong to this earth and are citizens of the earth every bit as much as you. Therefore we too have a right to feel and to say what we feel about the doings on the surface that damages so much."

***

2003
ON WRITING

As I stand at the top of the stairs, I feel I am in a flame, right inside a flame. I am not looking at it but am inside it, completely surrounded. It doesn't feel bad, it simply is. I don't need to walk down the stairs because the flame just flows down. No steps, just flowing down. I don't quite see what this is telling me at all. I stop at the bottom and am upright now. The flame is still with me – turning gold. Like a pillar of light. I move forward deliberately following my pattern. I look around – tall walls, glittering walls. It reminds me of a cathedral or church. It has a high vaulted ceiling. It echoes a little here. I walk in along – this IS a church or cathedral. I turn to the left down one of the many passages. This one is wider than most. It is gold and like being inside a huge cathedral. I turn to the right to a little door. It is not meant for the public. The public come into the cathedral but not through this door. It is dark, heavy stained wood. It is studded and heavy to open. It has a Ring to open it and I turn it and it operates a lift catch. How do I describe it?

I go in and it creaks a bit. I have to stoop to get through. As I ask to be shown what I need to see there are lots of men, all writing away at different tables. Busy, busy, busy. Some are from our historical times, dressed in olden days. Some are very modern, some are very science fiction, Star Trek type stuff. Others are clearly from the angelic realm, glowing as they too write. There are so many of them here. Ooh! I've even got some Gods from ancient times writing. This is telling me something. What is this telling me?

"All these words, all this writing is already done. They will come through you. You will write what we say, what we ourselves have written."

"I don't see this. The words are still on your side. They are not with me."

"Be patient. The words will come. When we begin no longer will you have your visits to other countries. When it begins no longer will you accept offers for readings in other countries. You may still accept them according to your own desire, for this will give you some release from the writing. Once we have completed our job and pass through you what we wish to say, then you will travel once more. You will continue to travel to promote our work."

"These are lovely words. I wish I could feel it. May I have some proof please that is not within my meditation? I need some evidence that what I hear is true."

"We give you evidence from the mouths of others. We understand this is not enough. The evidence will come when you begin."

"With so many writers won't the style be a bit muddled?"

As I watch all these writers stand up and put their pens down. They link arms. They don't hold each other hands but link arms. Impenetrable, unbreakable in the way they have done it.

"Strength in unity. The energy and the message will be the same from all of us. It will be the same and will run smoothly through the current we send you. The tenure, the tone will be yours as it comes through you in your words. The message comes from us. We intend this and it is so."

As I feel despair that I have nothing coming through in the way of writing they all begin to pound on the tables they were writing at. They are chanting, write, write, write. They are quite determined. They will need to impress me very strongly. I have no idea where to start or what to write.

I see myself again as the pillar of gold flame and they begin to circle me. The flame goes right up into the sky. They keep circling, circling clockwise. A great circle. As they do their own light forms a band of light around me. It is all very nice but what is it telling me? A band of light surrounding me.

***

2003
LEAGUE OF NATIONS

My stairs are more like a ship's gangway; the sort one uses to get on and off a ship. I am in long white clothes. It is not exactly flowing but is strong cotton. I go down the gangway. There is a car waiting for me, a black shiny one. I get in pulling my long clothes in so that they don't get trapped in the door. I don't know what this is or where we are going except that I am expected.

"You are going to The League of Nations."

"I didn't know that it still existed. I thought it was old and finished."

"You are going to a meeting of the League of Nations. It has been re-formed to meet a common occurrence. It is not a threat but a happening, a global all over. This is why the League of Nations has been re-formed, for this does not affect only one country but all countries, large and small. You and others like you have been called upon for it is finally recognised that you are the ones who can communicate with non-human beings on the planet. You can communicate even though you do not know the words. You are able to understand the thoughts and intention and are not fazed by an (odd) appearance."

We arrive and there is an armed guard all around. I am escorted inside the building. I don't know the building, but it is not important. Armed guards are everywhere. It is not necessary, but people might come in and they don't want that. On the platform are many different interplanetary species, humanoids all. Many different kinds and they are all twittering and communicating with each other in their own way. They appear to be in harmony, though some would be frightening to others. I have an impression of arms and legs and different heights. It is weird looking at them for they are different, very different to us, except for one or two who are similar and who have voices and can speak as we do. They have the mouth and throat structure the same. They will be the spokes people for the others. What am I doing here?

"You will act as a kind of interpreter, an intermediary reassuring those in power in the world, assuring them that there are more benefits to be gained by co-operation and inter-action than by denying access to the general populace. This will go in the media while these visitors remain in safe custody until the general populace become adjusted to the idea of their presence."

"This sounds all very well but if, and we know that this is ahead of this time, I don't see how I as an ordinary individual can come to the knowledge of those in power."

"They will have heard of you through your talks and your books."

"I don't have any books published."

"You will write of this."

I am currently speaking many different interplanetary languages and understand the gist of it. I am not alone in being able to do this.

***

2003
THE OVERSOUL

I am sitting with a picture of Alvadeon (a powerful guide) before me. I need his energy. I am holding a crystal, a long one. I feel the presence of my guides and energy of them. I am simply talking so that I get the energy going. I decide to do the stairs. They are flimsy, almost made of wire. There is nothing very solid. It is a thin rail like wrought iron but is just wire instead of iron swirling round. I look down – it doesn't look as if it would bear my weight. I go down carefully and holding on to the bits of wire even though they would not support me if I fell. Everything is in silver, silver light. That reassures me for to me the silver is always truth. I keep going down. It is dark on either side of the staircase. I can't see anything. Whatever might be there is not important else I would see it.

I bring myself back to the stairs. What am I dressed in? A silver gown, flowing, draping. I am very tall, not the me that lives this life. I am extremely tall and fine, almost regal looking. Very straight and upright. I have a purpose here.

I get to the bottom. It is all in silver. It is fairy like in the sense that there are tall walls, gleaming. All this has an unreal feel. I keep walking forward and turn off to the left. The passage is very narrow, and I can touch both sides if I put my arms out. This is not meant for a lot of movement but for one individual to pass at a time. The ground is solid, at least that will not give way. The walls are solid too; cool to touch with the occasional rough edge here and there. It is like walking through crystal – rather nice. Let's hope the crystal walls don't move or I would be squashed. Silly thought!

I almost glide forward and come to my opening on the right. It is not exactly a door but a panel that is glowing with light played over it in different colours. I can't see any means to open it. It is a patch on the wall with the different colours marking it so I can see it. I suppose I could try walking through. I step into the glow that comes from the colours and walk through. It is a portal. That is what it is. I am out of time here.

I pause to go deeper. The energy is building. My eyes are hurting. Both my eyes are under pressure here. I wait, knowing I must go deeper into this…time passes and questions surface in me. So many things I want to do but without one particular drive to get started – scattered.

A voice says, "You know that you have the ability to be inter-dimensional and to be all those things that are seen by others. This is proof to you and to those others that one particular life is simply just that. Each is many personalities (My head hurts) You are multi, you are many things and when you are seen as such. It is all aspects of you making it clear (to others), bringing forward all you have been and all that you will be in one. You are demonstrating to others your Oversoul. Or to put it another way, you are demonstrating the unity of all consciousness in one. You do this by connecting with the records of all time, for this is when it happens, does it not?"

"I want to know the purpose of all this. What about the books? What about the Cards, what about the workshops? I am living in this world. I need to make an effect on this world. These small meditation sittings are not sufficient to do that."

"If you wish to make an impact then you MUST write the books. You must get into it. Do not procrastinate further. You have done this long enough. You have rested overlong."

***

2004
AFRICA & BEINGS FROM OTHER WORLDS - PROOF

My stairs are steps down the side of a mountain or hill. I hold on tightly to a bamboo rail. It has been placed there, not grown there. The steps have been made too with all natural things. It is hard on the feet as I go down because the bamboo pole that holds the earth in place has sunk down behind it. The bamboo ridge is still there. It is not easy, quite steep. Steamy jungle, insects, the sound of insects, shrill. Oh my head hurts as I go down. The energy gets stronger and stronger. At the bottom it is a very narrow space. It looks like a pool. I wouldn't want to go in that. It is not clean water. I look for a way round it and step around the outside holding on to various bits of trees and twigs. I don't want to fall in, as it is deeper than it looks. It is not just a puddle but is a very deep hole. I don't want to fall in the hole. I work my way round, holding on. On the other side there is a well-trodden path. A lot of beings have been this way. Whether it is people or animals, animals probably who don't mind drinking from this water. It doesn't feel safe but it is the only way I can go and I know I am alright.

There are two men, natives with spears. Not much in the way of clothes. They are not short, but tall. They have been waiting for me to arrive. As I draw close to them they stand on either side of me. Clearly, I am to go with them. I am being escorted. The path widens out now. It is getting brighter. We go to a village where they have been expecting me.

"This isn't answering my question whether to focus on the cards or go abroad. This isn't telling me."

"Well this certainly isn't England, is it? And if it isn't England then it is abroad."

"I don't know where this is."

"You have already been told that you will go, and you do know where this is. This is why your plans to go to Australia, to America are not being fulfilled yet. We are leaving the way clear. We are leaving the way clear. This will be arranged."

"Am I to do nothing then? Am I just to wait? Africa is a big place. Do I do nothing and just wait?"

"Just wait."

The men take me to a hut. Bending low, I go inside. It is a round hut. It is not Maasai. It is a very round hut with a pole in the middle. There is a very old man dressed in his finery. He has been dressed up with regalia of some kind. He is sitting, as he is too old to stand. I don't understand this at all.

"When you do go to this place you will be under his protection. You will not be in jeopardy from any adverse contingencies. You will be under his protection and that will be strong enough."

It doesn't feel very comfortable, and what am I here for? What am I to do? I have lots of pictures now, dancing people. A white man. A lot of very rapid movement blurring with the speed of it. I don't quite trust this message for I can't see how it can come about or what I can do.

"It is here that you will meet beings from other worlds. It is here that you will record, take notes and provide evidence for the world to see at large. Not only are you under the protection of the old man but also those who are present from other worlds."

Shortly after this I was invited to Cape Town and from there went to Zimbabwe at the time of Mugabe. I was the only guest in the hotel and very soon I had a queue of local people lining up for healing. It was a humbling experience indeed. My flights to Florida were cancelled due to hurricanes in that area.

***

LAND SLIP/EARTHQUAKE

I ask to be shown what I need to see. They show me people going up what appears to be scrambling nets going up a cliff face. It is land that is fresh, not an old cliff. It is a break in the Earth and they are scrambling up so as to be on higher ground. There has been what you would call a landslip I suppose, but it is an earthquake thing. They are trying to get to higher ground for where they were will be covered with water. They must go higher. I don't know how this leaves people who are low lying.

"Where is this?"

"This is along all known fault lines and also in lands where there have been minor quakes in the past. These will become more than minor but not as great as on major fault lines. Excessive rainfall will also cause these slips and not all will be caused by earthquakes."

"When is this to be?"

"We are speaking of the next two or three years and not all happening at once. There will be enough happening to cause comment and concern."

"What can I do?"

"Go back to your original purpose, that of explaining that this life is but one. Explain that the continuation of the soul will always be, and that the quality of one's being is of the paramount importance. How one conducts oneself through life in the physical, internally and externally is of importance for a better continuation of the soul's journey, irrespective of conditions on the physical plane. Adhere to the Commandments, in particular to that one of Love one thy neighbour as oneself.

"Write about the continuation of the soul of one individual amongst a group of souls. Write about the soul's journey through one lifetime after the other in a continuous thread. Write from your experience and you may entitle it "The Thread of Life."

***

2008
INTERGALACTIC DELEGATION

I am standing on red artificial carpet, the sort you might have outdoors. It's a bit rough to the feet. I see steps going down, no walls, nothing to hold onto, just steps pure and simple. I am perfectly safe. They are not wide steps. The carpet, where I said artificial, is plastic – most odd. Ah now I see what it is. These are steps going down from a craft, I don't know if it is an aeroplane or what, but it definitely is a craft that flies. These are steps that open down onto the ground. This craft is quite high and there is nothing to support the steps except the actual craft itself.

I go down and although there is nothing to hold onto it is safe. Weird! I am at the bottom now. It is concrete and open space like you would get at an airport – very much a landing area. It is just open space so I am looking for a way to go. To follow my normal routine I turn left because it is my patterning. I can't see anybody or anything just open concrete space. I go to the left hoping to see something or somebody. Oh! I see on the ground little arrows, just like you get at some airports. I follow the arrows and they indeed do turn right.

They lead me into a collection of buildings. I am reminded of Bournemouth airport. Nothing big, nothing grand. The doors open as I reach them. There is a welcoming committee. Groups of men, only men. It is a committee of some kind for they all look as if they belong to each other. They are all happy to see me. I am led by them into a vehicle, one of those long sleek jobs that you'd get in a city. We all fit in. I haven't got a clue who I am or what I am or where I am going, except that it is very organised.

Again this is really odd. We are driven to an official building of some kind. There is a delegation of people there all waiting for me. I still don't know what I am supposed to do or why I am here. It is a long drawn-out thing this but they all look happy to see me. I am expected. I am not arrested or anything which is nice, for that thought did go into my head.

At last I ask "Who am I and what is this all about? What am I doing here?"

"Don't you realise you are not of the Earth? In this scene you are recognised as a being from elsewhere. You are seen in your true form and respected for your true form, for there is now acceptance of such as yourself from other planetary systems. You are representing the Galactic Commands. You carry the insignia of the Galactic Command and as such have authority. In this you are recognised and accepted and are able to speak with authority to delegations from a variety of countries across your globe. The craft you arrived in is indeed a craft from space, all of which is brought into third dimension so that it may interact with those of you on Earth. It comes from your command of the Galactic Fleet."

"I want to know who am I, apart from being an Intergalactic Being? Who am I really?"

"In which state do you wish us to reply? If we reply for third dimensional understanding, you are a being from space. If we reply from the idea of consciousness and essence only then that is truly what you are, merely an essence, an intelligence, a consciousness that may interact at all levels, with all peoples when appropriately called upon."

"So in this scenario you've given me, what help is it? What help is it to Shirley who is currently embodied as an ordinary human being?"

"It will give her a deeper understanding of her role. It will encourage her to believe that anything is possible."

"That is a lot to take in and I don't now know what it is I am supposed to do at this delegation. I feel very much like the Shirley that is an incarnated human being."

"Open your box. Open your Shirley mind and extend it into other realities. Extend it into far reaching possibilities. You know very well everything is possible to the mind. All that is required is application to that portion which knows all."

***

2008

I am standing at the top of stairs. My clothing is a tunic which is tightly belted. I have sandals on my feet. The banister is like brass, highly polished. It is not brass, but it looks like it. The stairs are rough wooden ones – straight down but I can't see the bottom yet. I could be going into a cellar underneath a house, or a building. I go back in time here. I feel a weight on my neck, on my shoulders. The thought comes that it is a wooden yolk.

Thoughts are racing through my head. This is a period of tyranny, tyranny of power. Rome. This is the yolk of Rome. I have no idea why – this maybe just a symbolic presentation of what is happening today-oppression. When I get to the bottom there is a sweet stream. I call it sweet because it feels so light, fresh and cleansing. I have to walk through the water – there is nowhere else. I follow the stream at ankle deep. It is easy walking. It is beautiful. I feel different. I am released – I am free. I am free to go where I want, to do what I want, to be who I want.

"The choice is yours. The choice is always yours. You can be of service, or you can simply enjoy being who you are and living a pleasant life. To be of service requires dedication, application and sincerity of feelings, not because you should or because it is required but because you wish to. This must come through emotion, the need to be of service."

***

2008

TO A PAST TIME – ORIGINAL BEINGS – SPACE CRAFT

The stairs are covered in red plush carpeting and the banisters are set into the wall on one side. It is smooth like marble – nice and gently rounded curves. I am told I must continue talking and not stop to think, just let the words come. As I go down the stairs I am not thinking about anything. I go down, down and am not even looking to see where it is leading.

"Keep talking, keep talking, keep talking, it doesn't matter what you say. Keep talking all the way down."

At the bottom it is all soft and squidgy, a bit like stepping onto marshy ground. A bit unusual! It is squelchy, there is grass but it is squelchy and waterlogged. Too much water when so many have not enough.

"Look for your opening. When you do find it keep talking. You must keep talking."

There is an arrow pointing the way. I follow the arrow. It is very broad, this arrow. It has been placed there with natural means. Leaves, twigs. It is a native thing. This is native!

"Just keep talking."

Yes, I must follow It is undergrowth, a jungle walkway. Ahead of me is a little man. He is beckoning me. He is a little, I was going to say aboriginal, but he is not Australian. He is a pygmy perhaps.

"He is an original of the Earth not from another planet. He is an original of the Earth"

That is strange. I don't come across them very often.

"They are originals. They don't come from another planet. They are descendants of ape. They are the original beings!

He is beckoning me now. I follow and don't know where I am going.

"Don't think, don't think!"

I am still in undergrowth and must follow the little man. He sees me as from the future or from somewhere he doesn't understand. I am from his future. I see a space craft. I no longer call them UFOs for they are identified by me. This is where I belong. I go up to it. There are others like him around it. I know how to get in. I think myself in and at once I am inside. It is big inside, bigger than you would expect. It is a bit like the Tardis idea. It is all constructed by mind. This is a mind, time and travel machine. I have been brought back to it because I got lost. I was lost in his world. I am now found.

"What am I like? I am not very tall. I can shape shift."

"When we travel we can confine ourselves into small spaces, when we arrive we assume our natural physical forms."

"That's a clever trick!"

"Anything is possible."

"So what is my original form?"

"We would have to take you somewhere else to show you that."

"Do it then."

Immediately I am taken onto another planet. It is a long journey.

"How is this helping me to deal with the planet Earth?"

"You asked the question, what are you usually like? We are simply reacting to your question."

I look at myself. I am a bird being. Tall, if I put my arms out I am very wide. Wingspan! I AM a birdman and yet a humanoid as well. My face is not that of a bird but is similar.

"Take me back to where I was. I want to know how I can be of help on the planet Earth."

"You must broaden the minds of others. Tell these things are possible."

"They won't believe me."

"Tell them anyway. Tell them as a story, a make believe. Actually sow the idea in their heads. Even as make believe you are a shape shifter. In your current life you retain human form every time your consciousness is with the planet Earth. When you work for us you retain that other consciousness so that the two do not mix and confuse things. You are more things than one. You can be many things."

"So how can I be of help on Earth for that is what I am there for?"

"You must speak. You must continue to draw others to you. Do not sit down and waste your time."

I am back here, very quickly, very quickly.

***

2008

I go down. At the bottom there are a lot of corridors going off in different directions. I am in a circular space with entrances fanning out. I don't know which one I am supposed to take. The floor is tiled. I choose the second entrance from the left. It has a greenish tinge to it. It is a small corridor, not wide but just enough room for me and perhaps one other. The floor now is smooth, cool to the feet. The walls feel close to and are smooth as well. It doesn't look as if it has any openings. I come to my expected doorway. Again it is very narrow with no bumps or lumps. I don't see any means to open it but I can see it is a doorway. I look hard and notice a little indentation. I put my finger in it and as I do it clicks, and the door swings open of its own accord.

As I step inside I know I am not alone. It is a bit dark, and I can't actually see anybody yet until my eyes adjust. I know I am not alone and am straining hard to see. I can feel the odd movement and the odd rustle. I feel the place is full of spirit beings. Then somebody takes my hand and the hand that does this is soft and pulpy. It is squidgy. It is taking mine so I don't have to worry about taking his and hurting him. Somebody takes my other hand and pulls me forward. I am obviously not intended to see. We move forward and I am trusting because these two know where they are going and can see in the dark. My eyes are not used to this. I ask for more light which they obviously don't need.

It becomes a little clearer as I ask. They have forgotten that I need more light than they do. (recorded over by mistake so is not finished)

***

2009

CONTINUE MY JOURNEY

At first, I thought the stairs were artificial grass but with a bit of exploration I realise it is carpeting that looks like grass, close woven matting. The sort you would get to go down to a swimming pool to make sure you don't slip. It is very artificial and green. There is a rail on either side. They are making sure I don't slip. There is a pool at the bottom. It is flashing different colours, very strong colours- nothing weak about them. They flash blue, red, orange – all flashing as if they are lit from below. I have to walk through and don't have to submerge myself.

As I walk across I feel the colours shooting through me. It is not unpleasant but is like electric currents shooting through me. I am being charged by whatever the colour is. It is easy walking and there is a slope out on the other side. Someone waiting for me. It is the nun I was told about earlier on this week. She helps me to get out and puts a cloak around me. She is not the one I am to meet but is taking me there.

I feel this is to be an important meeting. We hurry along corridors and paths. We are outside now. There is a building but it is almost not real. It is there but you feel as if you could walk right through it, like a mirage building. But she knocks and something opens so we can walk right in. It is a totally different world inside. All colour. Nothing is very solid but wafting and waving about. It is like walking into a wavy dream. But I am real and so is she.

I see the presence of many high beings. They have an aura and blend with each other and move about. I feel they are masculine with a sense of authority here. I can't get them to slow down enough for me to see clearly. I know they are trying to present themselves in a form that is meaningful to me for they are pure light. To show themselves they must condense a little so I can see them. I feel honoured to be here.

One reaches out and touches me. I shiver. The shiver goes right through me and I feel deliciously charged. It is wonderful and another one does the same. Again it goes all through me. It is wonderful. They are coming into me now, similar to when I channel. I can feel them in my head.

Me: "I wish to know what I am to do in the future. I wish to know many things." The energy in my head is almost more than I can take. Very intense, almost painful.

Forcibly: "We cannot allow you to step down from your work. We cannot allow for you to sit back and retire. We would request that you stay in contact with us each day and not just occasionally as you have been doing. We wish you to communicate with us more often and we will then take you further. How can we do this if you decide not to contact us? We are working with you. You know that. Do not doubt it."

Me: "I want to know something more definite, more concrete."

"If we were to have your book published you would then be extremely busy and would not always find the time for the tasks we have for you. So we will programme the timing of this book. There are some elements in it which should be altered. But you know this already and that will come later."

We ask you to continue to be of service until the end of your days. If you wish for good health then we tell you that to remain in service is your best option. You do not need to fear that you are not strong enough or awake enough or physically enabled enough. We will ensure that you maintain a high standard of physical and mental wellbeing. We can only do this if you continue in our work, if you do not you will resume normal aging process. You will resume normal human activity, which in itself is satisfactory. But this is not your role in this incarnation."

Me: "I wish to do deep trance."

"We have covered this before. Deep trance is not always an efficient way, for so many safeguards need to be in place. We wish you to continue to travel, to continue to visit even those areas that you are not actively enthusiastic about."

Me: "Then you will have to put them in my way for I am not seeking them."

"They will come your way. What we have in mind will come your way. You will grow stronger. You will develop stamina that is required for these journeys. You will have resistance to all and any inconvenient illnesses, bugs and influences. You will be resistant to all these things and many will wonder why you never get ill. You will remain in good health at all times. This is dependent on you continuing your work."

I feel his arms around me and I am ushered into a crypt. There is a large book on a stone bench. It is like a book of ages.

"Your name will be inscribed in this book for the work you will have done, not only in this incarnation but in previous incarnations, many times. Your name will be inscribed."

Me: "What is my name?"

***

2009

"You ask for tangible proof. If we were to give you this there would be no peace for you. We could not then preserve your anonymity. This is to be preferred, is it not."

I do feel the presence of someone in me very strongly but this kind of proof I already have. So perhaps something that is tangible to me alone? I go down the stairs. There is nothing at the bottom. I look around until I see the entrance to the left. The passage is lit with little glowing lights. A soft glow, very soft, very gentle. The passage itself is small, wide enough for me to get through but not wide otherwise. The lights are a bit like the lights we get as emergency lighting – soft and just enough to see.

The opening on the right is another soft gently lit way. It is not bright but just enough. All I have to do is just push and the door opens. When I get inside the air is brighter. Rocky ground. Although I am inside what appears to be a cave it is very open. It is just an entrance or exit. Exit into something much bigger. I come out into glorious sunshine. I am on a mountain looking out over the scenery. Beautifully lit, not sharp but soft in glorious sunshine. Everything is there.

It is a glorious scene coming out of confinement into the open. Though my way has been lit enough for me to follow, where I have come out is absolutely glorious, another world. I feel my hand being taken. We walk together down a nice little slope, easy. This is a different world. I am in a different world, not the same as before.

"If we were to put you into this world too soon you would very quickly become bored. Although it is a delight there is nothing that you need to do and being a soul of action you would certainly be looking for something you could have an effect on. You would be looking for this or that and would not be at ease. So accept where you are in your world. Accept that it is giving you what is comfortable and right for you as a human being. That action is keeping you alive, keeping you vital and giving you a purpose for your existence. Here in this world where everything is easy, everything is smooth and a delight you would lose purpose for being. You would simply be and that is not enough for you. You know this. To be is not yet enough for you. Your life is one of service. Who or what can you be of service to in this world? That time will come even here, but it is not for you yet."

***

2009

I am dressed in a cotton shift, white full length with a sash cord around the middle. Bare feet. The steps are in stone, very worn. The handrail is a heavy chain threaded through eyelets. Iron I think – not a firm rail but it is something to hold onto. At the bottom is a flag/stone floor. This feels like a crypt or cellar or below a church. The walls are plain and unadorned. The opening on the left is a little door, it is very old. I think I am in a church. Through the door is a passageway. No windows, just a passage with stone walls. It is not cold and quite dry. It echoes a little. I must find the other door on the right.

When I arrive at the other door it is a bit bigger. It is like a c. door and has an iron ring. I twist and turn it to open the door. It is inside – not very well lit. There is an old man sitting at a table bench hunched over something. It is an old book he is writing in. He has robes on with a hood so I can't see his face. My bare feet don't make a noise but he looks up as I approach.

He is brilliant, beautiful and not old. He is blond with blue eyes and youthful. He is like an angelic form hiding beneath the dark robe. He looks at me and I notice even his lips appear to be red. He smiles as he looks at me. He has been waiting and knew I was coming. I ask him to tell me what I need to know.

"Sit down, sit down."

I sit opposite him. He takes his time.

"What do you think you need? What is it you wish to know?"

I take a little time to think about that. "Am I doing things the right way? Am I right in pushing the workshops and the books? Is this what I am supposed to be doing? If I am not, then I want it made clear to me in one way or another where I should be heading and what I should be doing with the few remaining years I have. I don't want to waste the years."

"Although you are fed up with travelling and we can appreciate and understand the reasons why, you will continue to travel in spite of the inconveniences and the trials that come with this. We wish you to move about the planet as before. Your energies even when you are not aware will have an effect on the land and environment and the people that you meet. We wish you also to continue to teach even when you feel it is not having a lasting effect. Even if you have one out of ten going forward as a result of your teaching it will have been worthwhile and will expand outwards for others to take up the baton."

I ask: "What is my connection with ET's and the space beings."

"You are one of them. The role you are playing on Earth is just a part of your activities in your soul. You are also active elsewhere at all times, not just when you sleep. We wish you to expand your mind and allow your mind and thoughts to embrace the pictures that come to it. Embrace them as being your reality and things will then become clearer. We will try to give you scenes where the other parts of you are working so you can understand what it is you are and what it is you do."

It seems I am to continue to put up with airports and uncomfortable accommodation.

***

2009

DO NOT GIVE UP

The stairs appear to be a kind of rattan, handmade, native made. It swings down like a kind of chute. It is very well made so that there are steps, but it is all enclosed in one. It is unsteady and not fixed to anything. I have a feeling of Malaysia or Borneo or somewhere like that. It is very hot and steamy with noises that you get in a jungle.

"There are so many worlds even on your planet. So many different environments from one place to another. Stop complaining about your life. Stop complaining. You have it easy compared to others."

It is very true, and I have been complaining. Eventually I get to my door. As I go in there is a blaze of light, so bright I can't see at first. So bright! There are figures in there waving at me, calling me over. As I become accustomed to the light I see those from other worlds, not this world. Osishoo comes forward. He is clearly so different from the others, so much bigger and more stately. He is beautiful and reminds me of an angel. He has a presence about him, a calming one, a gentle and loving one. He is very much in charge.

"Do not give up as you go forward. Do not give up on what you are here to do simply because of little difficulties along the way. If you give up now you will regret it as you go into your other lives. Now wouldn't that be a pity? Keep going forward, keep striving, and keep alight the spark in you. Do not be downcast by the Earthly difficulties or your age. Your age is nothing compared to what you have done before. Your age is miniscule in comparison to other lives. Miniscule!"

I feel as if I have been thoroughly told off for having my little concerns. They are insignificant things really.

***

2009
I MUST WRITE – RECORDS IMPORTANT

My steps are like circles cut in half, semi-circles – stone steps with the bulge outwards. They are a bit crumbly and I am reminded of ancient Egypt or Greece. They are crumbling and I see have not been well maintained. The ground at the bottom is rough, crumbly rock. Not debris exactly but broken up rock that used to be a building. That is what this is – rubble. It is uneven and has been here a long time.

I look for the opening and it is more of a pathway that leads away from the area of brick and stone rubble. The path leads down a hill so the building, whatever it was must be up high. We are now going into countryside, vineyards, tended places but very dry. I keep getting reminded of Greece, not that I know Greece very well. It is a hot dry Mediterranean climate.

As I walk I see a tall metal gate, leading to a dwelling I assume. It is old again, rusting. I can get through quite easily and feel I am in a hurry now. On either side of the walkway are statues of marble and granite in various poses. I am in a hurry to get to where this is leading. It has to be somewhere grand, or that was grand.

I suddenly realise that there are two people, one on either side of me. They are men in old costumes of scribes. This is to do with writing. I am reminded of people like Homer, Plato and those wonderful Greek philosophers who put pen to paper.

"They didn't just think, they put it down. That is what you need to do. It is not enough to just think and know. You must put it down on paper else how on earth can you pass this on after you have gone. You must put pen to paper."

My reaction was, "What a journey just to tell me that. I know I must write."

"Yes, but you are not doing it. You must put pen to paper. After all the events that have destroyed civilisations what is left but the words of the Record Keepers. The words that have been passed down keep going when they strike a chord. Those of your world are trying to decipher words still laid down thousands of years before. Still your Bible is in production. Words laid down thousands of years before. Words laid down in the records for all to see, they are the things that endure. Even the teaching that you do, even that does not survive beyond the moment or in the minds of those you teach. Words laid down continue onwards. Can you not see that the writing is important so that it may continue?"

***

2009
WAY STATION IN SPACE

I am in a silver, close fitting suit. I don't look like me and am slimmer. This feels like a space suit but very tight fitting. My stairs are modern looking – shiny and they don't look as if they belong on this Earth. There are hand holds on either side of the stairs which are extremely steep, almost to the point where I might be better going down backwards if I was in my own body here. I go down facing out quite happily because of the hand holds. I can see it so clearly but to describe it isn't so easy. It is like when you are on a small ship and you go down from one deck to the other.

"We ARE on a ship. This is a Space Station, not the same as NASA has. This is a Space Station for interplanetary beings. That is to say, not from just one planet but many of their inhabitants are here. It is a Way Station. Some might call this a Mother Ship but it is not that. It is a Way

Station, a stopping off point, embarkation for passages of interplanetary travel.

"You are one of those who organise and run this. You give the directions and organise. My goodness me you have many roles here because your mind is clear and can function on many different things at once. You are able to see what is required and direct. You are of course, not alone. You are not the only one running things here. There are many others who have tasks allotted to them."

"Why the close-fitting silver space suit?"

"This has properties that make it easy to enter the various chambers we have on board here. A variety of systems that you might call 'airlocks'. There are adjustment chambers for different species from other planets. Each one (chamber) is different to the other and is relevant to the species requiring an interchange or a preparation. The suit that you wear enables you to enter any one of these without harm, for you too are a species that cannot always interact physically with all or any of the others. Not all are giving off the same energy waves, emanations and radiation. So adjustment must be made before they can enter the rest of the ship, or travel as they are here to do. This is why it is called a Way Station and not a Mother Ship." (*note: I went on a Mother Ship later*)

"I don't quite understand how this works. No doubt you will tell me at some point."

"You might call them decontamination chambers for not all the wave lengths, the energies, the attachment in terms of physical emanations are compatible with the environment they wish to visit, that of the Earth. There has to be a decontamination process to avoid contaminating Earth itself or any they might meet. If we didn't do this there might be effects upon the flora and fauna and living beings. The energies are not always compatible. This is why we have a decontamination process in these chambers. We have chambers allocated to each species from certain regions of the cosmos.

The suit that you and we all wear when we engage in this work is impervious to the energies from a whole range of species from other planets. We are not adversely affected by the varieties that visit this Way Station."

"I would like to talk about my role on this planet Earth as a human being. How on Earth (excuse the pun) would it be arranged that I give talks around the world. At present I have no means or contacts for this."

"Hold it in your mind that this is possible and we will arrange it. You need to meet an individual who will take this on board for you."

"I can't help feeling that publication of the book is key to this."

"It certainly will help."

"I'm not getting any younger and if it takes too long I will be ready to

family I may add, that looks to me to be human in all aspects."

"You will not find it hard, for you have the memory of the human form that you took and all it went through including all the human mental and emotional aspects." *My note: Since then I have been given a new guide that is to help me with speaking and interpreting different ET languages.*

"Do you have anything more to tell me?" I ask.

"Your next journey, albeit for a holiday will also be used by us for you are going into troubled areas. Almost every step of your journey takes you into a troubled area. We will use you to change the energies there, to have a ripple effect wherever you go. Think of it as walking through a field of energy and your entry into that field sends out ripples in the same way that a duck swims on the water continually from one part to another. As it does it disturbs the energy pattern. This is what we require, for the energy patterns to be disturbed so that they may be regenerated. You have chosen this trip for a holiday but it has a deeper purpose than that. You are to change thoughts and energies as you go. It should be easy for you."

"You are not human, are you?" I asked this tall Space Brother.

"I was once."

"That's interesting. Who were you?"

"I am now, Serapis Bey."

"Ah! So Serapis Bey, you were human, - and now?"

"I am a Space Friend."

All of this was conducted on an equal basis with neither being more authoritative than the other. I feel I am one of them simply reporting and asking for certain conditions to be changed or met to make my job easier. In the meantime I must be human. I am going to leave it at that.

I had an amazing year of travel which included Egypt, Aden, Oman, Jordan, India, Sri Lanka, Thailand, Malaysia, Java, Indonesia, Cambodia, Vietnam and Hong Kong.

***

2009

SURVIVAL OF THE FITTEST

I am in a long shift gown in green. The stairs are narrow with a rail on either side. There is just space for two people side by side. It is rough hewn, nothing polished or marble. As I go down deeper and deeper I hear rustling on the side. I know we are outside and I have the feeling it is like being on a forest treetop walkway with wooden steps coming down from here. I am at the bottom now and it feels like the bottom of a sink hole. Not much space. It is earth. Just discernible is an opening that I can get through. It is covered with branches, brambles and if I was any taller I would have difficulty and I would have to bend over. I walk along looking for another opening on the right. And there it is, just an opening in the undergrowth.

As soon as I step through I am in another world. It is a completely different world and nothing like the one I have left behind. I almost forgot to ask:

"Take me where I need to be, show me what I need to see." As I ask I see a row of little lights on the ground, marking the way. It is just enough to see and no more.

"Where am I going, where am I going?"

"You are entering another world, another time, another dimension."

As I ask again there is a barrier, a wall, an unseen invisible wall. It is enough to stop me. I have to ask permission.

"May I enter through this veil, this barrier?"

"Enter."

As he says the word I find I can walk myself through it. It closes behind me. I can't see it do that but I know it does. I am in another time. There is air and everything is shimmering blue. I expected it to be sharper but it is shimmering. I think it is because I am not used to it. My view of it has not settled.

There are large human beings here. I didn't expect humans; mostly male, though there are some females.

"This is a vision of what can be for your future. This is not fixed. It is an aspect of a possible world which is why it shimmers. For this time has not been set yet. The size of those you see relates to the strength required to exist in this world. Only the strong will survive, and we mean STRONG physically. Those who are not strong cannot endure this reality and so will pass on. What you are seeing is a possible future. As we have said it is not set.

"I had hoped to see a future that was more likely."

"There are many possible futures. You know this already. This is but one. Know that if things do not go well those who survive will need to be strong physically for it will be survival of the fittest and not according to the mentality or technology or the ability to see ahead. It will be survival on a daily basis."

"Can you not show me another possible future for us as a human race?"

"You will need to go in a different direction."

"But you led me on this path by following the lines."

"We showed you the way but you did not have to follow."

"I am asking now to show me another way." My mind will not accept anymore so I come back. I come back.

***

2009
TUNE IN HIGHER

I have a picture of lots of young people all going in a hurry in the same direction along a street. I am caught up in this and I am young too. I don't want to go with them.

A voice said: "If in doubt, don't."

I realise they are all heading in the wrong direction and I don't want to go in the wrong direction. I turn and face the other way, against the stream of people. Looking ahead I see peace, serenity and empty countryside. All the masses are going in one direction, into hordes of people. My direction is into peace and solitude. I want to know why now.

I am getting huge pressure in my head which tells me I am making a high connection here. The pressure I am under now is getting me readjusted. I am being re-tuned to higher forces. My way is not of the masses, not with the herd. I must tune in once more to the higher communication.

***

2009

The stairs I have are wooden boards. It is like pre-war houses. I can see the sides of the stairs where it has been painted but there is no carpet. Someone is either moving in or moving out. I feel it is moving out. There is a brass railing. It has been nicely cleaned and is not dirty at all. A lot of people have been up and down here. At the bottom I am still in the old house. It is not grand, just old. It echoes because everything has been taken out of it. It has been emptied and whoever was here is leaving. I am in the corridor now which leads to the front door.

I step out into the street. There are lots of people waving in jubilation, celebrating. They are very happy about something. They are dancing and laughing and joking. It feels like when the end of a war is declared they are released from all the fears and troubles.

I step out into the crowd. They are slapping me on the back and hugging me as I am part of it.

"It is jubilation over release from fears and they are happy in the moment since they do not know what is ahead. Nobody really cares for the past has gone. The past has gone. All that can lie ahead is better than what has been."

"What has this got to do with me? I can't see a connection with my desires"

"The past has gone for you too. Rejoice in the moment for where you are. Rejoice in the jubilation that is in your heart now. Know that ahead is better, much better."

A very tall man takes my arm and pulls me out of the crowd. He leads me to a quieter part. We go up some steps in a higher building. He holds my arm as we go up together. I know he is alright. He has the sense of someone with authority, someone who knows what it is all about. He even knows what the future holds. We keep climbing the stairs. They are softer and do have carpeting. We go up floor by floor.

I ask:" What are we doing? Where are we going?"

"This to be your new hall of residence. From here you will see far. You will oversee the activities that are going on below. From here you will receive higher messages. From now on this is your hall of residence."

***

2009
ENERGY HOT SPOTS

I am going down a twisting chute like a candy bar that curls round. I land at the bottom where it is all cushiony and soft. I get up and dust myself off. Clouds of shimmery dusty stuff swirls all around me. I look around me and see an opening just visible above the swirling clouds of dust. I can't see what it is like but walk in that direction. The floaty sugary stuff stays behind as I walk into the corridor. I am clear now and hear bells. Some are light and some are heavy. Sounds like the sort you would get in a monastery or church. I feel I am more outside than I am in. It is a bit like a cloister. I come to a few steps up to the right into another door. There is a huge vortex in the middle. It is absolutely massive and is an energy that I would previously call a hot spot. This one I can see and is swirling round.

"Why can I see this when previously I just knew it was there?"

"When you find a hotspot of energy if you had eyes to see you would see this very thing. It is a vortex.

Knowing that I can step into an energy hotspot absolutely safely I do that now. I am stepping in now. The only sensation I feel is in my body. My head feels as if it is going to explode. My total focus is on the body. There is someone or something pulling my hair up so that my spirit body is pulled up out of the physical. I leave from the top of my head and I am free to go up wherever I want.

***

2009
KEEP WRITING

My stairs are like a corkscrew. A corkscrew penetrates more easily than anything else. There are walls on either side to stop me getting giddy. I can put both hands on either side to guide me down a very narrow stairway. I make no noise as I go down because there are rubber strips on each edge. I can't slip and it makes no sound.

At the bottom now. The ground, the floor is like glass. Very shiny, unblemished, and totally black so it reflects like a mirror. The shiny floor flows into the gap I must take on the left. It is seamless like molten rock that has solidified into a perfect surface. It reminds me of some black crystal, but I can't think of the name at the moment. Obsidian?

The walls on either side of the passage almost feel as if they are alive. It is as if there are faces looking out from them but not distinct enough to say for sure. It feels as if they are behind the wall looking at me, like in a one-way mirror. I come to the door on the right which is like glass and reflective. Everything is reflective. I give the door a little push and it swings open easily.

I look around me at a large space. There are wall hangings. I am not sure if they are paintings, tapestries or other objects. It feels ceremonial where one enters an old place and all things of the past are hung up there as a record of memories.

It is very grand and palatial. I stand there wondering what to do next and how this can relate to my current concerns. There is a figure at the far end beckoning me to go over there. The far end is quite a long way. It takes me a little while to go there. There are no obstacles and everywhere is smooth, shiny and clean. It is just a question of covering the distance between us.

I stand before him now. He is depicted as a figure from a pack of cards like the king or knave. It is just a depiction for I know the real him is behind or inside. It is a façade. He takes me by one finger – the forefinger on my left hand. He takes me forward into a little room at the back. A room at the back is very much more enclosed. I want to know the answers about the books and whether I should really bother my time with anymore.

I ask the question. He points to what I can only call a forest of pens stood on end like trees.

"A forest of pens and like trees each pen produces branches. Each word that they write produces more growth, more branches which spread and drop seeds. Then new growth appears, all coming from the pens. I think this is a clear answer to you. Write even if you feel the books are not going anywhere. Continue to write."

"What am I to write? If feel I have done all I need to do. Where is the inspiration coming from?"

"The first thing is to sit down and write and inspiration will come. Ideas will be put into your head."

"That is all well and good. I have been given encouragement for so long now and still nothing is happening."

"It is happening all the time that you are writing. Every time you sit down and write and go over to look for subject matter your own growth is proceeding. It is never ever a waste of time."

***

2010
PREPARE FOR FUTURE

I have been given a rope and bamboo stairs. It is flexible and not rigid like a ladder but are stairs. I have to go down backwards. The bottom is rush matting. I turn round to see where I am. I appear to be inside. It is a flimsy rush matting type of building. I walk along on soft ground and go carefully. I come to the door on the right. It is very quiet. I push open a matting door. It is very dark inside. There are people here, Africans or at least dark-skinned people. A whole group of them. They have been waiting for me. They have met in secret as if they don't want anyone to know they are there. There is a huge gathering of them. I don't understand this. Tell me what this means.

I feel the weight of something on my hand – very heavy and solid. It is placed in the palm of my hand. It is a heavy book. What is it?

"It is a record of our nations, not just one nation but our history. We have knowledge that goes back much further than your history books. We know much more. We know of the events to come and yet you worry about insignificant matters when the world is at a turning point. The order of priorities will be reset. We understand the need to focus on the present so that you may carry on, enjoy and endeavour. But look further and prepare. Prepare well in your mind and in your heart. Prepare in delightful anticipation"

"I don't wish to ignore the present for that is not living in the now and we have to carry on. We have to carry on and experience the presence too."

"Yes, but hold in your mind delightful anticipation so that your thoughts are not in the negative. You can prepare in this way and send healing whenever you can and to those who need it. You will continue to speak."

I ask if it is important that I travel and do the books.

They unroll a map of the world on the floor. They are pointing to all points of the globe which I take to mean that I must still travel.

***

2010
INNER SPACE BEINGS

The stairs I have are covered in a sisal type of matting, very worn. The banisters are of wood. It keeps coming to my mind that it is a colonial house in America. The door to the right is heavy with a very heavy latch. It is in dark green. As I step in there is a big hole in the floor and is not at all what I expected. There are steps going down. I must descend into this hole. I go down several levels. It goes deep into the ground, and I realise the house is just a cover and one would not expect this here. The hole goes right the way down, a long way.

I already sense in advance what I am going to meet. I know I am going to meet beings not of this planet. They have been told of my coming and there is a lot of twittering and noises. Somebody is going down to them. I just know this because I have been before. I recognize I have been before, but it is the first time I have realised it. I am a friend and they know me as a friend. Their twittering is comforting. I don't know what this is all about or why I am here.

I am now at the bottom. It is very modern, very high tech, lots of instruments all very clean and furnished. It is high tech and clearly very advanced. It is massive. I am one of them. It is very busy down here with lots of beings doing things. Some are humanoid or human looking as I am. They are tall and in wonderful shape and in good condition considering where they are. I want to know who they are. The name is given but I really don't know if it because it has been hinted at by somebody else. Nefelim! I could have this totally wrong and there are other names I can't pronounce. (there followed a lot of their language which is impossible to write or put names to) I will have to learn their languages. I accept that it is friendly and they all have a job to do. It is something to do with preparation for underground activities. They have been here a long time. (more of their language)

Eventually after some procedures I realise I must leave straight away.

***

2010
MORE TRAVEL PLANS

I have made my journey down and am in a business centre. I arrive at a door and. There is a name on the door. It says, 'The Director'. I knock before I go in and someone from the other side calls out: 'Come in.' On the other side is a panel of people, all men. It feels like an interview board. I feel there are six people but I can't get a fix on their faces. They are in control. I ask them for direction and they push a file over to me. I open the file and inside there are flight tickets. What a surprise!

"You are still to go to America and also other countries."

I am looking to see what countries. It is not clear and I feel Japan.

So I ask: "Will you make the preparations? Will you put things in place for me?"

The men from the table come round and slap me on the back, shake my hand and congratulate me. It would seem they are pleased with me and I don't know yet why. It is their assistance I need if I am to go. I need the doors opened and the invitations to come. That is what I need.

A long trip to the Orient and Texas was in store for this year.

***

2010
TEXAS

My stairs are a bamboo ladder. I am going down a rock face. I appear to be in a typical canyon area. My path to the left is a gap between two high rocks like a pass. Soon I come to a turning to the right. There is a little figure beckoning me just in case I missed it, because I could easily have walked by. It is an obscure pathway which I could easily have missed. He is beckoning me on and we come out to a drinking hole. It is not that big and is a watering hole. Water in dry lands. Very precious. He is pointing at it. I have to drink it.

"It is very precious."

As I get down to drink from it, as I drink it disappears. It just isn't there anymore. It was there just for me. I stand there between the rocks and wonder what to do next. High above me there are eagles. Hugh big birds flying around and circling. I know they are eagles and not vultures because I can hear them screaming.

"You are standing in a vortex of energy. They are circling above for they feel it. They know where the energy is strongest and where they can soar on the thermals. You are standing right where it begins. You *ARE* to go to America even if you do not make your compensation financially. It is Texas that is more important to you than Washington. You might even if you wish skip Washington altogether. Just do Texas. Remember the energy and where it starts and that is you. So being there, you are the fulcrum of the energy that we can use in a place where it is much needed.

***

2010
TO THE CENTRE OF THE EARTH

I seem to be wrapped against the cold. The stairs are ice stairs, cut into blocks of ice. I have gloves on and spikes on the soles of my shoes so I won't slip. I don't understand why I have ice. I go down very carefully. There are walls on either side so I can hold onto those although they are ice as well. There is a reason for this. As I go down it gets warmer and I am now getting too hot in all these clothes. The ice has melted showing bare rock. I get the feeling we are going to the centre of the Earth where it is warmer and closer to the core. I begin to take my outer clothes off and my boots. I sling them around my neck as I probably have to come back the same way.

Someone has been here before because there are lights strung up. Yellow, white, some are blue as I go down. Down to the centre of the earth. It is easy going. I have a lot of questions. I keep going down, down, down. Soon I am at the bottom. It is solid ground and a bit rocky. There are crystals and minerals but they have the dirt on them and are not all in their polished state but as one would find them in a mine. I am walking carefully so as not to damage any of them.

I find the tunnel that must be here. There it is! This has been designed for it is clear cut, smooth, used quite often, quite polished smooth. I look for the entrance on the right. In fact it is just a bend to the right so I have to turn right any way. I don't want to get lost. It is comfortably warm. Not too hot. Living quarters? That is what I see, living quarters and not just for one person but for many. It is big, big!

The energy in my head is increasing a lot. The thought in my head is here I am wondering about how to promote the books, how to get the word out and yet there are things so much more important to focus on. So much more.

"Your desires that you are worrying about now will fade into the background as the other more important matters take over."

The big Indian guide that I was told about appears. A big muscular man. He takes both my hands and puts them together and draws me to him so that both my hands are touching him. It feels nice and comfortable and warm. I am to take his energies. It is to be one with him.

"You are one with me. You have always been one with me. Whatever happens you will be under my protection and guidance."

"I still don't know how my work is going to change. I really would love to know."

"Don't you see? When you begin any work with connecting people together call for me and think of the unity so that we work together, so that healing, clarity and explanation of things come through me to you to them. Use me. You so often forget to use us who are here. Call on us. Call on us and it will flow through you. Use us more."

***

2010
ARABS AND TEXANS

I am in deep velvet. Everything is in velvet including my clothes. I feel strong powerful energy. It is very deep blue velvet. I can't quite get the colour. Beautiful! At the bottom of the stairs it is soft, plush, like a very special place. Everywhere is hushed, quiet and reverent. The passage off to the left is small, just enough for one person. You could miss it if you weren't looking. It goes to a secret place. There are a few steps up with a handrail on either side, again just enough for one person. The door opens before me. I don't have to touch it.

There are several men sitting on the ground in a circle. I am reminded of the Arabs, my Tuaregs and all those tribes that came once before. They motion me to sit. I do but I am not very comfortable sitting cross-legged anymore. Somebody brings a cushion for my back which supports me. I am the only female here. They have all thrown their hand in; the cards and what they had in their hand are now in the middle. Someone has shuffled them all.

I don't understand this, but I am to take a card out of the pack and that is the card I must go with. It turns out to be confirmation for me because it is clearly an American with a big Texan hat. No mistaking that. I asked for confirmation and that is how they have given it to me. So clearly I have to go there, even though I don't know the reason.

"Stay a week, not three or four days."

Thinking of this later I have put two and two together. Oil – Arabs and Texas. Oil is the connection, but I feel a stronger meaning here.

***

2010
THAILAND

I have a beautiful turquoise green. The ladder they have given me is a rope ladder. Straight down. I feel the roughness of the rope as I go down. I see myself going down holding on to the rope. I see myself as a figure rather than me. It is a person without details. I can feel what that person feels. I can feel the rope under my hands and beneath my feet. As I go I feel the energy increasing. I feel transformation in my face and am entering another state.

I land quite heavily, solid and with shoes on. No bare feet. The ground is solid and it is an empty place. The ground is solid and smooth and I don't feel enclosed. I must look for a turn off to the left. There are little markers set in the ground to the left. I follow those. The pathway is laid out for me. I can't see anything around me, but the markers are there. I walk quite confidently and soon come to an archway on the right. It is an arch made out of wicker and bent into shape. Quite pretty! I have no door, just an entrance under the arch.

I stop because I know there is an invisible wall. There is an energy barrier here. I can feel it with my hands. It is to see if I can pass through; to see if I have the energy that is right. I walk through it very easily and am now in a different world. A world of light, gaiety and light. Quite a different world. It is like walking into another time.

"Show me what I need to see."

There is an elephant all dressed up like an Indian elephant in finery. It is painted, festooned. There is nobody on it. It is ready for some procession or something. The elephant is from Thailand not India. The elephant is picking things up from the ground and throwing them all over the place.

"He is demonstrating his own right. He is demonstrating his own will. This elephant represents the Indonesian countries who will demonstrate their own will, who will not be led and used. They have the right to lead themselves."

"That is not what I expected but it is what I have been told (in this meditation)."

***

2010
ON TEXAS AND CROP CIRCLES

I was in bed with spirit urging me to get up and meditate. As I was clearly in conversation with them I said: "Why can't we do it here?"

"Because you will forget what we say if it is not recorded."

I argued a bit because I did not want to get up then. However they persisted. My head was very full with energy. It clearly was important.

My journey:

The stairs are jagged rock. These steps have been put in a long time ago in order to go down a very steep mountain. They zigzag and are made of very strong rock. I don't know if the rock has been there already or has been carved and put into place. It doesn't matter. I am going down in sandals. To do this in bare feet would be foolish. The sandals are firm and just enough to cover the soles of the feet, kept in place with leather thongs.

I am not in too much of a hurry because it is quite steep and at almost every other step there is a turn. It is a real zigzag down. I wouldn't like to be going up. I keep on going.

I have to state that I have been urged to go into meditation for the past hour while I was in bed having a real conversation. They were insistent that I get up and meditate because I would forget it without a recording. My head is very full, so full I can hardly think.

Still going down as I am thinking all these things. There is a grassy plain at the bottom. I naturally turn left instead of going forward. Doing this I am going round near the base of a mountain. I know there has to be pathway or something to the right at some point. I can hear cows mooing and birds singing. It is warm and pleasant and not at all dangerous or threatening in any way.

My right turn is a path. A beaten path. It leads me into…oh I see what it is. I was struggling to find a word for it but I recognise it now as a crop circle. It is a proper circle not one of the odd shaped ones. Being low down I can't see a pattern.

"Go into the centre." A very strong voice tells me. I go into the centre of the swirl and stand quite still. As I do a great shaft of light comes down. I can hardly think or speak. I have difficulty in speaking but my training is such that I must. I am disappearing.

I then have a long bout of coughing which keeps my focus on me and not what is happening. I have arrived. I have arrived. It appears to be a space craft. Now whether this is my imagination or real, I am not sure. I am not alone. There is a lot going on. It is a very busy place. I am not speaking of one of the tiny pods that I would normally see or have been on.

For those who don't know, this would be called a mother ship. Osishoo appears:

He says without speaking: "You will be returning home soon."

I don't quite know what that means, and he repeats it.

"You will be returning home soon."

I wanted to ask about Texas and what has this got to do with me going to Texas? My mind is in a turmoil now of thoughts.

"Do you mean I will die? Do you mean that my soul in this body will return and there will be an exchange? What do you mean?"

"It is tied up with Texas. You must prepare before you leave."

NB: I had a great time in Texas.

***

2010

A WRITER SENT

"Why can't you let me sleep?"

"Well you said you wanted to write. That was your declared intention. We sent you a writer and you sent him away"

"Yes well it was 1.45 am and I preferred to sleep."

"In that case you had better give yourself time in the day when you are not taken up with other things so you can listen to him then."

"It seems to me that the things you are telling me have nothing to do with the kind of work I do. In fact it has no real subject at all. That is no good, is it? So here I am sitting downstairs at two o'clock in the morning hoping to make sensible contact. I have to say feeling a little foolish talking to myself."

"You know very well that talking to yourself is not foolish and is where you get the most information."

"So who is my mystery writer?"

"Now you know that if we gave you a name you would be looking up his works and then you would be just a copy editor, a copy writer. It would not be fresh; it would still carry the old style. You need to get into the habit of allotting yourself a set period of time where you can sit and let the thoughts come without interruption from elsewhere, without having to go off and do something else. If you are serious about writing then you must put your part into it. You must find the time."

***

2010
CLAIRVOYANCE

The stairs I have are broad. It is the size you'd get at a theatre or cinema. The carpeting is rich green. I am going on my own but there is plenty of room for others. I see myself tripping lightly down. I am a lot slimmer than I am usually, younger. At the bottom there is a door facing me, a big door, double doors. They are right in front, so it is clear I have to go in. I push them in the middle and they open quite easily.

On the other side are lights, high up as you would get in a theatre but very high. They are so high they are not casting a lot of clarity and are not fully on but dimmed. I realise we are in a theatre. People are already in their seats. The place is packed. I walk down the centre – I have been here before – I know this. I am the one that has to go on the platform. I know I have done this before and am not nervous. I go up the steps at the side and out to the front. I am a lot younger than I am in today's life. I have done this before.

Someone hands me a mike. It is a handheld mike, not one of the modern behind the ear things. I look very calmly over the big audience. Spirit comes swirling into me from the back. It actually enters and I simply observe this. I am watching it happen. I am doing clairvoyance. Then I start to lift off. I am floating. They know this is going to happens as they have seen it before. I am spirit.

"Why are you showing this to me?"

"You have done this before and because of that you can do this again.

You know that. It is time to put it into practice. It is time to open yourself to what you were."

***

2010
LISTEN

The stairs I am on are alive. They keep moving in differing directions and are moving while I am on them, very like the Harry Potter films. I am holding on to both sides, on a rail. It is like a fairground this. I don't know if I am going up or down or where I am on the stairs. It is a fun ride, and nobody can see where it is ending while they are on it and can see only when they have left the stairs. I keep holding on. It is pointless trying to walk and is enough just to hold on.

Then I see I am at the bottom of somewhere and I step off onto firm ground. They continue the fun thing for there are little lights along the way on the ground. That is all I can see, little lights. I follow them and they lead along passages with firm ground. Coloured lights everywhere. They take me to what I now call my space. No door just an opening with little lights all around it. It is a definite invitation to go through.

Inside is vast emptiness, but is not really empty, only for sight. I can hear thoughts. I can hear everything that exists, a cacophony of sound in what appears to be empty space. There is so much going on here – so much – the entire world. No, entire worlds all are making their sound. Making and leaving forever their impressions on everything. I listen to this for a while until it becomes too much. I ask for an explanation.

"Everything that occurs in existence remains for it to be found (discovered), sought after, ignored or whatever you will. It is all there for you to make use of, all of it. Speaking of sound, even your clearing of throat is a sound. Even that remains if you wish to anchor to it. You can let it go, as all beings have learnt to let go of sounds that do not serve them and yet can tune in to those sounds which please them and makes them feel whole again. Listen for the sounds of angels. Listen for the sounds that you have tuned out, the Celestial Beings, listen for them. Listen to the innermost workings of your mind. Each thought also has a sound. Every thought produces a vibration which is felt somewhere, sometime, in some manner. Be sure your thoughts are pure and of love."

I have standing before me what I can only call an angel. It is very still and just looks at me. Beautiful, golden, shimmering, giving off a light all around like a glow. One hand up, as if blessing me.

***

2011
BANDING TOGETHER

I am at the top of my stairs after a conversation with the guides. I am wrapped up in some kind of fur outfit, like an Eskimo. The stairs seem to be ice. I am in a very cold climate. There is no worry about slipping for whatever I have on my feet is a nonslip sole. I am going down a long way. I still need warm clothing even though I know it isn't so cold now. I don't feel cold.

I get a strong sense that I have gone back to past life in a colder climate. This is a journey back and I am told maybe a journey forward too. I don't like the sound of that. At the bottom are ice tunnels. Perfectly calm and smooth. There is no door to knock on, just another entrance. I see a guide, also wrapped up in furs.

He beckons me: "Come forward, come forward."

I feel I may have been related to him in a past time. I am a female and he is a male. I am not sure if I am his daughter or wife. He has the commanding position. I do as I am told and come forward.

"In past times we all banded together. We gathered together to support each other no matter how difficult things became. We survived by this means and people of today will do the same. You will also use the animals for your survival as we did."

I stroke the outfit and it is soft and silky. It is no horse skin but possibly bear.

"You need it to keep warm. If you don't do that you will die. **We knew that**"

***

2011
JAPAN/NUCLEAR

I am wrapped in what looks like an orange jumpsuit. I am standing on plastic kind of flooring – smooth and shiny- very hard. It is like a walkway with a slope down. There are handrails because it is not that wide. A gangway? I don't know what the word is but it is like plastic. I am wrapped in a working suit, orange.

"You must use the mind as it is a protection and notification to others". It is a winding pathway. It goes round curves. There are no angles, just soft bends as it goes down.

"I can't understand what this is about."

"It is so that you can't see what is around the corner. It implies a certain trust in carrying on, knowing this is leading somewhere."

This is really weird as I don't know where I am. I am going down but not steeply. There is protection. The curves are also a slowing down device for anything that might be coming up because it is harder when you can't go straight. I don't know what it is talking about but I must follow the thread they are giving me.

I am still in orange. I feel quite strong, much younger. I feel much younger than my current age. Then I come against a thick wall, blocking the way. Remembering that I am only mind I just walk myself straight through it, no problem at all. But the wall is there for others too, not just for me. Not everybody will know that it is not an impediment.

I am in a different place now. It is softly and gently lit. The few lights there are, if they were not there it would be black. Oh, these are emergency lights, the sort that are put on in a plane if there is an emergency. There is a soft gentle hum. I don't know where this is leading me but it is going into somewhere that requires work, specialised work. Oh I see! My mind keeps going to the nuclear disaster in Japan. This is something to do with that. That is why I have a protective suit but this is a mind job. I must remember I am not physical.

I am in the heart of things now, in the very heart of things. There are a few things I must do. I see a few disconnected pipes. I put them together. I do this with my mind but using my hands. I am snapping them together and am tightening the rings, like a screw on. I am tightening it and making sure it doesn't come off. There are quite a few of these and I must do them all. I am now opening a flow which allows the coolant, whatever they use, to come through. I do this now and it starts to flow all around. It is a coolant and is designed to bring the levels of danger down. Where all this is coming from I don't know, but this is what I must do.

I stand here watching it take place. This is a place no one has been to before, not even in the mind. Nobody has been here, nobody would go there. I know I am alright. This is a massive place, there is nothing small about this – disturbance of tape – there are switches, I turn some of them on. Things are starting to happen around me. There is a glow and a vibration, a physical vibration such as a noise would make. It is a noise that is produced by the vibration.

I am just here. I don't know what else I must do. I must stand my ground. The gentle hum continues. Things begin to change, more organised, if I can use that word. Now it is time to leave. I turn round and see another way out. There is a thick casing of a wall. I am to walk straight through this. This is to tell me and remind me that I am not physical even though the experience feels physical. I pass through easily. It is thick and seems to go on and on and on. Then I plop out the other side into a much cooler environment. Air! I am out of there. Then some hands come and pull me away. These are spirit guides, the angelic realm. They pull me and are attending to me. I feel that is quite sufficient for now.

***

2011

SAFETY IN THE EARTH

I am going straight down on a bamboo ladder all tied up with twine or creepers or whatever is natural. It has been constructed by those who know how. It goes down on what appears to be a rock face from the surface down into the earth. I get the feeling there will be many such ladders down leading to deeper places which will be safer from whatever is going on at the surface. It is not permanent but is a safety measure for a short period of time. For example, against strong winds, hurricanes, tornadoes.

"You are much safer down in the earth than on the surface."

I follow my usual route left then right. There are a lot of people, indistinct but very busy. They all know exactly what they are doing. It is a comfortable warm cosy feeling in here. I don't know what this it telling me. I am reminded of gnomes such as you see in a Santa Claus thing when they are sorting out the presents. They are happily going about their tasks. They are short, round, happy.

***

2011

SAFE PLACE WITHIN EARTH

I am standing on purple velvet, very thick and rich velvet. It is like carpeting in velvet. The banister is knobbly so you can't slide your hand down it, metal like gold or brass. As I go I realise there are a lot of people watching. I stop and take my cloak/coat off and put it over my head so I can't be seen. That is a bit odd. As I get to the bottom there are people, energies, intelligences, whatever. Some of them are interested, some are just going about their business. The place is absolutely packed, seething almost. I work my way through until I come to the passageway on the left. I can just about see it through all the others that are here. I slip into it. Nobody seems to notice that I have done this.

It is calm, quiet and dark. Not too dark so I can still see where I am going. It is a narrow passageway, very narrow, almost both shoulders are touching either side it is so narrow. I push my way along. The passage almost feels like a crack, something that has broken apart and has allowed entry into it. Like a crack or fissure in a rock. It is still quite dark and I have to feel my way along on the right to feel the opening. I turn into it not knowing where it is going. The only place I can go is down a ladder, fixed to the wall so there is no fear of it falling.

I keep going down. It is well hidden for safety, for security.

"You are allowed for we know you are safe (to know this)."

I come to a big open space – well lit. There are a lot of people here. I am talking about human beings as well as those who look like human beings but are not, not in our sense. This place is very busy with everyone doing something. It is enormous and well-lit but with no shadows. The light is everywhere. Everyone seems to know what they are doing but I don't know what I am doing here. There is machinery, lots of dials and controls. It has been here a while because it is so orderly, so well-practiced.

"What am I supposed to do here?"

"You are to observe and know that this exists. Know that we have plans to accommodate many."

"My question is how are people going to know about this? It is so far down. I don't even know the way in."

"When it is important for others to know there will be an opening which will show them the way."

"My next question is, who are these people you will show the way to?"

"We will show the way to those who will have something of benefit to offer the planet without thought of selfish gain. We will know which ones genuinely wish to assist planet Earth and genuinely wish for a better world for all, not just for themselves. Those who feel they have earned a place because of position or power will not know of this entrance."

"I feel you are talking of adults here but what about families, children, innocents?"

"We look at the soul. Even children have a soul that can be seen for its true purpose. Therefore it will only be for those who at soul level have intentions of assisting planet Earth and the continuation of the human species. Even children may have evolved souls or inferior souls, and we will know for we have access to their innermost being when the need is there."

"My next question is, why are you showing me this?"

"This is so you can make this known. So that others will look to their soul condition and take heed of what we say. We know you are safe for you do not know how to enter this place on a physical level. It will be clear when the time is right."

"It sounds a bit fancy to me but there are so many people down here. They are men down here, not ladies or children."

"These are the operators, those who are maintaining this in good order. The time is not ready yet."

They then showed me to another part, a different area. It is there that I see beings who are not humans. I can't say Extra-terrestrials for they are of the Earth but not as those on the surface.

"They too belong to the Earth and it is they who have assisted in this project. Without these beings from in the Earth this project would not be possible."

***

2011
PREPARE AND RESOLVE DIFFICULTIES BEFORE CHANGE

"When you go into a higher state such as the Earth and humanity is going to enter there will be a sluicing, a cleansing even after the event of any dross, anything that is contaminated, unwanted or unclean. The cleansing will take place before as well as afterwards. There will be much of this going on. It is a sort of halfway house and not a sudden transition. There is to be an interim period, not a no man's land exactly but an area beforehand, before stepping cleanly into the new world. There will also be a quarantine area – you can call it decontamination if you like.

"Family members will stay together in the changeover process and in the interim period this is where they will resolve any difficulties they may have had between them. They have to be resolved first in this so called no man's land. I do not have the correct word but I can't think of a suitable one. It is a second chance for everybody to sort out any family or relationship problems. They will sort them out before they can step cleanly into the new world."

"I can hear you ask, how long will this take? As you know time is not relevant. It may take a long time, or it may be done very quickly. Each situation is individual to that grouping so there is not one set period allowed.

"We would recommend that you try to resolve difficulties well in advance and get it sorted out sooner rather than later."

***

2011
RESCUE OF GREYS

I have finished my descent which is quite steep. I am dressed in grey, unusual for me, and am in tight fitting clothes so that there is no flapping or anything to catch on something else.

"They are in grey so it blends with its surroundings and is also a cloak, a mask."

I must mask my light so it can't be seen. I look around. Not much to see. It is a bit empty like being in a big tunnel that has been made but is just an entrance and is not itself important. I must walk along it because it obviously leads somewhere. As I go I realise that my outfit also covers my feet, padded. My feet are padded so I don't make a noise. As if I could make a noise because I am just a consciousness.

I keep going forward as the tunnel gets narrow and then widens. It is an hourglass shape. I squeeze through the narrow part and get into a lighted area. It is huge, massive, and really big. It will take me a while to walk around the area. There are lots of lights, very bright. They are artificial lights not daylight. There is a lot here, not in the middle but around the sides. I come to one area which I can't call a room but is an enclosure of some kind. Inside are many, many what you would call Greys, little people all jumbled together, all interacting with each other. I can't make out what they are saying. I am so much bigger than they are. They see me and call me, trying to get my attention. They are fingering me. They are very small and I have to be careful I don't tread on anybody. But they get out of the way as they are nimble as well.

They look at me and every time I look their way I see their big eyes looking back at me trying to impart some information. There is not just one trying, they are all trying together. I must unify a little and I might get what they want – so many all clambering. Whichever way I look there is someone trying to tell me something. I know it sounds ridiculous I know I am to help them get out from here. They feel physical and I am not, I am just consciousness. I know that but I feel physical here. I am so much bigger than they are.

I deliberately expand my energy field. I know this is what I have to do. I deliberately increase my energy field so it covers them and surrounds them so they are now enclosed. I can excite the field so it is more powerful and they are included in this. Quite interesting! With the energy field completely enclosing them I walk out of the enclosure and back along where I have come from and through the gap. It is like squeezing a balloon through, but my energy field is intact and they all come through with me. They are still with me, all of them. Some are clinging to me. I go back up the steps dragging this load I have with me and get to the surface. I stand with the huge energy field around me and the beings inside the field. They are protected and invisible while they are within the field.

Then it is odd, and it sounds so much like science fiction – there is a beam coming down from I do not know where. They all join inside the beam, collect in it and it is as if they are vacuumed up into it until my energy field is empty of them and I can bring it back to normal. The beam they have gone up in begins to fade. They have been rescued.

I feel good. I have a headache, that's all. I am on my own now and have done what they have asked me to do. I don't know where they have come or where they have gone. They are so small, like children and very vulnerable. I had to protect them. No-one is ever going to believe this but I must transcribe it just the same. Whether anybody believes it or not is irrelevant. It happened.

***

2011

SPACE CRAFT IN JUNGLE

I go down on what appears to be a bamboo ladder, the sort you get from a hut in the jungle set up high in the trees or built up high. This is a ladder that can be pulled up to make the place secure and let down when the need is there. I am going down the ladder. It is not very steady. I am going backward until I reach the ground. It is not exactly jungle but is native type land, a clearing, beaten earth. So now I am on the ground. Where do I go? I wander around a little bit, but I do not see anybody.

I see a pathway off. I take the path which soon gets into undergrowth. It is like being in the rainforest. It is more rainforest than dry arid land. I keep walking but I can't see much on either side because the growth is quite high and dense. I come to another path so I follow that one. I don't know where it is taking me. Very quickly, very soon I come to a huge clearing. This hasn't been cleared by natives. It is massive. This is nothing to do with clearing the jungle for anything minor. It has been done for a specific purpose.

There is a craft and men who are nothing to do with the jungle. They are watching the craft, patrolling and safeguarding it. Very odd! I am trying to describe the craft, but my mind is going in all directions now. I call it a craft because it is not an aeroplane. An aeroplane couldn't land in this jungle. It is not a helicopter. This is different. I don't know what to call it. You can hardly call it a flying saucer, but it is very similar to that. It is humming and is active. That's the word. It is not dead. It is not a craft that has landed and is still. It can move at any moment, I feel.

I walk past all the guards ,and they don't see me, or don't appear to. They are military because they have that sort of uniform, camouflage uniform. They are all around this thing and I walk straight through them. I go up to the craft. As I do a portion of it opens. Oh God, it sounds so science fiction! It opens and there is a way in for me. I walk straight in. I get inside. It is a bit cramped. The Beings, for they are not from this world see me. They do see me. They beckon me over. They are tall and what I would call gangly. They are not the short, tiny greys. I feel very nice with them, very comfortable with them. They show me to a seat. I almost recline in the seat but I feel OK. I feel fine.

"What is this all about, please?"

"You are to go on a trip. You are to go outside of your world and see the bigger picture. This is why you are here. You are here to see the big picture, not the little events that everybody is concerned about. So many on your planet are concerned about their own portion of their existence, their own private worlds and are not truly bothered about the big picture. They may say they are but when it comes down to it they are not. As long as they are alright, as long as it doesn't touch them then the rest is unimportant to them, or so it seems. That is how it seems (to us)."

So I am in. I am lying down. It is odd because I know we are travelling but I also know that this craft is still there in the centre of the clearing. I just know that. To those guards outside it appears as if nothing has happened. Yet I know it has. Very odd! What I am doing now is looking through a screen, an all-round screen. I get up and go close and can see our planet and the colours from it. I see areas that are muddy and grey, that need help, that need healing.

I am not sure if I am seeing reality or an illustration of what can be because the planet is entering a beam from the sun, from other influences. I don't know the words for them. Rays of this, particles of that – entering a field of all manner of interferences and influences. The whole planet is in this, going deeper and deeper and deeper in until it is totally immersed in it. It will come out of the other side of the beam but this will take a long time. While we are in it things are going to change. It is a regenerating beam. Things will change but it is not an overnight process because the beam is very wide and vast. I'll be long gone by the time we come out the other side.

"We are showing you this so that you know that this is just a period in your Earth time. It is an age it goes through. When you come out you humans will be more responsible. What happens in your future is that you will be even more responsible than before. You will take greater charge and greater care of the entire body of your planet instead of being self-interested to the extent that you ignore external events."

I think this is already happening now on the planet.

"Yes, people are being disturbed, which is as it should be. They have been complacent and stagnant for too long. We need agitation to get things moving. To change things we need you to come alive and put things where they are meant to be."

"I don't understand why you are showing me this because I can't really do much."

"Yes, you can. You can help people to see what is happening. You may feel it is only in a small way but small things have a way of growing, developing and spreading. Whatever you do or say will have an effect and will spread. Don't give up. Don't give up. You will be travelling more."

"I don't think I could travel more this year than I have done already."

"You will be directed, and the ways will be opened for you so do not be concerned over where and when and how. We are opening the doors and you will walk through into where we have planned."

"Ah, a mystery tour, eh?"

"Don't worry about it, it will work. There is no alternative for you."

"What do I do now?"

They release me from the seat and point to the door which is opening. I go down past the guards who have not noticed a single thing happening. As I go back down the pathway the whole thing disappears. I am back here recording this. How very weird! A true mind journey. I didn't get a chance to ask all the questions, but I feel that is my fault. I could have asked more.

I don't know if that was a flight of fancy or real. I feel spaced out. I feel it happened but is it odd.

This was one of many visits to space craft but as they were not recorded I cannot include them here.

***

2011
EXPECTATIONS OF OTHERS

The stairs are wide and clearly not meant just for one person but for many. There is nothing terribly grand about them but is an entrance for many. There is nothing to hold on to. It is a huge wide staircase, similar to steps you get outside a church or cathedral where the steps are wide so that masses can go in and out. I am to go up not down. I get to the top and there appears to be what I would call ushers welcoming. They are inviting me to go in. It is the dwelling of the Council of Nine. There are many avenues I can go into from here in the entrance hall. It has a vaulted ceiling, so high I can't see it clearly. I am drawn to the left which is my normal way anyway. I am just going to follow my nose. I can hear sweet gentle music. I follow a corridor which feels OK. There is a rich feel about this place. I am drawn to go into my right – another pathway. It has a church like feel.

As I go in I ask: "Take me where I need to be, tell me what I need to know. I am looking for confirmation of my abilities that everybody seems to think I have when I don't think I have them at all. Expectations are always great and greater than I think I can deliver. I need some sort of encouragement, confirmation, something of that nature to reassure that I can deliver, even when I don't know how.

"I feel uncomfortable with the promotion side of things of what I do. I would rather just do. I can't get to grips with promotions. Self-promoting doesn't sit right."

I am feeling very emotional as I say this. I am really emotional over this as if I am baring my soul.

***

2011
BOOK IMPORTANT

I am down now standing on rush matting on an uneven floor. I suspect it is an earthy floor underneath the mat. There is nothing constructed here. It is as if the open space has been made out of natural surroundings. I look for my passage. There is a sort of dug out tunnel which extends into some sort of habitat. I go along and know there has to be another opening for this is how I enter. It is smooth. I am reminded of Coober Pedy where it is dug out for opals underground. Nice living quarters can be dug out this way. It is all very comfortable even if it is a bit rugged. It needs finishing touches.

I now enter the right turn. This is where I need to be to get some resolution to the things going round in my head. I see a central figure with an extremely long exaggerated quill pen. He has a pointed hat. He is trying to write but he is being bothered by others with their pens. They keep nudging him, trying to take him away from what he is doing. He keeps fending them off. They are all interested in writing but my attention is on the main one because he is clearly central to my work as well.

"Who are these others?"

"These are those who would write their books and who are trying to get as much attention for themselves. They are not looking at the bigger picture but their own particular journeys."

"I suppose there is nothing wrong with that. That is what I am doing after all."

"The book you are working on now will be more important than the ones you have already written, even though you cannot see that this may be. This is true."

***

2011
PUT YOUR TRUST IN US

I have gone down a very long way on a vertical ladder. It is a bit like going down a drain but a long way past any drain level. The last step I have to jump off as the ladder doesn't touch the bottom. There is not much space, a bit like the bottom of a well. It is like being at the centre of a wheel because there are passages going off like spokes in all directions. There are seven of them. I don't know which one to take because they are fanning out from where I stand. I am looking at each one in turn to see which passage can be different. I can't possibly go down them all. I have done a complete circle and come back to where I started.

I detect a very faint glimmer down one so that is the one I am going to take. It is not right or left but the one where there is a glimmer. It is not a big passage, and I can get through it, no problem at all. It is quite closed in. I have my usual coughing fit which seems to happen when I am going somewhere special. I wish it wouldn't! I pad along because either I have something on my feet or the ground is soft and doesn't make any noise. It is smooth as you get in caves when water has been through.

I go along carefully because it is not very bright. I keep my eye on the glimmer ahead. It has a green hue to it. As I get closer it gets stronger. It fills the passage and is not just a speck any more. It is circular, a pale green. It reminds me of something and I can't think what. I reach it and it is a bit like a mist.

I have come this far so I walk into the green mist. I am surrounded by the mist now. Walking through. It is long. Walking through. I am free of it. Suddenly I am in a completely different world. It is outside.

It is a completely different world. There is activity, a bustle. I am outside and the air smells sweet, sweeter than I have ever sensed before, ever. There is sweetness about it, pure. It is a long time since the air has been this pure. Yes, there are birds singing. Quite a lot, not like the silent spring we have these days. There is re-growth, fresh and pure. It feels happy.

I entered this meditation asking if the direction I have been led to is the one I should go. I don't know if this answers. I don't think it does but is another journey. Three people come towards me. I don't know if they are men or women. It is difficult to tell, but they too are sweet. The centre one is definitely a man. He extends his hands towards me and takes mine and draws me into an embrace. Ooh it's lovely! The other two stand and watch.

"What does this mean? Should I go down this route?"

"We will provide on each occasion that which is expected of you. You need not fear of not coming up to the expectations of others. You may feel you are on a knife edge at times. If you put your trust in us we will be there giving you what you need. Not just what you need but what the world needs to see and to hear. Trust in us then you will not need to worry about trust in yourself. For we are united, are we not? We work through you, do we not? So yes, you will as you say, 'come up with the goods' for that is what concerns you. It does not concern you the effort and the time which you must put in, only that you provide what others are seeking and what the world needs to hear. Maybe what they hear is not what they expected but will be what they need. Put your trust in us. Do put your trust in us for we are many. We are many."

***

2011

I have plain wooden stairs. As I begin to go down I see a picture of me when somebody grabs me. I am watching the 'me' wanting to go forward and yet someone is trying to hold on to me to stop me. The person I am looking at, the me pulls hard and pulls away. He/me is determined to go. I am determined to go and can hear the steps on the wood, the odd creak. Pressure is building in me, building up as I go down. I feel pressure. It keeps getting bigger. I feel male. I am a male.

I am observing me. As I get to the bottom I see I have boots on, working clothes and sturdy boots. I land on a path through a dense forest. The path is narrow. I don't understand this. It is straight ahead, no turnings when my usual way is to have turnings. I still feel very determined, to keep going and not to stop.

"Keep going and do not stop. Do not be diverted. Keep the goal in site."

The forest is still dense and large. It is still. Not much going on. I keep marching forward. I am not taking it slowly but as fast as I can go. It is urgent that I get through this.

"You must not be put off whatever happens to you. Keep your goal in site."

I am trying not to think for if I think I will get diverted by my thoughts. I keep going and there are things on either side clutching at me, trying to stop me.

"What is this referring to?"

"This is referring to your work of course. What is it that you have in mind? Whatever it is you must keep going towards it. Do not be afraid."

"I am not afraid."

"You are afraid of many things. You are afraid that you cannot deliver. Why do you not trust us more? We will make sure that you deliver when you arrive out into the public world."

My head hurts. I can't seem to relieve it. My head hurts.

***

2011

UNSAFE RADIATION BOXES

The stairs are old and worn with no carpeting. There is a sort of lino, broken in parts and uncared for. I am in a derelict place. It echoes as I go down. There is a wall on either side painted a horrible green in painted plaster. I keep going down quite a long flight of stairs considering wherever I am it is in an old building.

At the bottom it is like being in a warehouse. It is big with huge empty spaces. It could be used as it is quite dry, painted floor like concrete that has been painted smooth. It has been used in the past. I look around for my exit from this. Yes, there is a passage going somewhere else. We are rather deep below ground somewhere. There are no windows.

I walk along. Gosh this is not a nice place. It is old, uncared for. It has been used and is not now. I am looking for my door on the right-hand side. I come to a door that has wooden slats nailed across it to stop entry. It has been boarded up with wooden planks. How on earth am I going to get in there? I start to tug at the boards. They come away quite easily. I finish pulling them all down. The door inside is rotting on its hinges. As I push it falls inwards.

I clamber over all the bits and pieces to get inside. What an odd journey this is! Oh, that is interesting. There is something glowing. Not a celestial glow but which feels radioactive. I don't know if it really is radioactive but that is the impression I get. There is a glow from some element. I don't know my element table, but this is not a safe glow. I suddenly realise that this is why this place has been boarded up. This is why a perfectly good building is now unused. It is because there is an unsafe radiation in it. Nobody would dare go near.

Well, I am only a mind so I can go near. It isn't going to affect me. I move over to whatever it is, a fairly large box. It is difficult to see through it for it has a reddish haze over it. It is not safe for most physical beings. What am I supposed to do with this? I haven't a clue. So I ask for information.

"What we are showing you is not an isolated place. That is to say there are other areas, other houses, other buildings that contain unsafe elements within them, that we have isolated, forbidden entry to. That is authorities have forbidden entry to. This is much more widespread than this one building and the general public have no idea. They are in areas of the world such as Eastern Europe, China, even the Philippines. In many other parts of the world there are these buildings which we have boarded up and restricted entrance to."

"I want to know what I am doing here then. What can I do?"

"You must now use your mind. When you complete this one task it will have an effect on all these other places we have told you about. We want you to use your mind. Put out both hands and lay them on this box. As you do with your mind the glow will subside. Send your thoughts so that the danger element in this box is nullified. It reduces the radioactivity. This you must do. Create a mind picture of the other aspects of yourself doing this in many other places. You are not restricted to one place when you use your mind."

I have a picture of me many times over laying hands on the bock, container and see the glow diminishing, fading, fading and leaving the box completely free. I see pictures of me everywhere doing the same. It takes quite a long time.

"When this is done we can use these buildings safely. All these areas will become safe as a result of your action."

Well it is done but I don't know how I can put that into my book. It is too difficult to put into the book.

"You can type it up just the same for it needs to be a record of the actions taken by those such as yourself for reference later."

"Why couldn't you do this yourselves?"

"You are very well aware that if change is to come about on your planet the change must come from those who inhabit the planet whether they use their minds or their physicality. You human beings have to make the changes, not us."

It is obvious that changes are taking place and that we as human beings need to take responsibility for our actions. We need to realise that we are more than our physical bodies and can travel wherever our minds take us. It is clear that whatever travel we take we can change things using our minds. We are more connected with other intelligences than we ever thought possible.

These journeys may seem unbelievable and fantasy to you but to me they have been as real as my everyday existence. I recommend you try for yourself using the method described at the end of this book. Enjoy the ride.

***

2012
GROUP MEETING

All those great ones we know about such as Plato and the great philosophers, mathematicians, all those who have left their mark on your world, they have all come from the stars and have incarnated down to assist Earth. When you talk about your society and say that we have been manipulated and used, it is only because you have allowed it to be.

It would help many if they realised that even though they are minute in comparison to the whole cosmic universe that the minute part that is an individual will still continue and continue and will still exist wherever it may end up. It will not disappear and get lost in the mightiness of everything else.

Then I was given a picture of rabbits. "Reproduction will not be so prolific among humans. The advancement that will come after you have made this great shift is going to be so far ahead of what you have today. You think the last hundred years have been rapid, huge growth, huge innovations, but is as nothing compared to what is ahead. Earlier you were talking of vaccinations and illnesses which are being eradicated. All that is small in comparison.

If you happen to sever a limb it will grow back. There will be the ability to re-grow parts that have been damaged in some way, and that means internal organs as well. Bodies will be precious for they may be used and reused particularly when reproduction is not so prolific. Bodies will need to be maintained."

They are not talking about ill health so much as accidents. Not ill health caused by such things a stress or the usual things that create bad health. These are by accidents."

"The angels, the Ascended Masters and all those in spiritual high esteem will be as important and as valued as ever. What we are saying is because of heightened ability and technology to take care of yourself does not mean that there is not also the importance of connecting in a spiritual manner. It will be as important to maintain that connection because you will just be on one step of the ladder and there are many more yet to come."

***

2012

I slip down until I reach the bottom. I am slightly damp. I get up a bit shakily and am not steady on my feet. I am disorientated. I can't keep my balance and am holding on to a wall. It is as if I am giddy. I don't know where I am going or where I am and am confused. I hope this is leading somewhere. As I put my head into an opening there are a lot of students sitting at desks, studying quite hard. They are all engrossed in what they are doing. I am directed to a desk where I too must sit and study. I am still very giddy. I sit down and papers appear.

"You like these others are learning to be new again. You are starting fresh into another world, a new environment from what you have been in. It is confusion. Things will soon become clear, and you will have no doubts whatsoever."

***

2012

MAN'S JOURNEY?

I seem to be clad in furs, brown, shaggy natural furs. I seem to have become a creature of some sort, very large. I go down a mountain side. I am out in the country. It is very odd because I have my own mind and yet I can see myself in this form. I jump off the last step onto stony ground. Not smooth stone but gravelly stone. As I land the fur skin I wear falls off me. I am still not myself. I feel very bare. I know I am not naked, but I feel naked and still do not feel like me. I am very much of nature.

I go ahead not walking naturally. It is very hard to describe. Like a monkey, Mowgli type figure or early man almost on all fours but not quite. I am in forest. I ask to be shown what I need to see and to take me where I need to be. I need guidance in this. The path stretches ahead of me so that is where I must go. It would be stupid to go off into the undergrowth. There are lots of creature noises around me. High whistles as well, high pitched screeches. Some of the whistles appear not to be from animals – more like signal sounds. Somebody knows I am coming.

As I go along I begin to straighten up. I stand straighter, taller and more upright. Oh I see what is happening, yes. They are putting clothes on me. Clothes are appearing on me and I am very much upright now. I know where I am going and am purposeful. I keep on walking steadily. The screeching has stopped.

There are beautiful melodic sounds which are angelic. There is celestial music as I step forward into bright sunshine and open grassland. There are blue skies and everything is beautiful. It can't be paradise, but it feels like it. As I continue in a strong and determined way I see two angelic figures. They alight on the ground and take me by the arms and lift me up. I go up with them into a Celestial world. It is beautiful. I am so different from the animal skin person of before.

They take me up and we keep going up together until we arrive on a platform. It is all beautiful pastel colours. They leave me and I am left alone though I know I am not alone for there is much going on around. I continue to walk. The walking is no effort. My head feels wavy and I can't focus clearly any more. Everything is waving in beautiful colours. I feel I am being absorbed into the surroundings and becoming part of everything here. I am joining with the colours and the music. I lose myself into bliss.

***

2012
LOVE ALL

I am putting down my thoughts. When I say I love everybody I mean it. Is it wrong to love those and still feel love and compassion towards those who do dreadful things, who act in ways that we would not condone? I am thinking more of the politicians, those in the black governments who are still human beings. If I were to look at them individually I still feel love for them even though they knowingly do dreadful things. I can't help but still feel that love. Is this wrong? It doesn't mean I condone but still see that humanity, the vulnerability inside, the doubts, the fears. All those things that drive them on is as if they can't help themselves, as if something has taken hold of them. How dreadful!

Is it wrong to still love all? With these words I feel great emotion I didn't expect to have. It is as if love itself makes me emotional and I can't help it. In thinking all these things I have a vision of a wonderful light going down to the deepest part. In front there is a great enormous pool of light. The thought of throwing everybody, no matter who they are, no matter how bad they are, just gathering them up and throwing them all into the pool of light. It is an amazing image. They have no choice as they are picked up and thrown into the pool of light. It is wonderful and joyous. They have no choice but to be transformed.

***

2012

The stairs are silk and I am sliding down easily. My turning to the left is an archway of flowers. I can smell the sweetness of them. Beautiful. There are flowers all the way along, petals on the floor where they have dropped. There is the sound of birds. It is like being in the country but in the grounds of a country house where these have been grown. I am looking for my turning to the right. I see it, steps going up into a raised part of the garden. It feels like a country house garden with big grounds. I go up the steps into what looks like a kitchen garden with vegetables. It is a big plot, a big wall with fruit trees trained along it. This is a proper working kitchen garden with a large staff for this.

There is a gardener working away, tidying up and doing things. He looks up as I come up to him. I hear a real country accent.

"There is a lot of work going into this to make sure people are fed and nourished. It doesn't just happen you know. There is a lot of preparation, seeding, watching it grow, waiting for the harvest, it all takes time. But at the end of the day everybody is happy, everybody is fed. This you know is your work too and we are not talking of vegetables. We are talking of knowledge and speaking of all the preparation of the ground that you have put in to provide people with nourishment of ideas, thoughts, teachings. It is hard work and it takes time. You can't rush it; you can't expect it to happen overnight. This is true for you too, the nourishment that goes into bringing you along, encouraging you and helping you to grow. This too takes time. It is all one big chain."

I have now got the usual big build-up of energy in the head that says they are taking me elsewhere now.

***

2012
MASTER HERMIT IN A CAVE

I am all in green, a fresh spring green. I am not a clearly defined shape but a green whirling column. I am looking down the stairs as I have decided to use the stairs method again. They are green too. It is outside and the steps are green grass. I move down rather than walk down and at the bottom the whirling that I am like a mini twister is moving towards the entrance. It is very weird. I have not done this before. It/I move to the left to the entrance there. As I go whirling along it lights up the way. Everything parts as if I am moving through matter and is swept to one side. Then I come to the entrance on the right. They are just following my patterning. I could go straight there if I wanted to but somehow this is the deepening process. I move into my space. Immediately as I move in I am me again. The spinning green column disappears, and I am left standing as me as I am today.

Where am I? It is not exactly a cave but similar. It is not closed in and has rock underneath. Smooth rock. The entrance to this looks out over a big scenario. I am high up and it feels good. I couldn't have got her any other way apparently. There is no way up and no way down. This place is not visited by human beings. So what do I do? I have so many questions in my mind.

I notice a man at the back end of this cave. He is a hermit and has been here a long time. He cannot be real because nobody visits, so how does he eat?

"It doesn't matter," he says. "It doesn't matter."

I sit down in front of him and ask if he knows what is ahead for me. What really am I to do? I feel as if I am changing direction, even changing contacts, which is not nice for me.

He says, "New faces, new personalities, new contacts who will become firm friends. Much movement. You have no need to search for it for it will find you. Sit back, enjoy and wait for these connections to be made. You have enough to think about in the meantime although you will be busy, It is getting things in order busy, settling your house and doing all those things which you might consider to be mundane things. Relaxing, relaxing and getting your book around."

"Yes, yes."

"There is to be a gap, a pause in the programme you have set for yourself, the ones you have been doing for so many years. There is to be a shift in arrangement. The shift is coming for you."

The little man, the hermit gets up and steps backwards into the wall. He disappears into the wall behind him. He is no longer there. Is he a figment of my imagination? But he was speaking to me, that much I know.

I turn round and look for the way back. The green steps are still there.

***

2012
CONFERENCE ROOM

I am in a big hall such as in a village or school. Great tall floor to ceiling windows. It is a public place or one that is hired out to the public. There are various doors going off to little rooms or other places. I take the one to the left which has a door to it is quite easy to open. There are other doors in the passage. It is a bit like an adult education type building with a lot of things going on. I continue until I reach the one I know I must have. It is bright startling red. I step inside.

It is like a conference room. A long table with people sitting round it. They represent different planets. Human beings are here too, representing different countries. I can tell that by the clothes they wear. They are pretty much all men though there must be women here but I can't see any. These are the ones who control or dictate roles and strategies, not just for Earth but also for other planets and the interaction between them.

They beckon me to sit and I find an empty seat. I sit with them but don't hear what they are saying. This is not one of the huge G8 type conferences and there are not as many people as you might expect. This puzzles me but thinking about it but I see what they have here is a representative for Europe, another for the East, another for various sections of the Globe rather than for individual countries. They have been allocated or have decided to take this position. It is to do with events to come in the future.

Individual countries would fight their own corner. When it is seen to be more global than that, things won't happen just in one country, it will happen in sectors of the world, which will encompass all those countries in that sector. To avoid squabbling these men sitting here have been chosen from spirit and are higher than the individual representatives, such as a minister, presidents and so on running their country's affairs. These men have been chosen by spirit and are of a different level altogether. The interplanetary ones, many of them look much like us and those that don't are humanoid form.

"I don't see any reptilians here. I entered this meditation asking where I should be. This isn't including me so I don't know where. It hasn't answered my question."

"It has answered your question for you are to go to the sectors of the planet, the quarters if you like. The East, West, South, Asian, the Americas, Europe, all those areas. You are to try to cover them without worrying if it should be this country or that within the sectors. It is your presence needed within these sections of the Globe – oh yes and don't forget Australasia."

I am telling them that they need to arrange this. I don't want it left all up to me and want them to put things in place. I will go but they need to set it up. Once I am invited, I won't refuse.

***

2012

I have gone down. At the bottom there is a lot of water, dark swirling water. Somehow I move to the left – more water funnelled. I move along with this. I don't know how I am moving but my mind is moving with it. I come to my usual opening on the right. Here I come out of the water and come out into a round tunnel, a round opening. It is like a tube with walls of glistening iridescent colour. Beautiful moving colour as I move through the tunnel. Tube is the better word. It has to lead somewhere; I am reminded that it is the umbilical cord. Beautiful it is. I am being re-joined; I am being regrouped. I understand. It is that silver thread that connects us, that connects the physical with the spirit world. It cannot be severed until you leave the physical completely. And that is my tube and it is beauty. Incredible beauty. Of course I am still attached which is good. (faintly now) My head hurts like mad. My head hurts and I can't seem to alleviate it. It is the heavenly power of the change of dimensions and vibration. It is the change from physical to spirit. I feel as if I am going to faint. I don't feel good. It is a white feeling. I don't know where this is leading me.

***

2012
PURE ENERGY FORM

I am like a whirling dust devil at the top of the stairs. I, the vortex move down my stairs. I simply move down them. I am watching it as a spinning column moving down and down. It takes a few turns so there must be platforms along the way. It must always go down to the source, that inner being. I am watching it and am it at the same time. I / it gets to the bottom and it moves around to all parts of the space there. As it goes it gathers energy and is picking up energy from the surroundings. I find the left turn and it moves into the passage, gathering speed and energy. It is beginning to grow and gets hotter. Strong hot energy now! Moving along gathering speed and energy and getting brighter. It is white, a glowing white. It stops at the entrance to my space. I wonder what is going to happen now. It hesitates in front of the opening. I have to say 'it' because it is a whirling column of energy.

It moves in. I don't know how I am to become the 'me' again. It is odd because I recognise at last, this energy, this me, is just consciousness in movement. I am aware of all things. I am aware of taste, of everything. I am on acute awareness. It is hard to detach words I use to what is happening. I have to describe; it is my training. That is what my role is to describe being in both places at the same time.

"This is what energy does. It can take form such as you can recognise but at the same time it is aware of everything that the third dimensional world holds, feelings, all the senses, acute awareness but without using ears, eyes, and touch. Without anything that makes up a physical reality, the awareness is still sharp and clear."

Having realised this what it is trying to tell me is that all the energy forms that we connect with as a human being, all those forms in whatever way they present themselves they are acutely aware of what it is to be human. They understand emotions, all the senses, thought processes and it is as if they watch the synapses, the electrical impulses of these thought processes and understand them from their viewpoint. They are observers with complete understanding. There is nothing they do not know. This is why it is said that each leaf, each blade of grass is known because there is nothing they cannot be aware of.

I think that must be very hard for some of the things that go on in this planet.

"This is why we say we suffer as you do. We are not distant from you. We do not distance ourselves from humanity and this includes all spiritual energy forms. We are not specifically speaking of this form or that whether they be from your planet or elsewhere. Whether they be Masters, or souls in other dimensions. We as pure energy know all. We are speaking of pure energy, the Great Knowing, the Great Awareness. Put this out to others so they may not feel that they are alone or ignored in any way."

I was then interrupted by the telephone which shook me badly. I felt very odd afterwards as a result and it took two hours to get back to normal.

***

2012
EVENT AND A SPACESHIP

After a little preamble my steps are steep, metal like metal bars across. Quite steep and as I go down I can hear my footsteps on the metal in a kind of pinging sound. I am reminded that the only reason I am doing the stairs is to stop my mind going off on all the hundreds of things I have going on at the moment. This is keeping me focussed. There are rails on either side so I can put a hand out on either side to help me down the steep steps. Made out of metal and for some reason made of iron. There is nothing refined about these steps.

I can feel energy with me for certain. At last I am at the bottom – on stone. Not shingle but rocky loose rubble. I pick my way round to find my entrance and there it is. It is a pathway between two rock walls. It is the sort you would get in a canyon in America. It is narrow but I can get through. I walk along and know there has to be another turning. It feels a long way and there it is. It is more a cleft than a proper pathway but it is the only opening to the right so that is the one I must take. I go in there – pause – I don't know what I am expecting but I come slap bang against a dead end. Now that is stupid.

I remind myself that I am just mind and not physical and pass straight through it. Just straight through, no bother at all. It was just a reminder to me that although I feel physical I am not. I can hear music playing – it is a band – a brass band or something like it. It is not that close but I can hear it. I am in the country and I walk towards the sound. I don't know where this is leading me. As I go over a rise I see them on a bandstand. There are a lot of people sitting around listening. This is the last place I expected to find myself. They are sitting around enjoying themselves. What is this telling me? There must be a reason. The pressure in my head is enormous. The pressure is stopping me from thinking.

"The band is a prelude to some event. This is what we are trying to tell you. An event is coming up for YOU. This is simply an introduction."

"Is this soon, a long way off or symbolic?"

"It depends what you mean by soon. If you are thinking of the next few months then that is soon. If the next few months seem a long way off then that is not yet."

"You are playing games with me now."

"You know we do not give the actual date ever. That is not our way."

"Okay then. Is it in this country or elsewhere?"

"It is elsewhere as you already know that answer. Why do you ask questions you already know the answers to?"

Then as I watch I see myself stepping out of what is obviously a spaceship. I step out of this all clad in silver and it is me even though I am watching. I am in a silver suit and seem to be shining in a silver glow. I walk down the ramp to all the people sitting listening to the music. I have come to tell them something about existence elsewhere.

I am thinking this must be happening in another dimension as I can't see how this can happen any other way.

"Wait and see. There are extraordinary things to occur. We say beyond the normal that you can't possibly imagine right now."

"That is not true because I have just imaged it and it has come from somewhere."

"Yes, it has come from us. Now you can go about your day."

***

2012

MESSAGE FOR ALL from The Soul Whisperers

"To all, and this includes those in power, various governments, those who consider themselves to be the elite, those who rule in unseen ways, those who dictate your health in ways not seen, and those who would be in power without regard to others.

This message is for all. It will not save the world if you succeed in your personal and private ambitions at the expense of others. Every single thing that you do will affect all quarters of the world and you will also be affected by what you do. If what you do is harmful to others then you too will be harmed by the effects. Those who have in their minds to introduce life threatening things such as chemical warfare, nuclear warfare, do know that you will be included in the consequences and will not escape the damage done. Every single thing that one group does will affect that group also and will not save the world.

The only way you can go forward is by working together on all areas for the entire globe. Working together for the benefit of all is the only way that you can proceed in good health and sanity. This we need to tell you. No matter what your ambitions are if they are not for the benefit of others then it will harm you."

***

2012

DARK SOULS TO BE SMOTHERED BY LOVE

I have a very graphic picture of a creature such as a dog or animal that is being contained within an environment that is harmful to it, cruel to it and one that allows no expansion of the divinity of that creature, but which has learned to become part of that cruelty. I have the picture of it being released, but on release it still has the trappings that surround it and which has enmeshed it. It still doesn't know how to feel joy at the release for it is still entrained by that which has held it fast before. To some degree this is an analogy of people who have been held in an environment that is full of hate and hurt and damage. When they have been released, as they will be with the change that is coming, they still do not know how to express that divinity within. So there will be retraining, a gradual awakening for them through love, through compassion and through realisation that the world is not out there to hurt them, that there is something other than the dreadful conditions that they have been in. They will be retrained by love. Those who fear for those who appear to be dark souls need not be concerned for they will be smothered with love and attention until they too realise that all is wonderful and joyous to be alive.

"Thank you so much for that information for it makes it clear."

***

2012
RENEWAL OF ENERGIES

I am standing on a wooden platform. The steps are wooden boards, not quite like a ladder but broader than that. It is not difficult to go down. Rough concrete walls on either side. A bit crumbly, chalky. This may be going into a cave or something underground because the walls are like a rock face, only crumbly. It feels very closed in. The ceiling is lower so I have to be careful not to bump my head in a few places. This is going into a cave. Oh now I see what it is. At the bottom I am in a kind of grotto, stalactites, stalagmites, that sort of thing. Uneven walls and floor. Not many, if any have been this way. Water hasn't been here as it is so rough underfoot. I am deliberately looking for my turning to the left. It is different, smooth, polished, modern looking like polished granite. It dawns on me that the entrance I have used is not well known. It is a secret one to get to where I need to be. It isn't open to everyone. It is beautiful, polished granite. Everything is polished and not left to its natural state. There is soft lighting from somewhere and soft music too. Very relaxing, very gentle, and very soothing. I stop and see an entrance. A sharp corner turning. This granite has been cut and polished to a high degree. I turn into the right. I can't call it a door as it is just an entry. Sliding panels of dark maroon granite. The panels slide easily to one side, and I step in. There is a blinding blaze of light as I step in.

"Come here. Come over here."

The voice calls and although I can't see I walk in further into the light. There is an enormous figure which takes my hand, pulls me close. This figure can't possibly be real as it is too large. But I feel as it pulls me to him. It is very masculine. My mind is going off in all directions, wondering what this is all about, asking questions and for clarification. The clarification comes by a knowing, a realisation rather than being told. He pulls me closer into him so that I almost merge and we become together. We move into strong light. It is a regeneration chamber. This is what this is, renewal, energising, absorbing life energy. While I am In it my mind is trying to work and trying to accept this renewal. I hope it means what I hope it means. I must stay with this a bit.

***

2012

They have just said, 'Tinker, tailor, soldier, sailor, rich man, poor man, beggar man, thief. You can be anything you want as time goes on and you will meet all kinds, varieties will still be abundant. You won't all merge into one kind. There will be so many varieties to keep your interest. Otherwise it could get very boring for you.

I see the papers going up in shreds." It won't make a jot of difference what anyone does, for the programme has been set. Whatever individual countries or newspapers do now it is to no avail. The collapse and the programme is in motion. Accept, for there is a reason. You expect change to come about with no disturbance, with no resistance, with no upheaval and this is not how it will be. It is natural that those who are caught up in disturbance will not be happy with it and will wish things would be what they were. You know this is not to be. It is a moment or two in time of history. You will come out of it. The disturbance will be recorded but will not last forever. It is unreasonable to expect the change that is in the planning to have the change without any upset at all."

Me: I have the one who is saying this is very matter of fact, very much in charge. He knows what he is doing and is one who does not brook any nonsense. He is not without feeling but who will act with steadfastness. A strong character. I feel that where he comes from is very business-like.

PREDICTION RUSSIA

I have a picture of a bear, clearly symbolically it is the Russian bear which has climbed up onto the roof of houses and the people on the ground are trying to bring it down. They are trying to call it down, entice it down. But it likes it up there and feels it wishes to stay on top. The little people are working to no avail. It will not come down for them, only if IT decides. It is very large.

GAINING INFORMATION

A very helpful piece of advice for you is to have in your mind somebody you admire, somebody who has achieved greatness in one way or the other such as Leonardo, or maybe someone who has similar interests. Focus your thoughts on that one. It may be a scientist, a statesman or whoever it might be. Your thoughts dwelling on that individual who may or may not be in spirit but who may have incarnated back, the essence remains, the knowledge and the information that was gained during that lifetime is still there. Whenever you think about that individual it is like plugging in to that particular consciousness and withdrawing the knowledge from it. That way you will get the information you are seeking in whatever interest you have. Think about the individual that embodies that interest. This is for anyone who wishes to gain information. You will need to be precise. Focus on whoever is likely to supply you with the information you seek.

***

2012
CAPSULES OF GERMS ????

I have called on the Blue People and asked them what they need me to do. I go down what appears to be wide stairs, similar to what you get in a department store. I go into the right turn as an entry to a particular department and am aware this is simply a mind technique to get me to focus. Once inside I see a lot of packages all containing what appears to be bullets or little bombs. At first I thought they were missiles, but they are not directed as missiles are but are dropped from aircraft.

"We want you to alter the DNA of the contents so that they are rendered completely harmless. Each one is a capsule containing germs. In altering the DNA of one then all the others are automatically altered too. Because the DNA communicates with itself even if it is divided. Which is what has happened here. So whoever owns these, and we are speaking of more than one country, they will not know that what they intended will have no effect, or rather no harmful effect. Wherever these capsules land they will not be doing the job that the military, governmental organisations intend. They will wait for results and will wonder why. I don't know where they intend to drop these but it feels like places we are not thinking of.

***

2012
GOING TO THE FUTURE BLOCKED

I have asked to go to the future of planet Earth. I am dressed in bright red. Each step I take is going to take me forward in the future. That is what I have asked. As I step forward the red that I seem to be is changing. It is gradually changing as I step forward and is turning into gold. So now I walk forward in gold. I feel as if I am walking into the mists of time. Nothing is clear. Everything is hazy and wispy. Still I move forward and that means forward into time. It is not too fast but a step by step forward.

My head begins to hurt as the energy builds, very painful especially over the eyes. I try to relieve it, but it keeps coming back. Painful! But I must keep going for that is my intention. I feel as if I am morphing, changing form as I push through this pain barrier. I must keep my mind clear or I could easily lose it.

INTERRUPTED BY THE TELEPHONE

I manage to get back to where I left off with difficulty and time.

I ask to be shown what I need to see and I see figures walking about. People, but not distinct, just people. They are walking about calmly with no hurry. There is no rush. Maybe it is me but they are dreamy as if in a sleep walking state. I know this can't be and must be coming from my own perception. I ask for detail, something more precise. Colours begin to emerge. My head hurts again, my head hurts. It is as if my head, my thoughts, my mind is pushing into an invisible barrier that either I am not meant to go through or cannot go through. Perhaps this is why what I see is vague and dreamlike as if I am looking through a veil, a barrier. Clearly, I am not meant to see yet. I want to but if I am told I will then pass it on and this is not to be yet. This is why the telephone interrupted earlier. I am not meant to see that much yet.

***

2012
CONTROL CENTRE FOR SPACE

The stairs are of polished wood, stained wood in a nice rich colour. Somebody looks after this place. The stairs are going down but I must have started up high because on going down it seems to be at floor level, not to a cellar or anything. It is polished wood all the way, no carpeting but in a very rich chestnut colour. Going down each step, going down feeling the wood as I go. I have some rustling clothes on that makes a noise as I go. There is nothing special about them just that I am aware. I can't even see what they are, but I am aware that I am making a noise as I go. I don't know why.

I know I am going somewhere because my head is starting to feel painful now. This usually happens when I am going into a much deeper state. I continue down trying to keep a focus. But oh the pain in my head is increasing all the time. I must go through that barrier. It is going into a different state. I must keep going. I am at the bottom now. It is the entrance to a passage obviously man made. There is only one way I can go with no turning off. It is a passage that is sloping. I am still descending but it is a gentle gradient and not difficult at all but definitely going deeper into this. The walls have been clad in wood. Difficult to describe. There is lighting and I can see it is very deep underground here. I must keep going. It is a square passage and seems very contrived, deliberate passageway to something else.

Underground. I feel I have been taken to some sort of headquarters. I am not talking of spiritual headquarters but secret official headquarters. Secret service type stuff that is what I am feeling. I get the sense of cameras watching as I go. Very weird! Following me and I know I am being observed by eyes somewhere else, perhaps in a control room. I just know this but there is no way to know it, but I know. They are aware of me coming and it was important that I rustled as I came down to alert them. This is really odd!

Keep walking. Oh I see. I am dressed in what looks like protective clothing. Not white overalls but is still protective clothing. I don't know where this is leading me or what this is all about. I keep walking. It is endless this passage. Soon I come up against a blank wall right in front of me. But it isn't a wall, it is an entry. I feel around for something that will open it. I notice there is a pad on the right side, and I know I have been here before. I put my hand to it. It Is a handprint scanner. As I put my right hand to it the door slides open into the wall. I step through.

The passage is behind me now, closed off. I am in a very busy active area, so well lit, very bright. Lots of people and they are human beings working away, all at their particular jobs. There are monitors, screens, lots and lots of screens, wall charts. It is a hive of activity. I wonder what I am doing here. Nobody takes any notice of me at all. It appears I have been here before and I am familiar with it, though I can't quite get my head round that yet. I go over to what is obviously my desk. I sit down and start playing with the keyboard and watching the monitor. I haven't got a clue what this is about except it is almost as if I am watching me doing this.

This is an observation room for activity in space and they are monitoring –how they can do it down here I don't know – but they are monitoring spaceships, satellites and co-ordinating – it reminds me of traffic control. They are making sure that they each have their own particular lanes. There is so much space junk up there, so many satellites and the spaceships, clever though they still need to be mindful of all the stuff that surrounds our Earth. That is what we are here for, to monitor. It is very much like traffic control making sure people don't bump into each other. Sounds really weird! The ships they are monitoring are into physicality although they may have come from other dimensions and can blink out, once they enter a certain field to be able to interact they are then physical and can be affected by all the other space stuff that is going around orbiting the planet and that is dangerous.

So this is a monitoring station and I have no idea why I am here. Or this means I am watching for knowledge of this. There are all sorts of currents, rays, energy waves which could interfere with instruments so much. It is such a busy place and if you could see it with our eyes you would wonder how anybody could navigate their way around this planet. It is such a busy place. All the waves and magnetic influence, somebody said 'scalar'. I don't know what that means. Activity also from the Sun which has an effect on the other emanations, not just on our planet but also on Space visitors and individuals. We have to be sure nobody is in danger. Keeping it safe. Then we have the interference from the governments doing their experiments in space completely ignorant of the effect they are having detrimentally. They are ignorant like children playing with toys they do not really understand. So this is a control system to make sure there is not too much damage done by the ignorant ones who think they know it all. How peculiar this is!

What I am feeling is there is conscious me as Shirley observing this other me who knows exactly what he or she is doing – I can't tell the difference. The other part of me that is working here up to now has been kept separate for my own sanity. It certainly has given me something to think about. Do I put this down?

"Yes, you must put this down because at a later stage you will come to consciously interact with both levels and operate well. It is yet another opening for you, one you have had no conscious recording of. This is for you to understand at a later stage when your brainwaves have been reactivated."

I must come back for my ears are aching now. There is definitely a physical change when I do this at least for the duration. The whole thing begins to fuzz now. It is phasing out and that clearly is the end.

***

2012

My stairs are slats of wood. I am going down quite steeply. At the bottom I step into clean warm water. Ankle deep. I swish through this quite easily what seems to be an underground stream. Because of the heat it is probably coming from a volcanic vent or hot springs. It is clean and pure. I am comfortable. I follow the stream of water quite happily in. If it was dry would be a passage between rock or underground caves. This is what it will be, an underground cave, a grotto of some kind later in the years ahead when the water has gone. And the water will go and it will be left bare, but not yet. I look for my turning to the right. This will take me into my special place that I have no knowledge of until I turn into it.

As I climb up the slope at the side takes me out of the water which was very shallow. I climb easily into another passage which had previously been under water. Because it is smooth I know water has flowed through this before. "Why am I doing this? Why am I here? Show me why."

My head begins the usual building up of pain and tension which always indicates going into another realm, other dimension perhaps. I don't seem to be able to do anything about this. It happens and I must allow it. I feel I have become another person (shudders) and I know I must do this more often so it becomes a natural occurrence for the work ahead.

"It will be easier and easier as you continue. Do not neglect this exercise. For that is what it is, an exercise in smooth transition so that you may do your work."

My steps are wide, white with rolled edges. Not sharp but smooth. I have never walked down stairs like this before. It is similar to where they have rollers at airport scanners where the suitcase just rolls along. There is no effort. You just go on it and roll along. I arrive at a smooth clean area with colours. No walls just wavy colours, all kinds of colours waving about filling the space I am in. I am enveloped in the colour. I look for my entry on the left but is as if the colours are pointing the way.

I glide into the entrance and am wafted along with no effort on my part at all. I come to my entrance on the right which I expect and need to have. The colours open up showing the way through. I step inside not having a clue what to do now. The pressure is building in my head which to me always means a high connection. The pressure keeps building, and I must just allow this.

"You could leave now."

"What do you mean?"

"You could leave now."

Papers appear.

"You like these others are learning to be new again. You are starting fresh into another world, a new environment from what you have been in. It is confusion. Things will soon become clear and you will have no doubts whatsoever.

***

2012
DREAM STATE

The steps are not quite real, as if they are moving by themselves. I have a golden rail on either side for me to hold onto. I need to hold on because the stairs are moving, not quite like an escalator. I can't define how but I do not need to do anything because the stairs are doing it for me. I keep moving down and it will know when to stop. I don't need to do anything. It is a nice feeling (*big sigh of pleasure.*) It is a dreamy feeling and I am aware I am hungry which is unusual because I am never hungry. I am in a dreamy vapour state. Various parts of my body are beginning to hurt. My ears are hurting – a headache – something is going on physically which is most unusual. My ear is really playing up now – sharp, and yet I am still in a dream state. I am moving through just vaporous clouds, colours, nothing solid or precise. It is so odd because although I am in a dreamy state I am so aware of bodily hunger which doesn't normally happen. Maybe this is to do with the body, I don't know what. I am still holding on to two rails. I am being moved and I don't have to do anything. My gastric juices are really flowing, my various nerves are jumping. Something is going on but I have no idea what it is. Lots and lots of pressure round my head. Lots of something happening. I hear very faint music. Dreamier and dreamier as if I am going under anaesthetic and it is hard to concentrate and record this. Dream – dream.

***

2012
FROM SPIRIT

"Speaking to all. Whatever you do, however you conduct yourselves is important to your soul, for it is that that continues. It is how you are that dictates your future journey as a soul, although it is important how the world continues, but more important to you and to the Earth is how you as an individual conduct yourself. Words alone are not enough. Thoughts, actions, feelings, all play a part. Words alone are not enough. You need to put into practice, spiritual values, compassion for others, compassion for yourself also. That too is important. When you stick to these spiritual laws your heart will be joyous."

***

2012

What gets us started? What got me started were books and following up an impulse to find out something. Sometimes we forget to follow urges, those impulses when we have already travelled in a particular direction and followed a particular way of working. We stay with that, following our course of action and all those things that sound positive. But consider this; there is a particular question and you put the same question to a group of people. A scientist will answer the question according to his viewpoint and his way of working. A mathematician will do it his way, a biologist will do it his way, a layman will answer it in his way with his thinking. Those working in health will answer the question in their way. What is really happening here is that each of those specialists are staying within their particular field and are ignoring other avenues of thinking, other ways of seeing things. Lots of us are the same. Once we get stuck or channelled into a certain way of working, specialising then we do not step outside as a rule.

"What we are asking is that you step outside of your established thinking. Don't be afraid to look at alternatives. Expand your knowledge in this way, expand your viewpoint and you will discover many surprising things. The tendency is to stay with what you know. You can still continue to follow what you already know but don't be afraid to step outside of that band and look elsewhere for answers too. Go where your nose leads you. When something catches your eye, piques your interest, follow it, don't ignore it because you are too busy or bound up in what you are doing. These little impulses, these little attentions are brought to you to tweak your interest. These are the signposts that are sent to you. These are the indicators of what the spirit guidance; your own soul wishes you to investigate so you may spread your knowledge and understanding too.

Sometimes what takes your interest, catches your eye might give you a feeling that this is going to upset your status quo. This is perhaps going to give you an idea you won't be comfortable with because it might challenge what you have been doing. Don't you think this is all part of learning as well? This is all part of understanding. Not every individual is identical in their thoughts. Sometimes to have complete understanding you need to follow the thoughts of others and see what they have discovered and what they have written about. See how it may resonate with you in some way or at least challenge your inbuilt feelings."

***

2012
MULTIPLE CONSCIOUSNESS

I have gone down in yellow; everything is yellow. It always reminds me of using the mind. At the bottom it seems to be an office or library. Lots of books lining the walls. There is my door out of here on the left. It is a building, office, college or whatever. I go down the corridor. Lots of doors until I get to the one I know is mine. It is green. An ordinary office door with a knob. I am hesitant about going in. It is very business-like. I don't know if I will see anything but I must go in at some point. I can't stand out here. I turn the knob and go in. Yes, there are desks, more than one but with nobody sitting at them. I ask to be shown what I need to see and notice that one wall is like a giant screen. It lights up as if someone has pressed a button like putting the TV on. It is the entire wall. It is bright and takes a while for my eyes to adjust to this. Moving pictures which are big enough for me to walk into.

I see pictures of warfare, guns and battle scenes. There is smoke and lots of noise everywhere. This could be anywhere on the planet. What am

I supposed to do with this?

I walk into it. I am there on the ground in the middle of all this noise. I know I am alright because I am not physical here.

"But what am I doing here? I can't be everywhere."

"Yes, you can be everywhere. You know that. We told you that. Your consciousness is everywhere at all times and your presence here will change the energies. It will make a difference. Walk through this."

So I do and walk quite openly through all the mayhem that is going on. There is a knowing that the other consciousness of me is doing the same in other areas. I don't need to see the effect because as I walk through the effect is taking place. I don't need to see it. It is happening. Well that is good but seems a bit weird.

"Just keep walking through knowing that the very essence has an effect on this scenario."

Multiple me's. My gosh!

***

2013
NOT ONE OF MINE SPACE CRAFT

My pathway down is very wide. It is outside. It is similar to a wide pathway through nature. I am feeling more tropical, rattan at the side, rattan matting. It is like a village roadway, pathway down to the village. The steps are very wide and shallow. Nature made, basket weave just to make it easy on the feet so you don't tread on thorns or stones. Keep going down and feel the energy increasing as I go, as I get closer. At the bottom is the village itself. It is a hive of activity, smoke coming out of the huts, people running about. A couple of children send me off it the direction I need. I can't see what I am dressed in at all and am just conscious of me.

I follow the track and know I have to turn to the right because that is the system. Eventually there is another track leading me. It is very quiet and there is only me here. It is extremely quiet, hushed and not a single sound anywhere. I come up against what I can only call a stockade, but it is flimsy. It is just to stop the eyes from noticing it. It is natural but a barrier of some kind. I don't need an actual door and walk my way through the camouflage barrier.

It is so different in here. It is big and has been cleared. There is a hive of activity, but it is further down, I have to go down to get where the action is. I ask to go where I am needed. I know it sounds silly but I am not third dimensional but am still feeling physical. I slide and slip down the slope to where the activity is. My nose won't stop twitching, tickling and irritating. I keep going down, down until I get to the bottom.

Men are guarding a spaceship. It is a typical flying saucer shape. It is very big, maybe 30, 40, 50 feet across. It is big and would take a while to walk around it. It is raised up off the ground on something. It reminds me of when you are near an aeroplane, you can't reach the fuselage and have to go up steps to get into it. This is a similar idea. It is suspended by something, but I can't think what. There has to be a means to get in.

They can't see me. I can see them but they can't see me. Oh I see. I have to think myself inside. It takes a bit of doing but I think what it might be like inside and with that thought I am inside. This is interesting because it is not one of mine. This is one I have no real knowledge of. There is nobody inside here but there are passages, active coloured lights. Beautiful colours all moving. This is not one of mine. I understand now. This is one of theirs, manmade, not space made. It is one of those they have reversed engineered. They don't quite know how to use it yet. How daft is that!

There is something going on here. For a start it is miles too big. They should have started with something smaller. They should have accommodation.

This is why they keep saying, "This is not one of yours. This is a manmade thing."

What am I supposed to do, touch it, feel it? It is smooth, very smooth. There are far too many corners. There shouldn't be any right angles, it should all be round. Energy gets stuck in angles. Where is the propulsion? I don't know. This is making my head hurt.

***

2013

ON FIFTH BOOK

I have just had a long conversation with spirit where it has been made clear that I have to take more than one recording device. I am going to run out with just one no matter how long it takes. It is the only way I can get these thoughts down without interrupting the flow. If I had a tape recorder inside my head it would be a lot easier and wonderful. Dialogue is great and it would make good reading too. So here I am insisting on the stairs. I have a thick pile carpet in deep purple. It is so thick it is amazing. I have done almost anything not to meditate this morning and yet I have contact. Hay fever is starting up now, another interruption. I must stay on the carpet. Good!

The stairs are theatrical type, very wide, not steep, very easy going. Up or down it doesn't matter. It is the stairs that matter. No banister to hold onto and I am walking down the middle. Nice and easy in spite of the hay fever. At the bottom is a circular area with lots of corridors going off. I am going to take the one that is on the extreme left although the others look inviting. They are there to tempt me. The one on extreme left is quite dark. It could almost be missed and is not as grand as the others. Very narrow. Nothing on the walls, painted and smooth. No carpet here but a tiled floor.

Look for the door on the right. It is innocuous looking with an ordinary door handle. Nothing special about this but like a door to a broom cupboard or something. Not grand. Let's go in. It is the only door here. It is like a storehouse with lots of shelves, boxes. Not many people come in here. Boxes stacked high with just a passageway through. Tell me what I need to know.

"This is a storehouse of all things that have been and that will be. Whatever you do will also be stored here for someone to look into when you are long gone. So whatever you do you need to make sure that is to good effect, and you will be pleased that someone has looked at it, and not be ashamed of. You don't wish to go into the categories where nothing happened, where nobody is interested enough. Make sure it goes into the special category, something that would help others in the future"

"I want to be able to help them now."

"Well that is why you must be sure that you do what is right for you and what feels right for your soul. That is the most important thing."

***

2013
IMPRINTING ME

The stairs are wide, in fact they are so wide it reminds me of steps at the entrance to a church or a big official building. The sort of steps that people sit on when they are tourists, stone steps. I am reminded of the National Gallery where there are others using the steps, not just me coming and going. I get to the bottom and there is a little street on the left, a little alley way. Houses and buildings on either side. There has to be a turning off soon as my head is beginning to hurt, which is a good sign. I wish I could stop that, but I can't. I come to a tiny alley way with a bollard at the end. No vehicles are going to go down here. It is really narrow, just a gap between two buildings. Clearly it must lead somewhere, or it would not have been built in the first place. Oh I see, it takes me down further to some steps leading to a jetty where you can use you small boat. There is a boat. Clearly, I am meant to get in it. Nobody else there. I step in and cast off.

The current carries me. I haven't a clue where this is going to end up. There has to be a current, a flow or I would not be carried. I go down past other buildings, carried along quite steadily. To the right there is a man with a boat hook. As I go past he hooks the boat and pulls it in. Clearly this is where I get out. He gives me a helping hand. He is an ordinary looking guy and yet there is something extraordinary about him. It is his eyes. They are very big, very big and bigger than you would expect. I am quite happy to go with him. This is a meditation after all. He leads me and I follow up a slope. It is country but the steps are cut to go up. He clearly has a purpose. Where is this all leading me? I didn't come with any intention this time. We get to the top and it is flat.

There seems to be laid out big trestle type tables, covered with a cloth. It is long and there are people, different kinds of people. By that I mean different species of people behind the trestle tables with notes in front of them. Recording equipment, different contraptions suitable to their own level of communication. The guide I am with takes me to one end and I am to walk along the tables. There must be tables put together since it is so long. I have to look at each contraption that these beings have and examine them and either approve or disapprove. Since I don't know what they are I can hardly disapprove. I start at one end. There is a tiny little guy here, clearly extra-terrestrial. I handle what he is showing me and then put it back down. I move along to another contraption, I handle that and put that down. I do this all the way along, handling each contraption. It is important that I hold them first. It is not enough just to look; I must hold them. There is one very tall being here and he hands me something, I don't know what to call it. I handle that too. With this one I press a few buttons. I don't know what it does but the buttons are there so I press them. He is quite happy with that, so I put it back down and move on.

They seem to be anxious for my approval. I don't understand any of it. There are loads of them. I keep walking down the line. Some are very animal like, you would be reminded of animals when looking at them and all of them have amazing eyes. I look into the eyes of each one before I pick up whatever it is they are showing me. Contraptions!

"What is this about?"

"The purpose of this is that you receive the energy and knowledge that is contained with each device. Not only that, you have put your energy into it creating a link that will not be broken now. You have now connected with each different species from the Galaxy and would also receive as a result of you holding their devices. There is an electromagnetic connection, an energy connection. It is like leaving your fingerprint and it has imprinted you too. It isn't important that you understand, simply that you do what has been requested of you by continuing down the line doing this."

"There are so many here."

"Ah yes but there will always be more as time goes on. Just know it has been effective."

"I don't feel any different."

"You won't notice the difference, but it has been imprinted into you now. That is sufficient. It is not the same as having an implant, but is an imprinting."

"I don't quite understand."

"It isn't necessary for you to understand. It is reinforcing the connection, the electromagnetic connection which creates a mind connection. So when the need arises you should receive the knowledge that these imprints give you. It is reinforcing your place in the order of things."

"I don't understand it but will accept it quite happily. I don't appear to be doing very much these days. "S*ee book trilogy 'Calling Earth'*

***

2013

CONFERENCE RE THE NEXT BOOK

I have used a different countdown method to the stairs. Time for a change!

I am in a room full of people sitting down as at a conference round table. They are all officials of some kind: no, that is the wrong word. Representatives is what they are of various states. I am not sure if this means states of species or the council or what. I am not sure. There are females here too, but the majority appear to be male. I am a guest, a visitor and I am at a table in the middle. I am not sure what my purpose is here. They are all watching me and waiting to see what I will say or do.

I start by saying: "Thank you all for coming. I am going to depend on you all to put forward the information you have to give. It does require it to be put in context that will be understood by the human mind. That is important. Information on its own is not enough. I will need some gifted writer who knows how to place this with an understandable scene. Information can't just be dropped on the pages. There has to be padding to make sense of it otherwise it comes out as a factual textbook. That is no good. It has to be easily assimilated by the human mind. That is important. I need your help in this. You are asking a lot of me and I need your assistance in making sure that this goes down in a palatable manner, one that is sort after and not seen as yet more non-sense.

The public are fed up with platitudes and need your help how to do and not how to be. They are usually told what to be and not how to be. They will need more information that will grab their attention and something that will hold their interest. I am pleading you to transmit in an easy manner to me. I will give the time and the focus, and the rest is up to you."

They are now standing up and applauding.

"I haven't done the job yet. Don't be too eager. It is up to you."

***

2013

PROTECT THE WATERS

I have been led underground down a ladder to like the bottom of a well. Only like a conduit. The water is pure and beautiful and fresh. Sweet water. I follow where it is coming from along the conduit. As I move along I know that this water is really fresh and pure. Nobody knows it is here; eventually I come to what I can only call the source, the spring. It is outside, well hidden by bushes. It is a spring of beautiful fresh water. I am told that this must not be discovered. The source of all spring waters must be kept hidden from governments, councils, official bodies, water boards, if they discover a new source of fresh water they will commandeer it, use it, steal it, take control, pollute and use it for all manner of things for which it was not intended. So these natural springs need to be protected. Anybody knowing about fresh springs of water keep it to yourself. Use it but keep it to yourself. You need to keep it away from governing bodies, who as we have said will commandeer and misuse and very soon it would disappear.

"This is what you can put into the book. This is part of the message you need to put out.

The peoples of the world need protection from their own rulers. They need protection from those who are supposed to look after them, from those in power."

***

2014

Crystals in Japan – I asked my guides if what I was doing with programming the crystals to clear the radiation from the seas around Japan was doing any good or was I kidding myself. Their reply was that radioactivity does not affect them (the crystals?) and that they could easily clear up the mess of our creation. However we ourselves are meant to do that. What I am doing with the crystals while may seem a small thing is showing them that we are indeed taking some responsibility and willingness to do something, no matter how small. And that is important.

***

2014

I am walking myself to the stairs as suggested. Flat even ground. I feel rustling on either side as if I am being watched as I go along. Nobody in sight but I know I am not alone. I keep moving forward. I am going to the rejuvenation chamber for healing and rejuvenation. I reach what appears to be a sealed door. There are two tall Beings, my blue Beings one of either side. I walk up to the door and wait. Then it slides open. The two Beings put their hands under my elbows to assist me through. I am now in. They follow behind me for they are not physical and I am. Nothing is clear, waving colours, it is like being in a dream. I can't see much just waves of energy. I keep moving through what I call energy fields. Oh! That is nice I see Serapis Bey. I haven't seen him for ages. I am walked into the same chamber I was in in 1993. The same beds. Oh! That is a nice surprise. I lie down on one of them.

***

2014

I have been having a dialogue with those I have approached. I have asked for the stairs.

"What stairs would you like?"

"Polished stone, ebony I think. Polished and smooth in a beautiful russet colour. These are my steps. Steps, not stairs. I feel my way down very carefully. It is a long time since I have done the steps. I usually go straight into dialogue.

"What can you see there?"

"Water, swirling water. Not still or stagnant. It is moving in a circle, swirling not flowing. Vortex. I look for my entrance but the water takes me. The outer edge of the swirl takes me to the exit. I swish comfortably through the water. I am not in any danger. What sort of water is this? Clean, active and not stagnant. It is full of life. I move along the conduit. Concrete walls on either side to make sure the water does not escape. I come to my exit on the right in the way I have been programmed."

"This is a programming! You have been taught how to do this."

I look to see how I can move from the passage. As I look the wall disappears in front of me. I walk through the space that has been created by the disappearance of the wall. I am now away from the water. Lush green, verdant, alive, and beautiful. What am I doing here? Show me what I need to see. My books are stacked up high all around me. I am sitting down signing them. There are big piles of the books. There is a long queue. I am assuming this is my latest book.

"Tell me what I must do."

***

2014
STEP INTO A BRIGHTER LIGHT

My stairs are rattan matting. They are a construction from high up going down to a village. Steps taken by many people from a hut, a long house. You would have to call it a longhouse where meetings are held, where everybody congregates and listens to the outcome. The steps are going down back to the village where everything goes on as normal.

I must go down and as I get to the bottom to start my journey I am accompanied. There are many natives, local people following me as I go to see where I am going and what I am going to do. They are intrigued. I am still in natural surroundings. I walk along and am sent ahead so that the others can follow. They won't take the lead; they refuse to take the lead. They look to me to do that. I keep walking hoping to find my space.

The entrance to it is on the right and is like a hole in the undergrowth that I must slither through. I go down on my bottom and go through feet first. The others stay outside. They are still waiting to see what I am going to do once I am away from the main route. I had to be off the main path. It is light and airy. This is nothing like where I have just come from. It is almost magical. There is a sound, music in the air which I can't quite pin down. It is background music, very ethereal.

There is nobody here. It is so light and airy, like being in nothing recognisable. I turn all the way round looking for something. There is a brighter pinpoint of light so that is clearly where I must go. I walk towards it hoping it doesn't disappear. I am on my own.

Hands from either side of me are trying to grab me but they don't quite make it. If they caught me I would be pulled to both sides. But they don't quite reach, they are trying but don't quite reach. I keep walking. I am not afraid. I am being encouraged to keep going, to get into this extra bright light. I am being encouraged but I feel if I step into it I will be in a completely different world. I have no idea what that world is. I step in as I must and there is no going back. Once you step in there is no going back. So I do.

***

2014

My journey began with me laden with books. I threw them off so I could be uncluttered but there are still one or two books clinging to me. They do not want to let go. I take it to mean I must continue to read more. They are your books that you will write but have not already done so.

I get to my door and I have to knock. It is the first time I have had to do this. Someone calls out to come in. There is a man sitting at a desk, grey hair, learned looking, not young. He is surrounded by papers and books. He is looking at my book and at me to see if the two match up. He has a lot more to see. I am waiting for him to say yes or no. If he puts it to his left it is a no, if he puts it to his right it is a yes. He puts it to his right so I take it is yes. He has others to see but at least it is in the pile that will be looked at. That is a good sign.

I thank him and he waves me away. I go past him down a long corridor. Lots of rooms and people studying. Show me what I need to see and understand. Ahead of me is a wall or window. A whole window looking out. It is the end of the passage. There is no other way but to look out onto the world.

***

2014
MOVEMENTS

Their heads are all huddled together. There is a tall one, with a tall head. He waves me over and they all shuffle around so there is a space for me to come in and look at a map. I can't quite decide yet where I am to go. They have different ideas. Each one here has their own agenda which while they are working for the benefit of the whole as always there is a discussion, a deliberation and at last a final decision as to what my next move should be. It is like a game of chess because it is not only my movements that are important but also the movement of those I am to come into contact with. So there is often a shuffling of times and places. This is exactly why you are never given why and when."

***

2014

My stairs are metal treads with the holes in them, like an outside fire escape. There are rickety rails on either side to hold onto. The steps don't appear to be fixed to anything but they obviously must be. I clatter as I go down. I can't see the bottom. I am going with trust but it feels to be in the air. It can't be but that is how it feels. As I go the step in front of me appears, but I can't see the whole stairway. It doesn't seem to matter. I still feel as if I am in the air with nothing solid around, just the steps. Why metal. What is this leading me to?

It certainly is a journey into the unknown as I have no clues as to what I will land in. I am holding tight to the rickety rail, metal rods. Oh, they are nice metal rods. They are special. Surprise! They gleam like gold.

"They are conductors of energy." OK Keep going. My head is

beginning to hurt. This is a sure sign I am going into a deeper state or a stronger energy. I keep going down. I have now arrived. It is very steamy. Oh my head hurts. Oh! I must go through the barrier.

"It hurts because you haven't done it for a while. If you did it more often you would not have this pressure."

"OK, I have been told." I am in a steamy, fog like environment. Again I must trust because I can't see clearly. I find my opening by chance more than design. I walk though.

"These are the levels you must go through to get to where you are needed."

I walk along and it gets clearer and more solid, less vapourish. I walk strongly forward knowing there has to be another turn yet. I come to it. It is a downwards steep slope. At the bottom is a very little door. It is hard to describe. It is a small door for small people. I push on it and it opens by itself. The pressure is still there on my head. I must allow the pressure for that is taking me through the barriers. OK, I must allow it.

***

2014
USING COSMIC ENERGY

I am on a floating platform in mid-air. The steps down are like steppingstones, also floating. I step from one to the other. No rail. Although they are floating they are quite firm. It is as if symbolically I am going down from somewhere up there higher. Going down to Earth, travelling down through the cosmos. Using the symbol of floating platform stages. Keep going. I can't see the bottom; it is a long way down. I skip ahead to the bottom as it would take too long to do it step by step.

I am on the Earth, on the ground. Literally on gravel, soil, dirt, grass. The minute I touch down my coughing starts. It is as if being on Earth triggers the cough. There is a path, being formed by whatever creatures have been that way before. Well used path. I just have to follow the path for it I don't I will get lost. The path leads me to a cave, the entrance to a cave. I am hoping there is somebody or something inside the cave. I walk in. It is warm, a nice damp warm feeling. There is something in here, but I can't see what. The path is trodden through the cave, so someone has been here before. I wander around. I ask to be shown something, to go where I am meant to go.

At the back of the cave is a sheer wall. It looks natural but it isn't. It looks impenetrable but it isn't. I know I can see myself on the other side, so I do that now. The other side is completely different. It is a hive of activity. There is so much going on here. It is alive with activity. There are humans, there are extra-terrestrials. If one can call them that now for they are terrestrials. They have been here so long. They all have jobs to do.

"Show me what they are doing."

"They are manufacturing, using energy that they draw from the great energy that is available to everybody. It is energy that can penetrate rock, the energy is all around. They bring this energy into a denser matter, they condense it. I am getting the image of when you smash a cup it flies into bits. But when you bring the bits back, like when you rewind the picture it comes back to being a cup. This is them correcting the energy and bringing it back into a solid state. They can do this. This is all we are, condensed energy. So they are condensing energy to produce physical objects."

"What are they making? I can't see what they are making."

"What they are doing is providing survival equipment and nourishment and anything that a human being might need in the event of an emergency."

"I am not sure what you are trying to say here."

"They can produce whatever is required at any given time by this technique. We don't need equipment or machinery and we don't even need to mine for the metals. We simply condense the energy that is around with intent to produce what is needed. This is why we are doing this already for the events to come."

"Why are you showing me this?"

"Because with intent you too can do this. Start practising now. Start practising what you desire and call on the energy that surrounds you which has consciousness. Bring it into being. This is your next learning step."

"My God! OK."

***

2014
THE BOOK *ANCIENT WISDOM*

I have done my journey and have ended up in what appears to be an old shop, an antique shop full of all kinds. I am looking around at all the many objects. There is a very old book lying flat on the shelf. Nobody has looked at this for a long time. It is covered in dust. It is a thick book. Put my finger on the top and push aside some of the dust to see the title. It says Ancient Wisdom. It is going to be very heavy to lift.

I take it off the shelf and look around for somewhere I can put it and open it. It is too difficult to open it while standing. There is no space. I ask for somewhere and I notice there is a passageway between all the stores and stacks of stuff. It must lead somewhere so I carry the book with difficulty in my arms. I go down the very narrow space hoping to find another room or something. I go down a few steps to a lower level which has a table and a chair. There is nobody else here. I put the book on the table. Nobody has been here for it is covered in dust.

Where do I start? I feel someone is standing looking over my shoulder, not a real person but spirit. Because I have been thinking of Pythagoras he comes to mind, but whether it is him or not I really don't know. I haven't yet opened the book. I am hesitating.

"There is no turning back if you open this book. Once you have learnt something you must then use it and share it. Opening this book comes with responsibility. It is to do with journeys of the Mystery Schools which go back long before your time. Open it if you dare."

I know nobody has opened it for a long time and I feel this presence, who I sense is Pythagoras. I lift just the cover. There is a blank page so I turn the next page. It is if the figures there dance. They come alive. They don't keep still. I must keep moving.

"You must keep working through, taking each step at a time and the knowledge will be yours to use, or as so many have done before you ignore."

I feel the pressure of two hands on my shoulders. Suddenly I am extremely hungry. My gastric juices start flowing. Is this symbolic of me being hungry for the truth? I still haven't consciously absorbed knowledge, but it is there if I want it, if I keep turning the pages.

***

2014

SECRET ENERGY SOURCE

My stairs are padded. I am walking on air cushions. I ask why.

"It is so that your entry will be unheard, silent. Nobody will know you are coming. Everything is deliberately muffled. As I go down there is not a single sound. There is stillness all the way. At the bottom it is still deliberately padded, it is soundproofed, not for me but for others. I am querying this and what I am getting is so that the outside world, the general population is unaware of what is going on from the sounds. The soundproofing is to stop the sounds from the other side coming through. So it is to protect my ears and the ears of others and to keep it a secret.

"I am here for something, so show me."

I walk along a tunnel looking for my way in. There is a door set into the tunnel, almost unseen but because I am looking I see it. I push on it. There is no door handle or lock on it. It is kept shut by suction. I push and get myself on the other side. I ask to be shown what I need to see.

A pair of ear-mufflers are handed to me. I put them on as clearly there will be noise here. The mufflers are good and thick and I can now only hear my own thoughts. There are men in uniform here constructing an even deeper underground base. I have a coughing fit which is preventing me from delving further. I must overcome this barrier that is set up by another force.

"It does not wish you to delve deeper. But that is what is happening here. These forces are delving deep into the Earth to source as yet an unknown energy related to the core, the magnetic core of the planet. They wish to harness this but it is dangerous work. Once they discover how to harness it they will use it, not necessarily for the benefit of the inhabitants of the planet."

"Why are you telling me and what is the purpose of me knowing this?"

"You are, as you have been told, an observer and need to report this back to your home base."

"I would have thought they knew of this already."

"Remember you are an observer and your role is to report back, give confirmation if you will. The military on your planet are delving into matters which could if mishandled damage the planet and its inhabitants. They are playing with fire.

***

2014

The stairs are steep and curl round like the steps you would have going round a tower on the inside. There are walls on either side, no railings. I must watch my step because they are quite steep. If there was anyone coming the other way there would not be any room for two of us without squeezing into the side. It is not meant for more than one.

At the bottom it is circular and as I stand wondering what to do a huge gush of water comes and sweeps me along into a passage. I can't do anything about it and am just swept along. I feel safe. The current of it sweeps me to the side and into my space. I hear bells, tolling bells as for a funeral or procession of some time. A measured heavy tolling of the bell, not light. Calling. I listen and ask what is happening.

"It is the dying of the old. This must pass before the new can come in."

"I understand that but what about my direction? What am I supposed to do?"

"You are witness to the transition. You are a witness, an onlooker watching it happen. You will not be caught up in it personally."

I ask again about the book.

"Your friend was accurate. You will teach what you have written in the book."

"But I need to get it published."

"Wait and it will be. Wait.

***

2014

I have counted myself down. I see what at first appeared to be a mouth opening and shutting but I now see it is an entrance into a tunnel. It keeps opening and shutting. If I go through I must choose the moment while it is open. I must dash through and not get caught while it is shutting. I don't know what is on the other side so am watching and waiting for the opening. It does and I dash through. It shuts behind me. It is constantly opening and shutting. What does that mean?

"The energies that make you and everything are constantly in flux. You will never be here or there all the time. It is so rapid, so fast that you never realise that you have been elsewhere. You never realise that you have moved into another dimension. Even when you are there you do not remember where you were when you started."

Sounds very complicated.

"For us to slow it down would create confusion. This is what we are going to attempt to bring to your conscious mind so that you do experience consciously both sides of this pulse. It is a very rapid pulse."

***

2014

SYMBOL TRAINING

I seem to be in a party mood with glittering clothes. I am in my space. There are a lot of lights but triangles, shapes, coloured geometric shapes. Different sizes and moving about as if they are in themselves alive. Each shape is an intelligence. All kinds but all geometric. Some are symbols I don't understand, just pure zigzags, curly, lots of odd lines as well as the shapes we would recognise such as triangles, squares and so on. There are others as well. It is like looking at writing, not even hieroglyphics. These are a different style of writing but it is not forming a line as writing would but just floating around. Making an appearance then moving along for another shape. It is like each shape is a meaning on its own, like a word or even more.

"I want to know what this is trying to tell me. I need more clarification on this please."

"You must attach thought to the shape that appears in front of you."

"I now have a wavy form, not a smooth wave but with sharp edges."

"What does that remind you of?"

"It reminds me of stairs."

"Going up or going down? The thought that comes into your mind is the answer."

"It is going up."

"So, you have stairs going up. That has come out of just one shape. So you now have a sentence."

"Ok. So what is the next one please?" I get an oblong, no, no. It is an oval.

"What thought comes to your mind with the oval?"

"Given that I have just gone upstairs, my thought is a door."

"So, you are going upstairs through a door. You have already added more meaning to just two symbols."

"Ok, give me a bit more. What else are you going to give me? A triangle. So I have gone upstairs through a door and see a triangle. My first thought is a wigwam. That can't be right, can it? Can it?"

"You are entering the realm of Egypt."

"Ok. Upstairs through a door into the realm of Egypt. More shapes please."

"I get zigzags but horizontal. Like before but this time lying flat, so it is not stairs. What does that mean?"

"The ups and downs of life, that rise and fall."

"Alright! So I have gone upstairs, through a door into Egypt which is now speaking of the rise and fall of Egypt."

"You have got the story now."

"This is hard work."

"Keep at it. It will get easier as you go along. It is like learning anew alphabet."

"Hmm! What about these wavy lines that seem to float? Like worms in space, or bacteria?"

"These are thought patterns which are there for you to grab hold of. Grab an idea!"

I reach out and grab one of the floating things. As I do a charge goes up my arm. I have grabbed a thought and it has had an effect on me. I don't understand all of this.

"What it means is that when you have these symbols there is a thought that can be changed according to what is going on in the mind of the person or viewer who has grabbed that thought. It doesn't have to be you, it can be anybody. Anyone who grabs this can change the thought of whoever made the symbol and adapt it to their own will."

"Alright. So I have grabbed a thought which sent a charge up my arm. The thought that comes into my mind is an injection, like a vaccination into the arm."

"Why do people have vaccinations? Generally to cure them or protect them from something. So it is a protective symbol."

"I think that is enough for now."

"The interpretation is dependent on the mindset of the one trying to understand. So nothing is actually fixed in the way that a word in your language has a fixed meaning."

"That is not true because the word meaning depends on where in a sentence it lies. That can change the meaning."

***

2014
BEAM ME UP

I am at the top of my stairs and am wearing a suit. It is similar to the one I wear when I give talks. Having gone down there are many doors all leading to where the audience sit. It doesn't matter which one I take. Oh I see. I go down through the audience and end up on the stage. There are little circles on the stage. I stand in one wondering what I am supposed to be doing. This is a real 'beam me up, Scottie' thing for on each of the other circles appear human beings, ET's. They have been beamed down. That is the only word I can give it. They are here on the platform with me. They step out of the circles, so they are real, physical. We all stand together looking at the astonished audience. They are stunned into silence and don't know what to do. This appearance; in reality are creatures appearing from other places. It is no trick, it happened. I am as astounded as they are and I am also on the platform.

What we now do, there are no words. We group together holding hands and the energy that has beamed them down is now a group beaming. We are all beamed up and out so we are no longer seen. We are no longer there. The audience erupts. There is absolute confusion, pandemonium isn't quite the word. Some are sitting stunned, others are scrambling to get out, presumably to report what they have seen. It is quite staggering, and I am now with the group elsewhere on a ship watching what is going on down below. I feel this is a genuine prevision of what will happen. See Trilogy of Calling Earth

***

2015

I am going down in feathers. Not short fluffy feathers or angel feathers but long sweeping feathers. They seem to belong to an eagle or some other creature. They go right down from my shoulders to the ground. You can't see inside the feathers, so I don't know what form I have inside, underneath.

I am going down. At the bottom I am in what appears to be a gorge or cleft between high rock. There is only one way I can go. No turning off. It is a gorge, just rock, no water. It is very narrow such as you might see on a Western film. There is only one thing I can do and to go straight. Before I get to an end on the left there is a ladder – steps. Steep, going up out of the gorge. I climb. It is not hard, very light in fact as if I have no weight. So it is easy for me.

I get to the top. It is a plateau, in bright sunshine. It appears to be empty but I know it mustn't be. It mustn't be empty. I am thinking, these journeys, these stories are not necessary.

They say, "Remember you are a time traveller and you can travel into the future and bring back what you learned to your current time and pass this along. So direct your mind to gathering information from the future and bring it back to combine with the knowledge of your present day. This is what you must do now. You may forget your journeys for you may go immediately wherever you wish without the preamble that comes before."

"It is very hard for me to do. I have got into the habit."

"Forget the preamble that goes before."

***

2015

I ask to be shown what I need to see. There are a lot of women in older costumes who are weaving something on the ground, not on a machine. Threads of something, like a matting. Quite a lot of them. It doesn't matter who they are. It is just that something is being woven together.

"All the threads are coming together. You needn't be concerned. But it does take time for all the threads to come together. If we miss one it will not be strong. Continue to be patient. Everything must be in the right place for it to provide the complete perfect whole. Surely you can understand that."

"Thank you, I do understand." I ask now about the next book and I am given a picture of poles being erected.

"They are erecting a platform from which to promote and speak."

***

2015

I am in a silver suit, standing quite still in front of doors. I am strongly reminded of lift doors, elevator doors. They open as I approach. I do not need to press any buttons. I step inside and immediately there is movement. I can't tell if it is movement up or down as it is just a vibration movement. It is the energy around me that is vibrating. I have no means of knowing if the lift is moving up or down. No sense, just the vibration. It stops and the doors on the other side of the lift opens. I step out.

Green fields, a low very orange sun such as you would get with a sunrise or sunset. Very low on the horizon. It is very flat. I can't stay here so I must walk forward. I am still in my suit. Nothing has changed there. My senses are on full alert, my ears waiting to hear something in this unreal world. I hear clicking sound, like an insect perhaps or a creature of some kind. There is a little movement over to the right. I turn my head to look but I can't see anything, but the clicking is definitely there. Something pops out of the ground, a head of something. It is taking a good look at me. It stares. It is lizard like and it is this that makes the clicking sound. It pops back down.

I am not afraid. I go over in that direction and I can see the hole it has come out of. What do I do now? I realise there is somebody or something behind me. I hadn't noticed him coming up. It is another silver suited what appears to be a human being, much taller than me, much more male. He puts his hand on my shoulder. He is not unfriendly but just making sure I feel and know he is there. It is not a mirage, it is not a mirage. I turn round to face him full on. He doesn't have a helmet. His face is warm and friendly. He is difficult to describe. A sharp nose, bushy eyebrows, nice mouth, a little bit on the full side. The sort I wouldn't mind kissing. That is an irrelevant thought that pops in.

He steers me. No words. he steers me away from the hole and walks me over to what looks like a flight of stairs going down. How ridiculous is this! They are constructed steps going down into. ... If I was in my own world I would say this is a silo hidden from the surface. That is where we are going. We keep going down. It is not steps all the way. We go past the steps and then there is a downward path. He still has his hand on my shoulder, not that I am going anywhere. Where would I run to? There is lighting, we turn a few corners which shuts out the outside completely. I feel this journey is going to be long. There is another lift. We get in that and we go down. This time I can feel the movement down. I realise in this lift there are cameras. We are being observed, not because it is us for these cameras are in place all the time. So whoever enters will be observed somewhere in some control room. The lift shudders to a stop. The doors open and we get out.

***

2015

I am in a leafy green and am standing on wet dewy grass. It feels good to my toes. I look down for my descent. I am outside. No steps but simply indentations down an easy mountain slope. Going down until I reach level ground. It is very fresh with nothing dried up. I set off along a clearly marked out track through hedgerows. There is a stile on the right. I climb it and enter yet another field. I come to a wooden hut in natural surroundings. There are two angels, one on either side of the doorway. They are smiling.

I enter the hut. I have been here before. I know the hut. As before sitting at the table is Andreas, my own angel. I sit opposite as I did before.

"Tell me what I need to know and see and do."

"Your hand is in the honey pot and you will draw all the bees to you. The worker bees wish to have some of this honey."

***

2015
INNER EARTH

Go to viewing room and do as you have been instructed. Change it into something better. See the view as bad as it can be then change it for the better. This is what you will do on each trip. So the various scenarios will be individual, separate and each will have a reason to be changed. You have gone into inner Earth where the activities on the surface are viewed on a screen. Those who inhabit this inner Earth cannot or will not or dare not go to the surface. So you may do this. But because your mind creates realities it is your mind that brings changes. Teach others to do the same collectively and this is where you will be working once a fortnight or whenever a situation needs to be adjusted. Collect a group together for this. They constantly stress that we ourselves must make the changes and this is the way it shall be done.

***

2015
MY JOURNEY

I am in a green gown, in nature. My thoughts go back to the rainforest and the pure nature that is there. No interference, just pure raw nature. I am going down for that is my way. I am retracing my steps from where I have actually been but going down. I am taking time to actually look and watch the creatures at my feet and to look at the trees and bushes as I go. Impenetrable nature has its own way. I am at the bottom and get the feeling that we are not so important as human beings. Nature is. Nature will survive no matter what we do. No matter how hard we try, nature will always be the winner. At the bottom now. It is nice and easy along sandy shores. Easy walking. More air, more sun, more light.

I walk along and see to one side is a man. He appears to be a Shaman, a man of nature waiting for me on the path. He puts his hand out. I take it and help him to his feet. He doesn't need help but I do it anyway. He keeps hold of my hand and walks me along a very narrow path that I would not have noticed without him. It leads to a clearing as I knew it would. There are lots of families here, nature, children all living their lives with nature. They have no outside influence and are at one with nature. I want to know what this is trying to tell me.

"Everything has its place, everything is in order. There is no need to strive. It happens naturally. Nature being the key word. Whether you enjoy it or not is entirely up to you. There is no need to stress over anything."

"You might say, they have to catch their food, eat the right things, they still have to prepare the food, give birth and to clean themselves and do all the things that we do. They still have to pay attention to all of that. They still have their rules and regulations, and they must still have their emotions, hurts and the nature of man that upsets things."

"They do this, but everything is natural. It is not enhanced by outside forces. It is not interfered with by forces stronger than themselves, by other humans. They are responsible for themselves and are not responsible for those they have no knowledge of."

"I still do not know what this is telling me."

"What we are trying to put over to you is that nature will take its course whether it is interfered with or not. The cycle of events will continue as before irrespective of damage done by others from outside their cycle. The souls in this environment will live and die in the same way that you do. Their souls will have to account for the way they have behaved in their lifespan, in the same way that you will. In the same way that others who do not mean well have to account. So you see, nothing really is changed. Focus on the life that you have decided to live. Do not be so concerned that the Human Race will not survive for it will, and as souls will reap their rewards or account for their doings. Nothing has changed in that respect. Be more at peace. All is in order."

My thoughts stray now to the activities of those who would damage Earth itself through nuclear weaponry and the use of nuclear energy.

"We have witnessed destruction of habitation and ability to exist on other planets as a result of nuclear activity. We have learnt from this and will not allow the planet Earth to go the same way that others have in the past. Much damage has already been done but can be reversed. This may take time. The planet Earth will continue." *Interrupted by the phone*

***

2015
OCEAN SPACESHIPS – ANDROMEDA

The stairs are very steep so I have to go down backwards like on a ladder. It is like gangway stairs on a ship steep enough to go down backwards. At the bottom I realise that I am on a vessel or ship of some kind. Whether this is an airship or sea ship I don't know. There is still movement even though I am at the bottom. This means I am not on ground. Movement has to mean on something that is moving. I look around. It is a confined space, not wide. Walls are metallic. Not a lot going on. I look for an exit from this place.

It is a small place and I am on a ship for there is the sill that one has to step over from one part to the other. I step over the sill down a corridor which is lit. It is a narrow one, nothing ornate, very workmanlike. It is not a luxury ship, not a cruise liner. I walk past doors and there is one that says, 'come in'. So in I go, over another sill to get over, another small space. I don't know what kind of ship this is, a submarine perhaps.

It is odd because I am not quite steady. This place itself is a cabin and there are charts so it must be a ship, but I am the one that is not steady. My head is rocking. I feel as if I am waving to and fro, as if I am not really here. I am not solid. I am experiencing being an energy form. I am not third dimensional here so I can't keep my shape steady. That is what it is. But where I am is steady. I want to know where am I?

"You are beneath the waves."

"I figured that much out. That is not telling me where I am."

"You are in a restricted space."

"I figured that out as well."

"We mean, not known, not acknowledged even by the forces. This one is secret."

"OK. Whose secret?"

"It is not of your governments. It is from space. It is occupied and directed by human beings from space."

"What are they doing? What is the purpose?"

"This is a scientific research vessel. We are testing the condition of your seas. We are testing its ability to maintain a balance with the creatures and the system that uses the oceans for the health of your planet. If this system fails then your planet is in a dangerous situation. So we are here testing."

"Why am I not third dimensional and you are?"

"You cannot enter here in a physical third dimensional form so there is a dimensional shift to enable your entry."

"I still don't get it. Never mind. Is this the only vessel?"

"No there are others in all the major seas and all the major lakes on your planet. There are many and all are monitoring the condition of the waters. This is vital work by us for the benefit of your planet."

"What about those forces from space that are not well intentioned?"

"We are aware of them. They have their agenda, but we are operating separately from them and do not have interaction with them."

"Why are you human?"

"We are not all human but we are all humanoid. The Human Race on the planet has come from us. So we are the originators, or the originals as you would call us."

"Is this a small vessel? Everything seems very confined."

"It is a large vessel with many compartments rather than open plan as you would have it in your houses. The reason for the small compartments is that each wall is like the wall of a cell and provides greater strength throughout."

"Who are you?"

"We are a mix of races as you well know. Andromeda is our main base."

***

2015

I enter my space after a journey along a chalky path. I ask to see and I am not sure if they are statues or what they are. They are tall figures lined up. They have different colours and are close together. I can't see clearly enough to see if they are alive, real or just statues. I go in closer.

"Are you alive?" one of them moved a bit, so they are alive. They seem to be guarding something. So if they are alive they will move if I push. I push through two of them. I go through easily as if they are a living wall. The scene on the other side is beautiful, something I could call paradise. Everything is wonderful, fish playing. It is a beautiful scene, unreal, glorious. So why were they protecting it?

"We have to protect from the evils that are on your planet. We did not wish for any contamination to come through our barrier."

"What has this got to do with me?"

"This is the world you are going to create. You will not bring any contamination which does mean that there will be many who you will leave behind. Do not try to bring them with you for they will be contaminated, or rather, they are contaminated already."

***

2015

NOTHING IS A WASTE OF TIME.

I am not quite solid at the top of the stairs. I am in green but waving about and not clear cut. I am not even shimmering but not here, neither here nor there. The stairs are neither here nor there either. They are waving in and out of reality. I can move down, in between times, worlds, I am not sure. I am neither here nor there. At the bottom I am in a library of records of the past, present and the future. That isn't solid either.

My passageway is almost beckoning me. As I pass along it there are rooms full of books, full of records. I keep going past them. There are so many. I come to a full stop at my turning to the right. I am keeping to the routine. I push the door open with both hands. It opens easily. I step inside.

Inside there is nothing, like a void. I am in nothing. I am nothing but my mind exists. It is like being in space. I ask to be told something and I do get a response.

"Remember at all times that you are timeless. That you will continue for ever and ever. Any upsets or challenges or anything that appears to stop you in your tracks or gives you cause for concern, remember then that these things are not important. They are simply to be gone through. For you are timeless. This too will become history and will become part of the records. This will help you to go through whatever situation you encounter. Remember these will simply become part of the records as you move through time in a timeless state. It does not matter who you are, what you are but just how you feel about your existence at each moment of your timelessness. It all goes down in the records. It is all there never to be lost."

"Now I am confused. Does it mean then that what I do does not matter? That it is not important if I get this book published or not, that it really does not matter one way or the other? If that is so, what is the point of living and being here?"

"We see your conundrum. Do you not realise that as you pass through your experiences you affect others? This effect upon those around you can be positive or negative, that is up to you. So the purpose of your existence is to leave a residue of beneficial effect on all those that make contact with you in one way or the other. By so doing you can enhance the entirety of everything, or you can devalue it. It is a question of how you are. You can consider your actions as being of value one way or the other. Nothing is a waste of time."

***

2015

My space is what appears to be a basement of a building. I look around at stacks of this, that and the other. Boxes, tools and the sort of thing that you would stack away in a basement. You only come down here when there is a need for something. There is a dim light on, one of those overhead bulbs hanging from a wire. There is a group of men playing cards.

"What are you doing here?"

"We are playing cards."

"I can see that. Why are you in my meditation?"

"We are taking bets as to the outcome of your journeys."

"Mmm! Taking bets. So it is not a sure-fire thing."

"It depends on what you do. That has always been the case."

"What if I don't know what to do? What if I am wasting my time?"

"This is why we are placing bets. Nobody really knows."

"That is not very encouraging."

I see a tall man further in and he is waving me to come over to him. I pass the men at the table who I don't particularly like and go up to the beautiful man.

"Don't listen to them. They are trying to put you off. They are trying to create doubt in your mind. But we know that you will accomplish the task. We have already seen this happen. We know that everything is going to work out for you. Stop being waylaid by others, your own doubts, and get moving."

***

2015

I am in bare feet and am walking ankle deep in – I can't quite describe – it is like flakes, large dead flakes the size of slate. Not small, but soft, and not hard and brittle like slate. I am wading through. They are platelets of something shining in different colours. It is not hard to go through because they are only on the surface. Below that it is like liquid. I haven't got a clue what this is about. I am walking along what appears to be a cleft in a rock, like a gorge. I keep following. There is a flow under the surface of what I call platelets. You could call them leaves but these are not leaves. These are dead.

I come out of this rocky divide and can go either side now. I appear to be on a cliff face. I can't go forward so I have to go right or left. If I go forward it would be to drop off the edge. On either side there is someone beckoning me to go their way. I don't know which one to take. On instinct I go left as it is a much brighter colour. The one of the right is pretty heavy, rough, red. So I go left which feels heavenly in nice, bright and beautiful pastel colours. It is a very easy path and I am not wading through anything now. It is a sandy path but there can't be any sand up this high, can there? There is only a wall on one side of me, to the right there is a drop off.

I reach the individual. I don't know what to call him or her. He puts an arm around my shoulders and guides me by this means into a cave. As we go in I see there are steps going down a long way. So of course this is going to take us to the bottom and off the cliff face. I am being guided in the right way, safely off the cliff down to safe ground. Time goes on and we get to the bottom at last. It is green, like a paradise. Soft music, pleasant, birds singing. It is a new world; it is a new world. No heaviness, no darkness, a fresh and bright world. We have come off the precipice into a fresh world. Absolutely glorious. No dangers here, no concerns, just pleasure.

"For me pleasure isn't enough. I feel I still need to do something."

"You can guide people off the precipice using your judgement. Guide them off the edge when they can't see which way to go. Because you have travelled the path you can also show them the way."

"I need people to have trust and faith in me."

"Oh they will. They will."

"What about the book?"

"The book is another matter."

There is a lot of meaning in this. I feel it is to do with timelines and helping people to go along the correct timeline else they will be doomed.

***

2015

MY ATTACHMENT FOUND ON BEACH

My way down is a ladder. It is not exactly a normal ladder, but one that does down a cliff face. It is fastened to the top and is the only means to get down this cliff. I go backwards. It is not difficult and is not that far. There is no other way. There is no path to get down. It is not going directly to the beach. It is a little inland, that is to say where the sea comes in there's quite a bit of land or the tide has to come really high to cover and to reach this point.

At the bottom it's shingle. Something is going to happen. There is nobody else around because the only way down is using this ladder. It has been put there just for me and nobody else. I won't be disturbed at all or interrupted. There is something I must find on the beach amongst all this shingle. There is something here that will take me back to the past. But this something comes from the future. Maybe it takes me to the future. I don't know.

I begin to search and then I see it. It is a triangle. A blue metallic triangle. It's not that big and I can hold it in one hand. It's attached to something. It is a device. How long has it been here?

"It is there waiting for you."

I pick it up and put it against my forehead, on my third eye. That is where it belongs. It has come home to me. It's mine. It stays on my forehead. It seems to stay all by itself, like some magnetic attachment there. It's attached to what is in my head. What's in my head has always been there and I have found the component that makes it whole. Now what do I do? I don't feel real. I don't feel at all real.

***

2015

I have gone down wooden stairs. Going deep, a long way down. There is an entrance into the earth like a burrow. At the bottom it is all enclosed, not wide, not a lot of room. Like being in a burrow. There has to be a way out. There can't be just this hole. I look and find a burrow that goes off to the left. There is no problem getting along. It is big enough and I am small enough. There has to be a right turning. That is interesting because the burrow is going upwards until it breaks out until what looks like a meadow. Out into the fresh air and sun. I come onto the surface. It is green and pleasant, birds singing. Nice English pretty countryside, absolute peace. Everything is in harmony. I have crossed from one area into harmony. I am trying to analyse this. Going through the earth into harmony. It Is a symbolic message. I look around to see what else. Over the horizon comes a whole gathering of people, large gathering. All coming up, and spread out over the horizon, coming towards me. They are all very happy. Waving banners and flags and celebrating something. They come towards me, greeting me. As they get closer I see they are all holding copies of my book. They all have my book and are happy about it.

***

2015

CHANGING LANDSCAPES

The stairs are steep. There is a rail on either side and it is narrow enough for me to grab hold of both rails. It is very steep but not so that I have to go down backwards. It is not that easy as I go deeper and deeper. My intention is to meet myself from the future.

He has a briefcase and is in silver. He is standing there. He takes my arm as I step off the last rung. I want to know.

"Tell me what I have missed, that I should know. Tell me now."

"This is about the future. This is about the rising of land, changing of landscapes, changing of waterways. It is about massive change. More in some parts of the planet than others. There will be upheaval. You will survive it."

"I am not bothered whether I survive it or not."

"But you must, must prepare for this. Prepare for it internally as much as externally."

"I don't understand because knowing this changes nothing, so what good is it?"

***

2015

RENEWED FROM BLACK HOLE

I have made my descent. As I step off the last rung I see I am on the edge of a large hole, a big circular hole. There is a very narrow path that goes around it. If I take this journey I must be careful not to step off. If I do I will go into the hole. I can't see the bottom of the hole. It is just a big black hole. Then I remind myself that I am just a mind, not physical. I could step off and I would be alright. The question is, do I? Or do I walk around it until I find my exit, my entrance. I don't know what to do. It is not scary, the thought of stepping off, but if I do and then find nothing, I need to find something, but I have to step off.

So I step off and am sucked into what appears to be a vortex, a wormhole, a black hole or whatever word you need. It is like that film, 'Contact'. As I whirl through for a long time it is perfectly alright. I am still here and that is the important thing for me.

Part of me feels I am making this up, but I know I am not. I know I am not. I find myself now on steady ground. It is sand, it is warm, hot even and I am covered in sand as if I have been lying in it and it has stuck to me. As I look at myself, brushing off the sand, I am slim, I am young, I am very much in good shape, good condition, younger skin. I feel full of energy, vibrant energy. There is nothing I cannot do. As I wave my arms about I am renewed. That's the word. I am renewed, revitalised. New body, perfect condition. Why?

"You must have this for the years ahead. You need this vitality for the years ahead. You will inhabit this body in the years to come until the time you are released from Earthly encumbrances. Your mind is sharp. You drop the vestiges of age physicality. You are now vibrant and can do anything you desire."

***

2015

I am in a big orchard. It is a farmed orchard, not just a garden or random one. The fruit is picked by machine not hand-picked. What am I doing here?

"The fruits of your labours will be picked by many, not just by one or two. It will be on a manufacturing scale."

***

2015

REFUSE DUMPS

My stairs are made of paper, stacked paper that has been recycled. It is quite solid although it is paper. I step down over a great pile of paper and find my way down. All this rubbish! I eventually actually get back down to bare earth again which hasn't seen the sky ever since dumping started.

This earth is not nourished by sun, sea, air or water wherever there is a mountain of rubbish. It needs to be dealt with wherever dumping occurs. At the bottom on the bare earth I go walkabout. I seem to be on hills. The sun is weak and just about coming through as it does on a misty morning. The mist is rising up from the ground and I can't see that far ahead but just enough so I don't bump into anything. I lose all sense of direction but eventually I come to what I create in my mind, a door, a silver door. It is clean, pristine.

As I walk through the door it is like walking into another world, through a portal where the sun shines. It is warm and the birds are singing. Everywhere feels happy. What a contrast from where I have come from into the beautiful clean and pristine world.

"This isn't telling me anything or showing me what I really need to see."

"Those who seek can find their way into pristine, joyful and happy world. But they will not find it unless they seek, unless they look for it, knowing it is there. If they do not seek they will remain in the wallow of the dump where all things are spoiling the ground. First, they must seek and if they do they will find their way into another world. That is the message. It will not be shown them; it will not happen without them looking for it. It won't be something that is given freely to them. They must put their effort into finding it, whatever that means. For each it will be different.

***

2016

VISIT JUNGLE HOLE- REPLENISH SOUL

My stairs are like hand holds going down into the Earth, a cavern, a sink hole. I can't see the bottom yet. I keep going down. I am suitably clad, jeans, strong shoes, proper clothing for expeditions. This big hole has been here a long time because there is vegetation on all sides. Like the deep holes you see in the jungles in South America. It is soft, green and very much like a jungle, and it feels sweet. There are birds, it is nature completely untouched by the world on the surface. It is like another world, but it isn't, it's the same world.

Further in there is a stream with lots of birds of all kinds. Small birds, not big ones. I follow the stream which is very shallow. The water barely covers my feet, but I still have my boots on, and I need to take my boots off because I know the water is beautiful to be in. I sit to one side for a bit, undo my boots, tie them together and drape them round my neck. I get back into the water – oh it's beautiful, cool and lovely. The stream is gentle and not flowing fast. I come across a little pool, a whirlpool has formed. Again it is not deep. I don't understand why I am being taken here.

"It is Earth unsullied by man. It is nature as it was intended to be. All the vegetation purifies whatever is above, cleanses it. Here there are no machines, there are no industries, it is pure nature."

"Yes, but people need industries to be clothed, to have the various things that make life for them. We need industry for those. While this is very nice it is not practical."

"But you see it exists and can be reached by those who seek. I see your thoughts have returned to your book."

"Yes, because I need industry to get the book published, printed, distributed. That too requires industry. That service cannot be done down here."

"Down here, as you put it, can replenish your soul. When you feel despair over the doings on the surface you can be replenished down here. Visit often. Visit often."

***

2016

My stairs are sharp angles going down. Oh I see it is like stairs that have a lot of landings. A lot of hospitals have these kinds of stairs, or office buildings, sharp turns with landings every so often. I am in a suit, high heels, not too high, I am dressed smartly, a business office presentation. I don't know. I go down now, there are smooth round metal rails on the side so this is not a posh place. I get to the bottom and as I would expect it is some kind of entrance hall.

There is a door leading out, automatic doors leading out into bright sunshine. Lots going on here with people going about their business. This might easily be a town busy thoroughfare. There is a narrow road that is beckoning me so that is where I must go. It is a narrow road and you wouldn't get a car down here. There are buildings on either side shutting out the sun. Keep walking. I can hear my footsteps echoing as I go. No pavement, it is too narrow for a pavement. There is nobody down here except me. It feels OK. I come to the door I am looking for on the right. It is bright red and you couldn't miss it. There is a knocker. It is the first time I have seen a knocker on a door here. I knock and even that echoes. The door opens by itself. I am expected. The coughing starts and the itching too. Something is trying to stop me going further. Maybe it is me.

I am staying with it. I am inside the door. There is a deep red carpet. Again it looks very official and I am dressed for business. It is a long hallway, and the carpet goes all the way. For some reason I am reminded of number 10 Downing Street and it has that official feel about it. There are pictures on the wall. A quiet hushed feel. I start to walk forward and as I go along doors are opening on either side and somebody steps out of each door, looks at me, smiles and gives a little nod bow. A little bowing of the head as I pass, acknowledging me. Both men and women. It is as if I am going to some kind of celebration. I keep walking and at the end of the corridor there are big heavy doors that open in the middle. Big nob handles.

They are opened from the other side by two footmen. Clearly, I am meant to go in, so I do. The scene before me is wavering in and out. First I thought there was a queen, not our queen, a queen. Then I see behind her and almost appearing to be in front as well is a long table with men sat behind it. Is she superior to them or are they managing her? I don't know. But it is the men I must see. I walk around her and the men all stand up. They too give a little nod of the head. So I am expected.

They each push a paper and a pen towards me across the table. Each of them has a sheet of paper and a pen. I am to sign these documents. I really don't understand this, but I sign each one. I don't need to read. I go down the line signing. I turn round and see all the people that were in the corridor, in the doors are all clapping as if I have completed something. I have succeeded at something. The signatures are all contracts. I do feel it is about the book. Different parts of what the book is entailing. I don't understand but it doesn't feel bad. I am signed up now. No going back and everybody is happy. I am confused, that's all, but happy too, even if I don't really know why and what this means.

***

2016

Great souls will arise during this time of disarray. Great souls will surpass all others and those who wish to be great can look to them and receive inspiration in the sight. All will surpass and outweigh the evils that are occurring on your planet. Things will go well. Your soul has the opportunity to rise and not fall. God bless you all.

***

2016
SILVER WINGED SOULS

I am in a tight-fitting silver suit, a jump suit completely covering my feet as well. This says space to me. My steps are metal, no adornment. Actually, they are not steps but is a lift going up or down. It doesn't matter. I just stand and it moves. I am moved where I need to be. The doors open. I step out into a tube-like corridor. Clear, clean, no windows. It is like an empty tube. Everything is clean. I walk along and as I walk lights come on and go out as I leave. So I am lit just where I am. I am being filmed as I go. Somebody is watching my every step.

The tunnel slopes down gradually so it is not steep but descending into a lower area, away from interference or being noticed by any above. This has a very secret feeling, not known to many. The tunnel itself is not important, just a means to arrive where I am meant to be. The tunnel fans out and I am greeted by . . . it is difficult to describe them . . . they are winged and appear to be human, but I know they are not humans like us. But they have wings. The wings are folded so I can't see the spread of them. I call them beautiful creatures and have a good feeling of warmth and love and welcome from them.

I am paying note that their arms are not attached to their wings. The wings are attached to the back whereas with birds they would have their wings as their arms. These wings are separate from arms. I don't know how to describe it but I can see it clearly in my head.

"We know you are concerned about your books and we also realise that until that issue is completed you cannot put your mind to the book that Andrew spoke of. So we will do our best to get your books on the publication system. Then you may feel free."

"I notice this isn't a promise. You will try. I am looking for something definite. I am looking to sign a contract."

This human bird takes me over to a glorious chair and made me sit down in front of a console that I look down into rather than up at. It is glorious, sheer glory.

"This is reality," he says. "What you are in is not. For you it feels like reality but it is not the real thing. It is a part that you are experiencing. No more than that. You are living, breathing and experiencing. What you see on this screen is reality. This is the real thing. We show this to you to put things into perspective for you so you do not get too wound up over what is happening in your reality created life."

"Oh dear! I think I know what you are trying to say but the life I am conscious of is the life I have to focus on. You have told me that before so that is why I am focussing on getting these books published. And sorting out all those things that this experience is giving me."

I had a nod of appreciation at this.

***

2016

I see an entrance to a mine, quite easy to get into. There are lights so it is used, or the lights are there for me. I don't know which. It is a bit rough underfoot now. People haven't been here for a long time or it would have been smoother. I look for a lantern and see one on a hook. I take it off the hook and use it. as I go in I see a pile of coins. You don't get coins in a mine!

Tell me what this is. What does this mean?

"Bury your money so that it is hidden. Keep it hidden from those on the surface so that you may use it when it is needed."

Somebody takes my hand, a male hand holding mine. I can't see who it is but he pulls me further on until there is an exit from the mine. As we come to the exit the view is vast, looking over countryside. The sun is coming up.

"The world is your oyster. You can go where you wish, do what you wish, achieve what you wish or stay at home. It is all there for you if ou wish."

"So it is my decision after all.

"It has always been your decision."

"It hasn't always been my decision. You have instigated many things. I now need guidance. Do I need to proceed with this book? Will I ever get anyone asking me to work anymore?"

"First you decide what you wish and then we will put it into action. We will make it happen."

***

2017

TRANSPORTATION DEVICE

I am in gold and my stairs are gold, glistening, very wide. As I go down I can hear hushed whispering, voices on either side. So I am not alone by any means. I keep going down and listen to the whispers and the rustling. I am being watched as I go down. It doesn't feel unfriendly, just watching me. It is nice, nothing to be worried about. As I get nearer the bottom the whispering is more like proper voices. I am getting closer and closer.

When I get to the bottom the voices are echoing. Not exactly loud but enough for it to echo around me. I can't see who is making the voices as there is a big empty space. It is a giant empty space. I feel I am inside metal, not rock. It is metal. There must be a way out and there is. It is as if a hole has been punched in the side of the metal. A tube is coming out of this space. I go into the tube. It is not very big but just big enough for me to get in. If I was any bigger I would have difficulty in the form that I am. I walk along and can hear the sound of my footsteps on metal. I am on my own now. It is a metal tube – solid, nothing flimsy about this. I wonder what this is all about. I am going underground. There is nothing on the sides, just a plain metal tube. Because of my conditioning I am expecting a door on the right, and so there is. It is put there for me. I don't need it, but it is put there for me just to be comforting.

I stop at the door. I can't really call it a door as it is more of a flap. Someone is waiting for me on the other side. I push the flap and it swivels open and I step inside. There is a flash of colour. I am in big flash of colour, blue and green. Brilliant, it is a bit dazzling so I can't see. It has dazzled my eyes.

"Show me what I need to see please."

"This is something that actually exists. this is not a figment of anyone's imagination. It exists. You have walked into a manufactured space."

I feel these are living quarters and I see what appears to be beds, slabs, bunks? I don't know what to call them. Clearly they are for lying down. Beds is a misnomer for they are not going to sleep on these things.

"They are to lie on. They are to take you to other – it is a transportation device. You lie on the bed and it is plugged into all sorts of attachments and the lid comes down."

It reminds me of Avatar.

"According to your thoughts you are then transported"

I am not in one. I am just looking and getting a description. Some of them are closed and there are beings inside them. So they are off somewhere in their soul journeys.

"Do I need to go into one?"

"You can get in if it is your desire and because of your physical problem on your Earth plane, if you wish to get this resolved you will need to step into one of these platforms, lie down. It is your thought that will take you where you need to be. Do you understand that?

"Yes, I understand. I must be careful how I word things it seems."

"Correct."

So I think about my words before I get in so I don't make any mistakes. I ask for rejuvenation and for health for my body. Take me where this is possible. I think that will do. I get on the slab.

It is warm as if it has been heated. It is shaped. That is interesting. It is shaped like the body, allowing for the curves of the body so that it fits comfortably. Oh, it is comfortable! Before the lid comes down I ask, "Please take me where I can be fully recovered and healed and returned to a physical body in full health. Can you do this now, please?

As I ask this the lid comes down. I am inside now and the whole thing seems to fill up with – not steam, not vapour – but I am in a sort of mist. Cloudy. Anyone outside can't see inside now. I lie there drifting, drifting, drifting...

***

2017

I am in bright apple green and am going down through an orchard full of fruit.: Looking at the fruit is making my mouth water. Keep walking! I am going down into a sunken garden similar to what you'd get in a country estate, open to the public. Yes, it is open to the public, with tended roses. There is nobody else here. I don't know what this is all about or what this is telling me. It is solitary.

"We have told you before that your path is to be the lonely one and you agreed to this. Don't you remember?"

"I do remember, and I was happy to agree to it."

"This just for a brief spell and your books will change all of that. You will then have the choice to remain solitary or to engage fully. The opportunities for both will be there and it will be your choice not ours, to go in whichever direction you wish."

I am feeling something heavy in my hand. It is heavy, solid and something tells me this is the book.

"It is already in reality. You need have no fear. It already exists."

***

2017

I am standing on what appears to be a revolving disc which is big enough for me. It is interesting because I have my arms outstretched as if I am to jump off and fly. There is nothing to hold onto. I bring my arms down and then together, palms together facing forward as if I am going to dive into a pool of water. I give a little jump and I've left the platform. It is not quite like flying for I have my arms together, shooting forward – through the air? It is a bit like a dart. Keep going, things keep rushing past me. I need to know when to stop. I am not looking at anything in particular or looking down. Just going straight ahead. As I go

I hit a barrier, not hard, just an energy field. I go straight though it but I have definitely entered an energy field.

I can relax, put my arms down and alight. I gradually alight on my two feet and look around me. I am on land. It is sandy, coarse sand which crunches as I walk. Do we call this sand? I am walking. Everything seems to be a bit bluish. Not solid blue but as if the air is blue. I can't see anything yet. Show me where to go please.

The voice in my head says, "You have gone through to another dimension, another field of energy. It is a field of energy that you have entered. Some might call it a dimension, but generally human minds think of a dimension as spiritual elevation. This is simply a new field of energy. That is what we must make clear. It is not the same as dimension. Dimension is the wrong word. Your scientists are not aware yet of this new energy field. You might call it enlightenment because when you are in it everything is clear."

"I am in and I am confused so that doesn't make sense."

"Yes, but you haven't digested yet. Focus on what is around. If you focus and intentionally look then you will see. If you do not and keep your thoughts simply on yourself you will not see. Intend to see and it will become clear."

I must think first what to intend. The first thing that comes into mind in my focus is the sea and what is in the sea, dolphins, sea life of all kinds. It is as if I have entered into that world of being in the ocean. It is beautiful. I am part of it. I think this is just teaching me because I have now changed my intention and wish to see something different now.

I am in treetops, in amongst the topmost part of the trees, all kinds of tree, tropical as well as deciduous, native to England as well as foreign, all mixed together. Nature! I am in there and don't feel I have a body. My mind is in there.

"Focus is all and you can be in any world you wish, any world you wish."

My thoughts now go to babies, children, toddlers, young ones and suddenly I am there. They are an absolute delight to be with. they are interacting with each other in innocence and joyfulness. I am there amongst them. It is rather nice because I don't have a body to be concerned about. It is just observation and my eyes are clear, my mind is clear as if I have become the energy that is present in these situations.

"Yes, you have it. But if you put your thoughts on all the things that you do not wish to have and let thoughts stray on the horrible things that are happening you will be there too. You cannot change it just by being in the energy. That will come later. We will show you how to do that. For the moment, this is training and teaching you how to be in another energy field."

"How is this going to help anybody, and how is this going to be "presented in the next book?"

"We have made a start. This is for beginners, a beginning, more to follow."

"I must teach this. It is an important aspect of the next book, to teach, to assist others."

"You can teach this by example."

***

2018
ANGELS AND MAN

I have gold stairs and a gold metal bar to hold onto. The stairs are quite flat, not steep, easy tread, very gentle. There are angels waiting for me. They escort me and I feel their arms around me and behind me so that I don't turn round and walk back the other way. I go where they are directing me to go. Everything is in gold. I don't know where I am going as this is unusual and unexpected. There is a man sitting down, a beautiful figure. He bids me to sit down opposite him.

"Why have you been neglecting us?"

I nod. "I am sorry. There is so much else to do. I am sorry."

"Well catch up now. Be with us each day for we have much to tell you and we cannot tell you unless you try to connect with us. EACH day connect, and we will show you your next step should you wish to take it."

"Thank you. I know I've been neglecting you. There is always so much else to do."

He stands up and I stand too. He points forward to a vast expanse. This is your world which you have still to explore. The world is ahead of you, waiting, waiting. We have been waiting. We will tell you what we wish of you next."

"Why can't you tell me now?"

"You have much on your mind. You still have your events and have to get these things organised. There is much on your mind still and we cannot work with you until this is cleared. It will be cleared. We will facilitate it. we will sort it out so that you can give us your full attention which you haven't been doing recently."

"I have in a way."

"In a way is exactly it. but not in the way we intend for you."

***

2018
RESEARCH AND MAINTAINING EARTH

My way in are steps cut into the ground through what appears to be jungle or thick undergrowth. I am wearing on my feet hand stitched shoes, like moccasins but they are not American Indian. They are stitched together from cloth of some kind. I am going down a steep slope on steps cut into the ground, earthen steps. I mustn't touch any of the undergrowth for there are all kinds of things there, insects, poison bushes, ants, all kinds. Best not to touch. It is hot and tropical. I have got to a stream. I step over it and keep walking. I am not to follow the stream. I come to a tent set off to the side. It is not a modern tent but an old one, quite large and could hold many people. It is for research. This is or has been, I'm not sure which, used for an expedition, scientific expedition. What are they researching.

"They are researching plants for cures. Medicinal plants to cure the ills of man. Nature will cure the ills of man if man will allow. If man does not stamp out nature all manner of cures and assistance to heal the whole of man can be found in these jungles. Man is destroying himself by depleting these natural wonderlands, man is creating his own death by not research and maintaining full growth of these wonderlands that have not yet been tainted by the industries and the greed of man. Take care, take note, preserve all forests and your jungles."

"Who is it that is doing the research in these tents.?" I can't see anybody. It is an empty tent.

"It is not empty at all times for we from other planets visit your Earth and we too need to research to assist us in maintaining full health. We need your jungles and your forests as much as you do. Many of our visits to your Earth are so that we can also research cures for our ills. So you can see that your planet Earth is as important to us as it is to you. You seem determined to destroy the bounty that you have all around you. Why is this so? We cannot understand why.

"In your third book you need to introduce the need to maintain your natural surroundings. You must stress the need, the urgent need to maintain a balance on your planet. We know you are well aware; many of you are well aware of the damage that is being done and we are aware that many are attempting to prevent the damage, but it is not enough."

***

2018

PREDICTION? New people coming

Warm stone, it is narrow. I am wearing lace up sandals. It feels old. There is a wall on either side of the stairs, steps are more accurate. Smooth rock walls. I am don't know what I am going into. It is a cave with an earthen floor. I am guessing that it is one of those caves that lead out to the sea. The steps have gone down a cliff, but inside the cliff, possibly used by smugglers in the past. As I walk it is sandy, mixed with sand and dirt. Quite smooth, easy walking. I can feel the air coming in from the other end now. Fresh salty air.

I see men with black rubber suits. They have clearly been in the sea. They are putting down some instruments. A receiver of some kind, square. I can't see much but it is some instrument, and I would say, heavy. As I query this I just know that all along the coastline these same instruments are being planted in caves underneath the cliffs all the way along the southern coast of England. When the time is set they are all going to be activated. It is like detonation. I feel the cliffs will be blown up or demolished in some way. I am not sure, but there are many of these along the south coast. They are going to be detonated. I don't know what is going to happen here. They are all in line with something offshore. The reach, the signal will all come from one particular point out at sea, and they will all go off at the same time. It will cause a lot of chaos. It is a distraction; I don't know what from. My head is hurting so I know this message is coming from a source to be truthful. I don't know the purpose. I am asking for the purpose. (heavy input)

"Landing posts, landing posts."

"What for?"

"Easier access. There will be explosions. There will be landfall which makes it easier. While it may not appear to be so, it will be."

"Who is going to be landing?"

"New people to your shores. New people."

"I can't pass this on to the people. I have to hold this to myself. Can't you give me something more positive?"

***

2018
TRANSPORT TO UNDERGROUND INTELLIGENCE FIELD

I have stone stairs, polished, not marble. Constructed stone such as you might get going down into a public place. Constructed for anybody who wishes to use it. Going down. I am reminded of a railway station, the back entrance, not the escalators. It is a side entrance to be used when the escalators are not working. It is a safety measure. I am going down so I am not escaping, I am going into - - going deep underground and once you get down there is transport. The idea is to go where the transport is, not just to be underground. That's interesting.

I get to the bottom and how they are showing it to me as a transport system. There is nobody around, just me. It hasn't been used for a long time. It has been abandoned, not used for ages by the public. As I stand there waiting, I ask, 'Take me where you need me to be.' It is a variation on what I usually ask. As soon as I ask, this is bizarre – a vehicle – how can I describe this vehicle. It is suspended in air, not touching the ground. It is like a pod, similar to when you go up in a cable car or a sky lift. You get in and it goes off. This is not a human thing. As I look at it, the door slides open inviting me in – just space for two people. I get in and it zooms off down the passage, the tunnel. I am holding on tight.

It is comforting because as I get into the speaking mode, which I know from years is essential (for these records), the energy is increasing in my head to painful levels, the level where I know, I absolutely know I am making contact. It took a little while this time, but I am connecting as I am zoomed along. I can't see anything around me, and it doesn't matter. I have many questions buzzing in my head as I go.

I am being zoomed into a nonphysical area, just pure intelligence. Nothing I can see, nothing I can touch, just pure mind. I am in the intelligence system where I can ask and receive. I am being told telepathically,

"The reason for your extended travels, both booked and yet to be so, are so that you can detach yourself from all the distractions that are currently in your life and put your next instalment for the book. Do not fear that what you have done is not reaching enough. It is all a question of timing and once it reaches a certain level it will explode into publicity and the minds that need to be awakened."

I am grateful for that.

"Your trips are not just pure extravagance. They have been intended all along. Don't worry about it. Everything is planned and is in order."

I ask many more questions. "Will I be returned to where I started."

They responded, "You may remain in the field of intelligence." I quite like that. "Knowingness. Pure knowing.

***

2018
SCIENCE RESEARCH

I have done the stairs and have ended up in a really luxurious place. It is beautiful with lovely objects all around. I walk through and open the door at the far end. What has gone before is nothing like what I can see now. It is like a science lab. Lots of instruments. It is like a science lab, very shiny and very new. At the moment I can't see anybody.

"What is this laboratory for please?"

As I ask there are a lot of sparkly spirits appearing and dancing around. They are recognisable as human spirits, very light and pixy like, like fairies.

Magical.

"It is a magical world where many things can be achieved. It is a magical world where many things will be achieved and will be the source of improvement for use on your planet."

"I want to know why there are no beings here apart from spirit."

"Because we, with our minds, telepathically give and guide those who work in these laboratories so that they may discover or feel that they are discovering new ways, new projects, new advancement. In fact it is we who are sowing the seeds in their minds. There will be miracles occurring as realisation enters the minds of your scientists. It will be the scientists who deliver some relief to your planet and the way it is run. A lot of water must go under the bridge first."

"So why was I brought through all the luxury and the grand place to get here?"

"It is demonstrating that those who have the money, those who have the backing will promote and support the scientists. Do not ignore the importance of those who have the funding. Funding will be required. It will not come from the poorest areas of your planet. The ideas may come from the poorest areas but funding will be required to put the ideas into practice."

"Thank you. Will I see any of this or will I be long gone?"

"You will see the beginnings but not the full spectrum."

***

2018

MEDITATION 3.00am re 3RD BOOK

I am dressed head to foot in cobalt blue, a cocoon of cobalt blue. The energies are coming into me and I must start my journey now. I thank them for the energies which always begins when I speak. It is that I must speak to fetch the rest. I follow the system now registered with my being. The stairs are the same blue, straight down. As I go I feel invisible for I merge with the colour. The stairs and I are one. There is absolute silence. The last bit is a slide and I don't feel real here. It doesn't matter. As I arrive everything is the same deep colour. I don't know where I am going for all I can see is the colour.

As I move along invisible to anyone else I see little glimmers of light here and there. I am to ignore those for they are just to show I am not on my own here. The lights are guarding me as I go into the unknown. I ask to be guided and after a lot of coughing and nose blowing I know it will clear.

"It is just passing from one reality to the other. It is a necessary clearing of earthly matters."

As I move along there is a beautiful glow like the stargate cover on my latest book. It is brilliant. I must go through this. I walk straight into it. Into it. when I come out the other side there is greenery. I am real, and it is like a paradise. Perfection everything glows and has an aura about it. There is nobody about, just me, I think. I am not sure because I am contained within me. I feel I could take any form according to my will. So I see myself here as young, virile, superbly fit. Alive and perfection of body. This is a reality I will accept with gratitude as I walk through what appears to be perfection.

I can't see anyone yet and I must interact with someone who can lead me. I am told I must ask a question.

"My question is: do I write book number 3 while I am away? A practical question and how do I do that?"

"Take paper, find a space and simply let your mind flow onto the paper. You will not likely meditate in your cabin. You may if you wish but it is unlikely. Let it roll as you would if you were teaching someone to write. Let it roll keeping in mind the characters you already have. We will influence your thoughts."

"As a rival for Gork, you will have a gigantic figure in opposition to Gork. It is male but looks like an angel. Looks like an angel and is dressed in shimmering silver with gold flecks. It can morph into many forms. You must give it a name. You must find a name for it for it will become a companion whenever there is a need to protect you. This figure will have been sent by Joslene"

***

2018
THE THIRD BOOK AND MY DEMONS

My stairs are slippery, shiny and I need to hold on to the bannisters to make sure I don't fall. I am only just keeping my feet. It is as if I am on ice and I haven't any skating boots, just my normal shoes which have no grip. I go down anyway and if I let go of the banisters I will fall. As I go further down it is getting warmer and the ice is melting and it is watery now. I have ground covered in water. It is getting a lot warmer now and steam is coming off the water. I step off the last step onto rocky, gritty ground, gravelly, that's the word.

As I look around and ask to be shown I see two beings come forward and each takes a hand and guides me forward. They have got my arms so I feel good and safe. They are large beings, strong and muscular bodies. They are clothed but I can see they are brawny. They have strength and are taking me somewhere.

"Where are you taking me?"

"We are taking you to meet your demons."

"I didn't know I had any demons."

"We are taking you to show you that if you believe you have demons, then you have. If you don't believe you have then you don't have."

"So why this show? Why?"

"We are still taking you somewhere."

We seem to be going into a glade. Fresh bright green, trees, fresh grass. It is beautiful and there is loveliness here – no demons – no demons. So why am I told to face my demons. Where are they? The two beings turn me to the side, drop my arms and say,

"Go into the bushes alone."

I have done this many times, so I walk into the bushes and they seem to part as I go through.

"What is this all about?"

"You are going into new pastures. Your life ahead is going to take a different turn, one that you cannot see ahead so that you cannot plan. It will occur and you will face whatever it is as it occurs."

"OK. I have always done that."

"Yes, but you have no idea what this is."

"Is this anything to do with the book?"

"It is where the books will take you and you as yet have no idea where this will be. They will take you into different realities of your life on Earth."

"I still don't understand this but am happy if they have an effect."

"Oh, they will have an effect alright. Please be assured of that."

"It seems to be taking a heck of a long time."

"Things will happen at the right time as always."

***

2018
MIND CONSTRUCT

My steps are winding down a mountain side, winding down corners. The steps have been cut into the hillside so they are natural, stones, wood, earth and whatever can make a step. It is on a mountain, so it is open, not in thick undergrowth or anything. Lots of bends, as I know it is the only way to get down the mountain safely. I am dressed in proper clothes for being outside. Strong boots. Keep going down. It is not a high mountain, so it is not freezing. If anything it is quite warm and at a comfortable temperature. It is higher than the hills of Wales but not a real high mountain. I can hear the birds singing. I am at the bottom now and can see a flat grassy plain. There is a path. What have they done to my usual pattern of turn to the left, turn to the right. I have just got to follow the path to see where it goes.

I come to what appears to be a large hollow. Not a crater but a round large hollow. It is not deep. I go down a slope and right at the bottom is a space craft. It is typically round and is slightly humming, buzzing, a vibrational humming. It feels inviting, that is how I feel about it. I walk closer to it. There is a rim all around it and as I get closer I see the rim is wide enough for there to be windows. There are lights, it is very active. I don't know if I am meant to go into it, I am walking closer and don't know what to do. As I walk around looking for a door, which sounds ridiculous for I can't see any, I find myself inside.

I have no way of knowing how I got inside but I am. It is amazing for it is like being in a different world. It is now as I would expect it to be inside a craft. It is big here, alive. The interesting thing is that it is alive with nature such as you would have outside, greenery, bushes and I feel there could be creatures here as well. So it is not mechanical inside, it is another country, another place. How odd! I expected it to be a craft with machinery, instruments but there is none of that. I feel at home which is a huge surprise to me. It is as if the outer shell wasn't there and I just stepped through. No I didn't step. I simply found myself inside. I feel I could walk for a long time and not reach the other edge.

Two little creatures, humanoids come up to me. They are not Greys but have peachy coloured skin with a tinge to it. They are smiling and take my hands and walk me along - - - long pause, oh! I think I have crossed into another time, another place, another method of transport that you wouldn't expect. My mind is buzzing with the newness of this. The two Greys look at me and I understand what they are thinking, no words – at this point I begin to speak their language. I can hear this in my head. I am in their land. I am in their time. I want to know where we are.

"You are on another civilisation land mass."

"That doesn't tell me where I am."

"You are on another time frame, another existence." At this point more of their language but from them. "We are every bit as real as you. All you have done is split through from one time frame, from one area to another space."

They are trying to make me understand.

"It is a land mass on another cosmic body. We do not wish to use the word planet for that would not be quite accurate. We do not wish you to think of the cosmos being composed only of planets and stars, for there are other land masses. Even the word land is incorrect. This is a new, for you, existence, an ability to exist in a form. The land, though that word is incorrect, we use it for your sake only, the land is a construction of our mind. It does not really exist in a material sense."

"I am finding that hard because I am in a third dimension and you, I can see you, hear and touch you."

"Yes, but you see you have not stepped outside the limiting frame of third dimensional thinking. You can be every bit a construct here as you are a construct on your planet Earth."

"I want to know will I go back?"

"Of course, you will go back. We will return you back. We just wished you to have an expansion of understanding of what you term reality. Reality is a difficult thing for you to understand. This is an intelligent mind construct. Even the word mind is incorrect fir that implies a physical brain. The mind does not have a brain. It exists in and of itself. It doesn't need a form but constructs a form to meet a specific request or occasion that requires the form for clarification. You could say that we do not exist except in your mind construct."

"That really has thrown me because I didn't deliberately construct. Construct means, put together to construct something. But this (experience) simply happened without me constructing it."

"You are forgetting that we have done the mind construct and have included you within it. Are you happy with that?"

"I am perfectly happy with it. I know nothing can hurt me."

"That is the best way to view this, for the only thing that can hurt you is yourself, your mind if you so wish to be hurt. The rest is entirely up to you."

"I am not afraid. I find it difficult to get my head around this."

"You will come to understand for this will happen more and more. As we wish to show you things we will construct the means to do this."

"Is this going to be of help to the planet Earth?"

Pause "This is a very large question."

"One I'd like an answer to."

"You see, we can construct things for you, but it is what you do with the information that comes with the construction of the mind. It is again entirely up to you or whoever receives this information. It is time for you to go. It is time for you to go back."

Whew! I find I am standing outside this – I can't call it a spaceship – apparatus, construct? I am standing outside it now, as me, quite happy.

***

2018

I have crystal stairs, white and almost liquid, like clear ice. I can see through them. There doesn't seem to be a side to them as it stretches both sides as far as the eye can see. I am not slipping, and it is warm to the feet, so it can't really be ice. Glass? It must be glass. It's a very gentle slope down.

"You don't need to go deep because you are already deep."

"Oh, that's good. I've got to keep going." It feels as if I am not alone. In fact there's…I am going to call them souls going in both directions. Some going up and some going down. This is not what I expected. "Where is this taking me?"

"You are going into the depths of knowledge. Some (souls) have been before and then return to put it into practice. That is what you are doing, going into the depths of knowledge, grasping what you can understand, and then taking it back with further experiences, and to spread the knowledge that you gain."

"That's lovely but I must know what the knowledge is."

I have just reached the bottom and all I can see are little lights dancing around. The lights are intelligences and they keep bopping up and down, excited. They don't appear to have a body attached. As I move forward they part the way for me. They move freely. All these lights are intelligences, sparks of knowing. I need to know what they are knowing otherwise this is just words and not information.

"Hmm! The knowing comes from within, not from without."

I have a picture of hands coming from all directions, joining hands and doing it in unison.

"We all understand each other, and we all accept each other's variance, and still hold hands in love. There you will have the heaven you are looking for."

"This seems to be unattainable in this world."

"Maybe, but if you hold that vision of these, not just human beings, we are speaking of all sentient beings. Sentient beings will accept all for what they are without trying to change them to their own way of thinking. Then there will be peace, when each does not try to outdo the other, when each puts out a helping hand to another."

"I am thinking as I am getting this, we DO know this already, but how can we put it into practice? How can we help others to see this and act upon it? That is the difficulty."

"You must at least try to begin to see it happening in individuals in your head. If you can't visualise it how on Earth can it happen? So, visualise it. that is a start. It must start with you as it must start with each sentient being."

***

2018
BEHIND THE SCREEN

My stairs are very shallow, easy gradation down making it easy for me, but I don't know why. Going somewhere very deep, deep. Suddenly I see there are walls on either side. I didn't expect this. The steps are encased by the walls but there is no sign of where I am going. The walls are rough stone or cement. I keep moving. There are a few sounds coming in and I can feel them coming in. I thank them.

"Will I have to speak before you come in? That seems to be the key. You pick up on my sound frequency. The effect of sound. I am aware that you are here. I am looking for something important to share."

At last I get to something. It is very dark and leads into a tunnel. I can still see because there is just enough light to see, and they know I must see. I mustn't go blindfold to anything here. I go forward. The ground is very rough. I don't think anyone has been this way before as it would have been smooth. Unshod territory.

"OK! So show me. Show me where I must go, please."

In front there is a green wall, curtain. I don't know what to call it. I know from experience that I must go through this.

"It is a screen, screening from those who do not understand."

"So, why should it be screened?"

"Because they cannot cope with what is behind the screen."

"Am I allowed to go through?"

"You are to help them adjust to reality."

I walk forward, through it. I am no longer me; I am another being, tall, thin. But I still have a female feel about me. I think this is another part of me. As I walk through the scene is of desolation, destruction.

"It is how parts of your planet are becoming as a result of warfare. People are on the move, away from the war zones."

"I know that already."

"These places that were home to them become desolate. Nobody there. The land, rich in all that it had before, but the people have fled, hoping to find something more. As warfare increases and as they take with them their own inability to manage affairs they simply take these troubles with them. And so the effect of war spreads, even without bombs and killing. This must change if you are to save your planet. For people in these situations do not, will not ever have the ability or capacity to make the changes themselves, and so they spread and spread.

"Within these mass evacuations, mass exodus there are bright souls, new souls, special envoys sent from spirit to assist. All is not as dire as you might think. We are doing all we can in this respect. Warfare must stop. War is not only killing people, but also destroying the land and bringing it to destruction. This must not be spread like a cancer.

"After a period of time, when the desolate areas, by that we mean devoid of humans, then nature will take over once more and the creatures of the land will return. Then you will find people beginning to return. It all takes time. It is so unfortunate that this is the way your years have become. There will be light in these war-torn areas again, given time. Time is the important factor here. We know it will regrow, be reborn and people will continue to produce children who are wiser than they.

"Your real problem is those who wish to control the world. That is where the source of all this is."

"Why cannot we do something about those people who are ruining the planet?"

"We will not allow the planet itself to be destroyed. Each individual upon the planet is responsible, as always for his or her interaction, decisions and growth. That must be at all times.

You have a question? Please put it."

"What is happening to human beings, children, adults who suddenly disappear, vanish? What is happening to them? Where are they?"

"As you are aware there are many causes, not just one. Seeing it from our standpoint those who vanish are being kept clear of destruction. They are being taken to safe zones off planet. They will continue to be nurtured, to exist as human beings. Within this plan there are several bi-purposes that will - - -

"There are the others who disappear, who are indeed taken by your own people for their own dire purposes, and not out of consideration for the humans they take. This too is true. As you are already aware of the law of karma, those who do these deeds will receive the same treatment in their own soul journey. That too will be regrettable. That is another law that cannot be shaken."

LATER

I have a bamboo ladder. It is difficult to see if it is fixed to anything. It is going straight down, no curves. It is going down into what you might call the Amazon rainforest.

"But this isn't the Amazon but other parts of the world that are as dense and as vital to your planet. Look beyond the Amazon into other areas that are similar and which are not protected. Protection would be vital for once they are discovered their protection would be vital for the world that you inhabit.

***

2018

TUNNELS

The stairs are very narrow, going down into a cellar, or so it seems. It winds down, not up. As I get to the bottom it widens out opening into something. It has a gritty floor, not sand, the grit that forms on concrete. As I move forward there is an echo to my footsteps which is a bit odd. This place is quite large like a cave. But this is not a normal natural cave as on a beach. It is inside the mountain.

A hand reaches out from somewhere, a strong hand which grabs me and pulls me into a nook, a cranny that I would have passed by had the hand not pulled me into it. It is a side passage that leads to something much bigger. I already know that in advance as if my mind is ahead of what it expects. All I can feel is the hand pulling me forward into a very large space, still inside the mountain. It is very manmade, very set with regular proportions, there is not much finery about this. It is bare. I walk forward and whoever is pulling me along I can't see but I can feel. They are invisible to me.

I keep being guided. There is machinery, not that I would recognise what machinery it is, quite large. We walk past that. This whole area is the nuts and bolts of whatever is ahead. To ensure smooth running of what is ahead.

I am totally trusting as I walk forward, not seeing far ahead. The passage is now well lit, colour coded I'd say. The colours are direction links. I've seen this before. You need to know where which colour leads. The colour is on the floor so I just follow the colour that I am being brought into. It is an odd orangy brown. It would be difficult to see if you weren't looking. There are other leads off. It's quite a long journey, this one.

"Show me what I need to see please. Why am I here?"

We enter into a more civilised place. There is seating, desks, computers, all clearly indicating connections with the airwaves. There are screens. I am guided through the desks to an office.

"Wait outside."

I sit on a seat for a while. A door opens. That is interesting for a military person comes out. It is a female in camouflage uniform. For some reason I had expected a male. I can't see what country is represented. She is very much like any other human being and is not an alien. She invites me in, to what I can only assume is her office. She has a lot of instruments in front of her desk.

"What am I supposed to do?"

"You are now one of us. You have been enlisted as one of us."

I repeat: "What am I supposed to do? What does this mean? What am I supposed to do?"

"You use your psychic abilities to gain information and report back."

"I want to know, is this a 'set up' for the benefit of the planet or for unwelcome beings from space?"

"This is to protect and ensure the survival of those who can run this planet later on, when it is for the betterment of all people who remain."

"This seems to indicate that not everybody will remain."

"You already know this is true."

"What about the stories I've heard, that those who control the planet for their own interests have built these tunnels?"

"That too is true. But do you not think that we too have our tunnels and our operation set-up to ensure survival of those who will benefit the planet?"

"So, this indicates there will be a war between the two factions again."

"There has always been war between two or more factions. This is unlikely to stop."

"So, are you receiving help from our Cosmic Cousins?"

"We work together as always. This is where you are needed, for you can communicate more easily than we can. We can obtain their help through you."

"Bloody hell! Is what you are giving me now for my third book or is this as it is going to be?"

"It is both these things. You are playing a part, as you well know. At the same time you are bringing into reality what is required for the human races."

"What about the planet Earth itself?"

"That will always be safe no matter what the human mind will do to it. That need not be your concern at all. Your concern and ours is about the spiritual journey of the Human Race, the spiritual ongoing journey of the Human Race. You as advocate for a betterment can work with us and the Cosmic Cousins. Have we made this clear?"

"Yes, but why all this going through the tunnels? Why couldn't you just bring me here?"

"You know as well as we that you need your journey into an altered state to be here. 'Mind Travel' remember. Mind Travel journeys are as real as living and breathing n your everyday world. We simply bring you into contact with us. It is very simple."

"Can you give me some evidence that what you are saying is valid, is true?"

The woman turns around, opens a door behind her by pressing a button. Out step three extremely tall … I don't like the word aliens, … extra-terrestrials. Two are female and one is male. They are smiling at me and I feel a wave of emotion and love. They are so tall that I feel puny beside them.

"You needn't worry about size. It is inside that matters," says the woman in uniform. "Is this proof enough for you?"

At that I feel I have to come back because my chest is hurting now. Something is going on with me, physically. I feel it. I must stop.

***

2018
MULTI INTELLIGENT ENERGY

I see myself as an energy form, all different colours. I don't actually have stairs to go down. I am moving my way down on what appears to be a knotted rope. It is to count the knots that I need to do. As I count I go deeper and am going very deep into the bowels of the Earth. As an energy form I am entering where a physical form cannot go. At least not physically, not without a constructed means. As an energy I can go anywhere. I can be anything. So I go down…I don't even feel I am passing through anything physical. Oh I see. It is the energy of the Earth that I am entering in the same way that I am an energy form, so is the Earth. It does not need to be physical.

I ask, "As I travel, does the Earth… is it conscious of itself in the way I am conscious of me?"

"Of course, it is conscious of itself. The Earth is aware of every part of itself as are you when you are physical. You are aware of anything that touches upon you. So it is with the Earth. The Earth is fully aware of the damage that is being done by other intelligent forms. You are all intelligent forms, all of you, deciding what to do or what not to do. The whole thing is driven by decision and action so that there might be a reaction."

"I am a bit lost here, I am still going down the rope and I am used to seeing something physical, and not having energy."

"The energy affects every single thing and that includes you as you go down into us. We say us because we are not single as you might imagine. The planet Earth is a multiple as are you. As multiple intelligences you are aware of the other multiples of you, as the Earth is aware of the multiples of itself."

"This is all getting a bit deep for me (excuse the pun)."

"But you see, we can communicate, can we not, through intelligence. You are, as you have been told, an interpreter of the intelligence put into words so that you may pass it on. There is no other way for us to communicate with those who are not aware of the intelligence."

"It is so very hard. How can I explain this?"

"We, as multiple Earths will continue to exist, as you as a multiple will continue to exist. We as the Earth in a connection as a physical form is the one to be conscious of, as the you, as the being you have become in your multiple will always be aware of what is happening to you."

"How can all this knowledge help the Earth and its peoples to move in the correct direction?"

"What is correct? What is correct for one is deemed incorrect for another."

"That is certainly true."

"What is correct is that can the Earth that you are connecting with now can be damaged in any way?"

"I would say no, it is not correct."

"But that is from your perspective."

"Surely, you as that Earth have the right to an opinion on this."

***

2019
EXPAND THE MIND

I have wooden stairs and a wooden rail as a banister. As I go deeper there are bits of grass, weeds, growth appearing through the wooden steps. So I am going down into the Earth, top layer, as it is grass, not soil. Keep going down. I come to what appears to be a viewing platform, similar to what you get for bird watchers. What am I to see from this platform?

"Look through the viewing part."

I see vague shapes, not quite like shadows, but are in colours and more substantial than shadows. Moving spirit forms in various colours not doing anything specific.

"Why can't I go through?"

"Do you want to go through?"

"Well yes, I want more than just viewing."

"Just see yourself amongst them and you will be there."

I do this and they are milling around me and through me and are not as solid as I am. It feels nice. I want to be hearing their words, their thoughts so that I may act. They suddenly form a line and I understand, so this must be telepathic. I understand that I must follow them (the spirits) as they go in a line. I join the line and move along as they pass through – it sounds ridiculous – it passes through what appears to be clouds or something on either side keeping the beings in a line. I am with them and going through faster now, speeding up. Then that too fans out and I reach the bit that fans out. It is a broad space now, there is music, sounds of nature. Really strong lights. I am looking for some way forward please. Something to guide me.

A pair of strong hands take me by the elbow and move me to a seat overlooking a vast expanse of planets. Within the expanse is the planet Earth. I can see it quite clearly. You can't mistake it.

"Why are you showing me this?"

"You are a traveller of the cosmos, not only are you required to travel the Earth, you are also required to travel the cosmos and this is not restricted just to your solar system but other solar systems also. Spread your thoughts, your mind and your learning beyond the planet Earth. In so doing you will arrive at a greater understanding of what you are to do in your current incarnation. You must awake your mind, read more information. Look for more information so that your mind is directed in this way."

"OK. So it seems that reading, and listening will be the keys."

***

2019

I am wrapped in green. The steps taking me deeper. I am counting the steps as I go. The stairs are like green turf, looked after. It is comfortable to the feet. Trees on either side and I am reminded of trees that are on the path to a church and cemeteries in Italy. I am going along now, not down and am a level field now. At the end of this path is a church. A beautiful Eastern temple, someone takes care of this. Clearly I have to go in.

"Show me what I have to understand. Show me. "

There are lots of doors going in different directions. I feel that whichever one I take is going to lead me into the past. As I look into each room there is a person there. They pop their head round as if to say hello are you coming in? I don't feel yet that I have the right one.

"It stretches back in time is the message. All the knowledge that has been gained here comes from the past. The past when everything was known. It has always been known. To discover what is here you need to discover the past."

"I can't understand that."

"Time is irrelevant, but we use the word past for your benefit. In fact is still exists in the now. Think with the mind that is ancient. Don't think with your current mind. Think as if you were already in the halls of knowledge with the great philosophers, the great mathematicians, all on hand to reveal the secrets of the Universe. They are all there. You need to decide which one to delve into."

"I'm not sure where to go with this. So many choices and if it is well known in the past it will be in the books, won't it? So I won't be learning anything new."

"You are forgetting where human beings come from. You are forgetting they came from much further back than that. Look for your answers to knowledge way back in time, way back before the current human being."

"Can you do this now? I want you to do this now."

As I ask that an extremely tall, fully robed man steps forward. He appears to be ancient, but he is not. He has kind, gentle eyes. He puts his hands out to me. I reach forward and take his hands and a current runs through me as I do, heat passes through from him to me. I love it.

"It is a uniting of the mind. A passing of one time to another.

The meditation is now broken by noise from outside. I have to leave. Lots to think about.

***

2019

DREAM EXPLANATION?

I have been given a ladder with rungs. It reminds me of a safety ladder, one you would swing out of a window etc. So it is not always in place but there when you need it. I asked at the outset to be given a meaning of the dream last night when I was given a lift over a water stretch to attend a concert. The lift wasn't what I expected for it was with a whole lot of military men, navy people. They grouped themselves on either side of me and begin singing altogether. It felt to be a religious occasion. Then I realised I was a lot colder and hadn't dressed up enough for the weather. I hadn't put on enough clothes for where I was going. At that thought they grouped themselves in closer to me and gathered round me tightly, to make sure I wasn't cold. I am assuming that. That is all I can remember.

I ask for an explanation of this and they give me this safety ladder. It seems to be for protection. I am grateful that this is symbolic for as I get to the bottom of the safety ladder there are a lot of snakes, loads and loads of them. Not huge like boas but a lot of them. I step off the ladder into the snakes. They move out of the way. I am not worried about them, but it is an odd thing to have.

I walk forward and I see a twinkling light, like a lantern moving about and not steady. I feel somebody is either holding a lantern or it is hung up. I come towards the light and reach up and take it. It is dark obviously or I wouldn't need the lantern. It is a trail, not a proper path, through the undergrowth. There is scurrying on either side, so it is lively active undergrowth, not dead at all. I don't know if they are interested in me or not and nothing comes across my path.

It is very quiet now, dead silence. I would rather have the scurrying than this dead silence. BOOM, BOOM from somewhere up ahead. I must go towards whatever is presented. I am getting telepathic messages rather than my own thoughts.

"You are once again to go into unknown territory, unknown to you but not to others. You will not know of this in advance. As in the way you are walking you do not know what is ahead, but we do. When you arrive at the intended place there will be…we want to call it a large happening, an explosion but not of dynamite – an explosion of knowing and activity. It will all go on very fast and you will be in the middle of it.

Don't worry about it for you are protected."

I am thinking.

***

2019
THOUGHT CREATE

I have steppingstones, large, round, smooth, not slippery and quite easy. They are going over water as one would expect. It is flowing fast under me. I get to the other side which is a long way off and an aboriginal is beckoning me. He is an Australian aboriginal not an aboriginal from Africa. He is leading me as he beckons me on and turns around to make sure I am following him. He is speaking mentally. I don't hear his voice but I know his words.

"We are truly the Originals. We were left here in the very early days and we were intended. The objective was that we teach you our ways, that we teach the growth of the new people that you are. We were to teach you the ways of living with each other and with nature. As you are well aware things did not go according to plan."

"Why are you telling me and what can I do about it?"

"Wait, wait," he says.

So I stop still. He goes ahead without me. I feel like a dog that has been told to sit and wait. Then a very tall slim, silver clad man comes forward along the path the aboriginal travelled. He is very tall, much taller than I am. He stands before me and puts both his hands out for me to take which I do. He bends forward and plants a kiss on my head, on the crown of my head. I feel like a little one to him in every aspect, not just a question of height. He takes my hand and we walk together.

I feel the energy building in my head, building to that level of pain which signals to me that I am going into a much higher state of vibration. I wait now…

"My mind is all that is. My consciousness is all that is and I am going into memories, memories to which there is no end."

"There is no beginning and there is no end, for your consciousness holds it all and will always hold it. We are not speaking of your physical form, we are not speaking of your physical body, we are speaking of the Soul. (Here he came in very strongly) An electrical memory of everything. Electrical is not quite the right word. Energy, an energy that surpasses all things, that contains memory of all things. What not many realise is that creation is continuous. There is no end to creation. Each energy of mind constantly thinks, brings forward ideas, manifests, and since all this happens the creation continues. Therefore we say remember that your thoughts create, and if you wish for a loving, peaceful, contented world then your thoughts must be of that.

"If your thoughts dwell overlong on all things that are wrong in your mind, all things that are deemed wrong for spiritual growth, if your thoughts dwell on this you are creating more of the same. This is why so many around you say they do not watch violence or things that disturb them because their minds may continue to dwell on it and that dwelling creates the thoughts in their minds and the reality that follows. You are going to say, how can we change things if we are not aware of that which we wish to change? It is good to be aware. What we are saying is do not dwell on the negative aspects of those things. Change, change, change those thoughts that mill around. Find good in what you are viewing or hearing. Find some good and focus on the good. Do not focus or dwell on the negative aspects. It is simply a question on focussing on what you see in a positive light. There is good in everything. Seek and find it and then you may dwell on that. In this you are creating a better world.

"Things have already been done that you cannot undo. Create, Create, Create images of the alternatives. A reversal of that. A remedy of that which you say cannot be undone. Your thoughts create. So it is your thoughts you need to dwell upon. Given in your world that many let others think for them so their thoughts are not their own any more. They are manipulated, distracted. There is so much distraction in your world. Those who are distracting and manipulating, they have thoughts and are creating what they thought. You can accept or ignore. This is always, always your choice."

The tall silver man has turned me around to face a kaleidoscope of colour. Brilliant light.

"What can you see?"

"I can only see colours of light. Nothing of form that I can identify."

"This is because when you are in The Light, when you are enveloped by light there are no forms. There are no distinctions of being. It is all light and that is as it should be. Walk forward and be in the light."

***

2019

I am going down very narrow steps on either side. Walls closing me in. I am going underground and as I get there I see underground rivers. I say rivers because there is more than one here. By that I mean that they go off in different directions. There is a choice to be made. In can wade through these rivers. It is very dark, I can hear the water swishing as I wade through it. There is a ceiling, a cavern like roof, not quite like grottos, not that high. No stalactites or anything. We all know that water finds its own level and will eventually come out to be seen.

"This is pure water from deep within the bowels of the Earth. It has not come from rainfall or melted ice. It has come from the inner Earth."

"You said it was coming from the top but the idea is that it is coming out into daylight."

"There is light in the inner Earth."

"OK. I am a bit confused here. Underground tunnels from the inner Earth finding its level in the light? That tells me that it is coming from up high in the inner Earth. I have to get my head round this one. As I wade through I do come out and it appears to be very much like earth, grassy terrain, trees, bushes. It is like Earth on the surface."

"A replica."

"The term replica indicates to me that it has been made to replicate that on the surface."

"It is the other way around. The replica is on the surface. This here is the original."

"You are getting me confused now. Anyway, carry on. Show me what I must see."

"We have already been telling you many times that everything that comes to your mind is a construction of the mind. This too exists in your mind construct, if not now but at some point, which remains in your soul's memory."

"Memory again implies past."

"You haven't got it yet, have you? Past, present and future are all one and according to your mind's intention you can join it at a timeline at any point in your journey."

"OK. Tell me then what part of the timeline we are on now?"

"This is the past, the present and the future."

"This is not giving me the answer."

"But you see it is the past, the present and the future all as one, in the same way. This is why we have given you the river. The river exists no matter how much water flows along it. It is still a river and what flows along flows from one direction to the other. Timeless movement all existing at the same time. Have we got your attention yet?"

"I have to agree it has."

"You are now looking at time itself. You are looking at existence, existence being the same, past, present and future. All happening at the same moment wherever you put your attention."

"How is this going to help anybody."

"Whatever you do in your conscious moment will continue to exist, always. Nothing is lost. It carries on into what you might term the future. As we showed you earlier many avenues, many rivers going in different directions."

"So we are back here to timelines."

"Call them rivers of existence if it helps you to understand. Yes, they have timelines because everything is time everywhere in the whole of the Universe and can be related to time. Wherever you find your mind that is your moment in time. What you do with your moment at whatever level, whatever branch of existence, that too exists forever. It is never lost."

"How can we improve as we move along. It is very difficult. How can our present moment of consciousness improve our existence?"

"However you react, whatever you do with your present moment of awareness has an effect on your continued existence."

"I feel I've known that. Everybody knows that."

"What we are trying to tell you is be aware that everything you think, do and react to is important for your continued pleasure, your continued advancement. If you react in a negative way that too influences the continuation of your journey. Be in the moment in the best way you can."

"It is a lot to take in and understand. I feel it is enough. Thank you."

***

2019

A REPORT OF WHAT MY CHANNELLED COMMUNICATOR HAD SAID.

Time is running out on this planet but do not worry about it. Remember there are multiples, parallels. If we focus on the negative that is going around, even if this negative is of good intention, if we focus and put our thoughts along that line, we are staying on the timeline that this thought is following. If on the other hands we have a different view, while the facts remain the same, but where we have a positive outlook on it, then we remain on that timeline (lifeline), we follow that timeline and so on. There are many variables on what is going to happen to this planet. Where we as individuals end up depends on where we put our focus. That will be the timeline that we follow. There are multiples and there are parallels. We must decide what timeline we want to follow. So that means following our thoughts in the way that we want to inhabit (our souls). There was a lot about children and about seeding of the planet. The planet is being re-seeded. I feel they are not talking just about our planet but the planet that is to be. We are not to despair about the future of the planet, it is not to be destroyed. It has been reseeded before and it will be again no matter what happens.

So do not follow thoughts on the bad things for that is what we create in our timeline. Some of these things have to happen. They have to be disastrous, for those who are creating it have to put it right. It will exist on one timeline for there are several timelines and several futures and it is up to us to decide what one we want. So follow your thoughts.

***

2019

I have gone down very quickly, and I am reminded of falling into a rabbit hole. At the bottom I can't stand upright, it is a tunnel. I crawl along not on hands and knees but edging forward as a soldier would do. I am crawling along on my elbows, going forward. I am comfortable and not worried for it is a route I intended to take. There is only room for one at a time, but it is a route that has been taken and will be taken again and again many times. So it has got to lead somewhere, it has to lead somewhere. I keep going on until it leads to a bigger area, not huge, but there is water, fresh, drinking clean water. I have a drink and it is sweet. Now I know why they call it sweet water. I can stand up now and even wave my arms about without hitting anything. I move round the edge of the water because I can't stay here. It is part of the journey.

I don't know where the water is coming from. It is not coming from a river. As I move forward a pair of hands come from ahead of me and pull me forward, to make sure I don't slip perhaps. They are making sure I continue. I say they, because they are two males. They look human but it is difficult to tell. They are humanoid at least and are covered in a sort of uniform that is hard, shiny and reminds me of Star Wars. I can't see any features because they are cased in this shiny stuff. But it feels OK.

I am pushed forward, pulled forward. I don't know if I am outside or inside and it is hard to see very far and where I actually am. This has got to get to something else.

My head is beginning to hurt. When this happens it is always a sign I am moving into another dimension, another level of vibration. It hurts quite a lot so I must bear with this for a while…

***

2020
CHINA

I have steps of rattan – I am in a Chinese market, full of noise and people. As I walk along I realise the enormous contrast between the high tech tall office buildings, everything modern and the ordinary people managing their daily lives. There is nothing high tech about the market.

"What is this telling me?"

"When you think of China and how the virus affected the rest of the world and how those in high places and high tech are changing and influencing the world, there is this other China that simply manages to survive in ordinary, everyday activities that has nothing to do with the high tech. Don't lump the two China's together into one. With regard to the virus vaccine, it should be called an antidote to the virus. It is an antidote that China will provide for the world.

***

2020
PROPHESY FOR YOUNG BOY (ME)

I am a young boy. I feel young, not Chinese but from somewhere like Burma or Borneo. I am walking along with some lady I think is my grandmother. I am holding her hand. I am about 8 or 9 going to the village. I am being taken to what I am going to call a council, a gathering of men. They are there for a purpose and I am the purpose and am taken before them. I am waiting to hear what they have to say. One of them, an older person, looking like a Chinese but he is not. He has a long finger and points to me.

"This is the one. This is the one who will take things forward. He is not in a hurry right now but he will mature and act wisely for we have seen his future. This is the one that will change matters not just for us but for many others besides us in different times. You must guard this child and see he does not come to any harm. He will journey on through many lives and do many things. It is proclaimed. It is so."

I let go of her hand and run off to play with the other children around. Being mindful of what is given.

***

2020
LORD MICHAEL

I am going down giant steps. It is hard to get down each one as they are so big. I get to the bottom onto a big slab of polished crystal. I must walk, not stay here. I ask them to take me where I need to be. I feel huge pressure in my head which is a good indication that I have connection. I am happy that whatever will be presented will be correct.

I am presented with a fork in the path. One to the left is smooth and a continuation of the crystal path. One to the right is rough. It is still of crystal but is rough. I have a choice of which one to go on. I think for a moment. The rough one is more interesting with many things to do along the way. The one to the left is bland, smooth and easy and not much else. I choose the right, the one with lots going on, lots more to learn, lots more to take my interest. Give me a life that will keep me alive for I am not ready for retirement yet. I go along the rough path and it branches again. Many choices.

"This is your life, many choices that are yours not ours. Go on your instinct on which one to take. They may be all attractive, they may all give you something to learn from.

"But I can only do one at a time. Maybe I will come back and do the others after."

"This is your life. Do it with as many avenues as you wish to take until you are finished here. Each path will be rewarding and add to your knowledge. If you had taken the easy path on the left there would be no adding to your knowledge. There would have been no further enlightenment, no further challenges to teach you. You have chosen wisely."

"What does this mean?"

"It means that the rest of your life, for the continuation of life in this incarnation you will have much to occupy yourself with. You will never be bored; you will never feel redundant, and you will go to the end of your days feeling useful and also feeling appreciated. Others will join the path, for you will not do this alone all the time. There will be others to help you as you get older. You will still continue your work."

Thoughts create your life.

I am a kaleidoscope of colours which change as it always does. Each time I think, each time I move the patterns of colours change. I am simply a colour, many colours, no stairs, just what I am standing on is waving like a wave of colours. No particles, just waves. It reminds me of dimensions rather than solid objects. At the thought of moving I move through the colours as the colour. I am united with the colours.

"But I am here for information so what is this telling me?"

"Keep moving. keep moving all of you through your worlds. Interact and think and feel. React as you feel with the passing of your soul through your existence. Your aim can be as glorious as you wish. If in your passing through you feel anxiety or trepidation things will be brought to you to make this real. You will have created it with your thoughts. Equally, this is why your mind is still active, creating as you go. What occurs after your thoughts is totally dependent on what those thoughts were. So we cannot tell you life is to be this or that for you truly create it. you can decide to unite with others or to enjoy your own journey irrespective of what others feel. It is all dependant on your thoughts, your feelings. That is what we have to say."

***

2020

WE ARE ONE – GIVEN IN CONNECTION WITH SPIRIT TODAY

Re the global situation. We are all in this together. This is for those who are not quite so capable of saying what they wish to say. All races, all colours, all genders, are all in this together. We need to remember that we are all one family on our home planet Earth. This situation should unite us as one for we are all in the same boat, all of us, whether we are enjoying it or whether we are absolutely hating it, whether we are in pain or in love. We are all in this together. The outcome will be according to whether we unite with each other or whether we love each other. Or will we continue the pattern of fighting one with the other. Will we continue the pattern of one war after the other in one country after the other until there is nothing left but tragedy and destruction? If you are fortunate in living reasonable lives, may you remember that we are all one together on the same planet. Maybe, each of us, will suffer what we did not expect to suffer, or we may sail through. Look to your heart, look to the sense of unity that this situation has brought upon the entire planet and see that this can be a uniting force. God bless you all.

***

2020

NEW BIRTH

On my stairs down it is draughty, windy. It is not dangerous, just very windy, coming in gusts. I hold on tight to the bannisters though this must mean I am inside. Strange to have the wind inside.

"It is the wind of change and what the whole world is going through is a wind of change, buffeting, pushing where you have to hold on so you don't get blown over. Keep going down."

At the bottom now, there is green grass, new shoots as if somebody has sown a new lawn. It is very new, very fresh. I can feel the freshness and the wind is easing. It is becoming very light.

I ask, "Is this for me personally or global?"

"You are entering a new birth process. You are learning new things. Into your mind will come new ways of being with what you are faced with. You have new ideas now. We are connecting you with the next layer of teachers. When you connect with us you will receive a completely new set of instructions. Be patient with them for you will be taken into areas you have not gone into before. It might require courage from you for it is so new to you. All of what you have learnt before, we are not cutting you off from all of your knowledge but simply helping you into a new way of being. You will be a new you."

"When will all this begin?"

"When you accept the idea that what served you in the past of your work no longer serves you in the same way. You will be connecting differently. We will guide you through this. You must not be concerned over how others deal with their lives. If they listen to you or if they do not listen. That is their choice. All is in order. It is all in the planning."

***

2020

My steps are of green jade and China immediately springs to mind. You are going into the depths of knowledge of all things. The steps are quite steep, not easy. I get down them with a little difficulty and there is nothing to hold onto. It is a deep jade all the way. I can't see the bottom. I hope this is going to lead me somewhere. I go now swiftly to the bottom because it is such a lot of effort to go one step at a time. I can't see the bottom because it is such a long way down, so I think myself at the bottom.

The jade continues along a pathway. There are high walls on either side. The path is narrow and the walls are high. It is like being in a canyon. It can't see anything but the walls and the path. It is very narrow and I feel very tiny. The walls seem to be reaching for me as if they are alive, reaching out to touch me as I pass through. Reaching to touch me. I can't see where I am going but I have to trust.

Eventually I come into the light. There is a very ancient Buddha like figure. I am not saying it is Buddha but very Buddha like, sat there, composed and waiting.

"We are waiting for the world to reach knowledge. It is the world that must do the travelling to reach the knowledge."

"When you say the world, do you mean the people?"

"Of course we mean the people for that is your world. They live in different worlds according to their mind set. You have heard it said to you, 'you live in a different world to us' meaning your mindset is not as others. Do you see what we say? So if you want to know what the world is coming to, we say to you, 'What world do you live in in your mind?' what are your activities? What do you engage yourself with? Ask these questions and if you are happy with your world and prefer to continue, then that is also your future. That is what your future world will be, to learn a little.

There are others also travelling, wishing to know their future and so we ask again, 'What world are they living in now? Are they happy with it or do they wish to change and broaden their aspects, broaden their minds? Their world will be according to what interests them what engages them every day. There are many worlds.

When we say there are many worlds, some assume you mean global, actual physical, perhaps Earth like worlds. It is not like that. Your future world is totally dependent on the world you live in now in your head. What interests you and what actions do you take in your world? Can you see where we are going with this?

Those who have minds will think about this and will understand what we are trying to say.

***

2020

IN AWE

The dark forces cannot have a footing in this world. They cannot sustain themselves in the light that is being shown all over. They cannot endure in the light that is shown by all loving creatures, and the human race and beings of all kinds. The dark powers have no standing in this light. They cannot endure it. They will either leave or change so that they can endure and be part of the light. It will be as it is meant to be. But I have no fear of the dark powers at any time while we continue to be as we are, wonderful, wonderful beings of light.

Experiences of the last few days. What have I learnt from the experiences? What have I learnt from going into a hospital environment? What am I still learning in this situation that we are all in?

I have learnt and am in awe of people and have seen how wonderful they are, how kind and caring they are. I have witnessed absolute kindness and gentleness in all those I have come across. I am in awe in how they are dealing with this difficult period of time. I am grateful for my own position, where I live, and am aware that others are not so happily placed. I can only speak of those I see around me; I cannot speak for others. But where there are pockets where people are kind, generous and loving to all those around them I am grateful and am heartened as a human. I am in awe of how they deal with what they are faced with. I will never ever take for granted my own position in life. I am in awe of others. They are wonderful.

***

2021

ALL JOINS ONE

I have two rails to hold onto. I am going down as if I am not sure, as if I am not well or strong enough. The steps are steep. I go one step at a time and definitely going deeper. I get to the bottom and it is very light. There are lots and lots of butterflies as in a butterfly farm. They are everywhere, landing on me, not settling. It is easy walking and very light and colourful. I need to know what I am doing here. Take me where I need to be please.

As I ask the question there is a very small stream of water running down the centre of the path. I follow it to see where it leads. I see it drains into a river. It is not a big river but is fast flowing and there are other streams joining from other parts, different areas all flowing in into the one.

"Wherever your living comes from, wherever people are having their experiences, each little, tiny flow of their life is joining the bigger flow and that is how they become one. They cannot separate. It is impossible to separate from the rive for it flows too fast. That river is joined by other rivers who are in their turn having the lives of others joining it. So all these rivers, from different areas of existence of your planet Earth join together. It can do no other and join together to form one big, massive flow. That flow then joins, as all rivers must into the great sea of consciousness. All becomes one. There is no choice. It is not a choice but a natural thing that all becomes one. The choice lies in how each little rivulet is. Is it full of light and joy or is it full of misdeeds and harsh living? This is where the choices lie. Once you enter the great sea, the great ocean of consciousness, all will be one and all is natural and cannot be contaminated. Everything is cleansed in this consciousness."

***

2021

RE THE BOOK *LOVE BEING A HUMAN*

It is important to include some of my experiences with Osishoo and Serapis Bey.

I am dressed in a long flowing tunic/gown of many different colours. Colours of energy and they move, wave about. I am enveloped in the colours. I am moving, not walking, just moving along. It is like being static in the middle of a column of colour. Very pleasant.

I ask for something to uplift the world at this time of great need. I am given a picture of something in the form of a boat. Very symbolic! It is as if the world has been put into a boat and it is flowing along the currents of all the colourful energies. It is carried along without any effort. It can't help but be in these energies. I am asking for help to explain.

"Your world is being carried along in the movement of the Universes, the galaxies, the solar system. Everything is moving, the whole thing is moving into a new state of expansion. It can't do anything about it. It simply is what is happening. It is a continual flow into a new waveband of energy in which the current is elevated. It is a process rather than a sudden event. As everything moves into this band of energy it is affected by it. Energy affects all things and that includes the energies of each individual soul and creature. Accept it and enjoy it. This is the process of nature. You cannot change it."

"This doesn't make it clearer how individuals can be uplifted."

***

2021
FLOW TO THE ONE

I have been taken down into a fast-flowing stream, a river of some kind and although I am alone there are lots of little boats all being swept along on the flow of the river. They are all getting away from something. This is – I don't know whether to call it an escape or an evacuation. They are on separate little boats. Some do have couples in them, but in the main they are individuals. They don't seem to be worried as it is part of their journey and they don't even know where the river Is taking them. They are leaving behind what was their lives before. The sun is shining, it is not a scary thing, it just IS.

I ask, "I must know what this is about, please. Tell me. Show me."

"When they reach the ocean they will link together and sail the ocean as one big raft of souls holding in comfort the arms of the others. They unite to sail the ocean with ease and when they arrive at their destination they will together settle in their new existence, and because they all love each other and have helped each other that continues and although each is separate in themselves, they will unite as one and form their new world, their new land. It is joyous."

I thank them for that picture and am part of it. I am one of those joined and united.

"Can you tell me something else?"

I now see tall buildings. Constructions.

"They have always been there. You simply never saw them before. They are pillars of light. Each may enter a pillar of light."

I choose one. A blue one. I enter. There is such a comfortable feel. - - - I then speak a lot of Light language.

***

2021
TO LEAVE OR TO STAY

I have bare feet and bare legs and am standing at the top of the stairs which are all gold. It is a golden pathway and not stairs at all. I am trained to go deep using this method and it works. I move along the golden pathway. It is not just gold but is glittering, sparkly and I know each step is taking me deeper to my inner being. I walk along very happy. There is not much on either side that I can see. All I can see is the glitter and some of it lands on me, glitter dust which sticks to me so I carry it with me. I move along each step taking me nearer and nearer to my objective. I arrive and it sounds a bit bizarre as it is a golden gate. And no, I am not passing from this world physically, but I am passing from this world into another of being. I step through the gate into glorious light, different shades of colour and it seems to be moving. As I look more closely the colours are people, beings taking form. Not clear, not sharp but definitely moving forms. I feel the energies are welcoming, loving, peaceful and joyous. There is a part of me that wants to see them more clearly.

"Yes, you want them to be more solid, and yet solidity, 3rd dimension is what you have been asking to leave and then when we take you into this realm of non-physicality, not 3rd density, you then wish it to be more solid. It does not make much sense, does it? You cannot have it both ways. Think more clearly about what you want. Do you want this beautiful loving feeling with nothing solid or do you want to stay in 3rd dimension a bit longer and have the feelings, the interaction and the joys of living and anything else that being solid means. You must decide and as you are a doer, one that likes action, would this diaphanous realm really be to your satisfaction? You cannot know that until you are in it."

I am asking, "Give me more reason to stay where I am because I feel I am not doing enough. Give me more reason."

"While you stay in your 3rd dimension, in your solid state you are able to influence and assist others who do not understand reality, who do not understand what it is to be a soul. You are there to help them understand. You are there to help them realise that the soul journey changes as it moves from one dimension to another. It changes according to your mind. So be clear about your wishes and desires and be content in your NOW."

"I think there must be an in between, something that is not so diaphanous."

"Yes, there is an in between, the 4th dimension where you feel you still have a body, where you still interact with others very similar to yourself, who still have issues, who still appear to you to be solid but in fact are not. Is this what you wish?"

"I don't know because I haven't experienced it knowingly. I think I have to stay here in 3rd dimension and have my interactions as I have been doing with people and not worry so much about the future. I think that has to be my decision. It would be helpful if I didn't hurt so much physically and relive the pain from my body."

NOTE: It is at this point that I have been diagnosed with two types of cancer.

4 MEDITATION TRAINING AND EXERCISE

GOING INTO RELAXATION

It is important you do not try to meditate too late in the day. Your body is already programmed and conditioned to sleep at the end of the day and you may drop off instead of taking it further.

- Get into that state where you forget your body and where only the mind is alert? Remember this is an inter-active process. Being comfortable is a must
- Switch off any phones and ensure you will not be disturbed for at least fifteen minutes.
- Before you begin, say a prayer. This is your safeguard whilst you are in that open receptive state.

THE PRAYER

Your own prayer could be something like this, though it can be modified frequently according to the purpose for the sitting.

"Dear Father, I come to you in love. I ask for your help with the work I have pledged to do. (Insert whatever it is you want). May there be no invading negative influences, whether it be from within me or without. May the White Light of the Divine surround me. I invite all those guides, teachers, angels or any who wish to come to communicate with me for the betterment of all. Amen."

- Close your eyes. Relax. Feel your feet on the floor anchoring you, keeping you safe.
- Feel the tension ease out of your limbs. Starting with the legs allow the muscles to relax and the flesh to become loose. Mentally check that there is no tension in your thighs.

- Consciously relax the muscles.
- Go up the body and feel heaviness of your arms and hands on your lap.
- Loosen any tension.
- Breathe gently and become aware of breathing.
- Allow your shoulders to sag down with the gravity.
- Feel the energy increase around your throat. Allow your jaw to hang loose with teeth slightly ajar. Feel your cheeks sagging.
- Your eyelids are heavy. Feel as if you are just dropping off to sleep in a soft feather bed. You do not even want to open your eyes.
- Relax the forehead. Ease away frowns or tension.
- Loosen the scalp. Double check your whole body to ensure it is relaxed, heavy and loose.

MEDITATION TO CONTACT YOUR SOUL GUIDE

- Turn off the phone and get comfortable.
- Go through the relaxation process.
- Say your prayer to reassure you that all will be well and will bring an increase of energy to flow through you.
- Remembering that these are mind experiences, feel or see yourself standing at the top of a flight of stairs.
- Feel the ground beneath your toes. Mentally wriggle them to sense what you are standing on.
- Accept immediately what comes into the mind. Do not think about it beforehand. Be as sensory as you can.
- There is a rail to one side. Pretend it is there if you can't image it. Put your hand out to touch it. Is it a banister, rope or something else?
- Look at the stairs. Are they steep or shallow? Are they wide or narrow? Can you see the bottom? These stairs will take you into the space where your soul resides or where guides wait for you.
- It is time to do down. Use all your inner senses. Three steps to go - - one – two – three – At the bottom now.
- Look around. Take a few steps forward until you turn off to the left.
- Note the type of passage. Soon you will come to a door on the right. This is your door. What is it made of? Touch it, feel it.
- It is time to open it and step inside. This is your space.
- Step in and look around. Note your surroundings.

- Whatever you see go towards it, even if it is a drop of water on the wall.
- Inter-act with it. You might see a table. Go towards it. There might be a book or a small chest there.
- Open it. You might see a glimmer of light ahead. Go towards it.
- If you see nothing, ask to be shown what you need to see. Tell me what I need to see. Most of your input will come in the form of ideas, thoughts, impressions and images.
- Ask to be told what you need to know. Tell me what I need to know. Ask, ask, ask. Question. Make your requests.
- You might not see your soul or receive a guide at first, but he will be there.
- Keep asking. If you don't understand what comes to you, say so. Try not to edit what comes to your mind. Notice your thoughts.
- You might see an animal. Note how you feel towards the animal. An animal is often used for you to follow. It frequently is the guide himself.

Your mind will use soul memory to assist you. Trust whatever comes to show the way. When you see a spirit form it could well be your soul guide. Talk to it in your mind and ask to be shown more. You can use such words as; 'tell me what I need to know', or 'show me what I need to see'. This is giving your soul guide permission to work with you, which it needs.

CLOSING DOWN

When you successfully get into the desired deeper state and are having such a good time it sometimes happens that when the session has ended you fail to come back to a 'normal feet on the ground' vibration. You may feel floaty or spaced out.

It is easy to deal with this. You will be pleased to read that eating a piece of chocolate or biscuit is very good for grounding you. When you decide that it is time to finish, deliberately bring the energy levels down by telling yourself to do so. Consciously feel the weight of your body on the chair, feel the weight of your arms on your lap. Wriggle your fingers and toes. This brings your mind back to physical reality.

You may also say 'CUT' to indicate you are finished, as in filming.

OTHER BOOKS BY SHIRLEY BATTIE

Calling Earth – Superpowers fight for Dominion over Earth

Calling Earth II – Time and Space

Calling Earth III – Fight for Humanity's Future

Spirit Speaks – Questions and Answers on Life

Love Being a Human – Waking Up

Channelling – Use your psychic powers to contact spirit guides.

LITTLE OWL CARDS

Web - www.littleowlonline.co.uk

ABOUT THE AUTHOR

For over thirty years Shirley Battie has travelled internationally giving talks and workshops in mediumship, psychic development, meditation, and mind walking. She is a qualified hypnotherapist and competent channeler. The author of several books; Channeling Use your Psychic Powers to Contact Your Spirit Guides, Love being A Human, Spirit Speaks, Questions and answers on life and our spirit connection.

Printed in Great Britain
by Amazon

10535509R00129